T0304923

CAPTAIN
DE HAVILLAND'S
MOTH

Also by Alexander Norman

The Secret Lives of the Dalai Lama:
Holder of the White Lotus

The Dalai Lama: An Extraordinary Life

CAPTAIN DE HAVILLAND'S MOTH

Tales of High Adventure from the
Golden Age of Aviation

ALEXANDER NORMAN

abacus
books

ABACUS

First published in Great Britain in 2025 by Abacus

1 3 5 7 9 10 8 6 4 2

A CIP catalogue record for this book
is available from the British Library.

Hardback ISBN 978-0-349-14644-7
Trade paperback ISBN 978-0-349-14645-4

Typeset in Caslon by M Rules
Printed and bound in Great Britain by
Clays Ltd, Elcograf S.p.A.

Papers used by Abacus are from well-managed forests
and other responsible sources.

Abacus
An imprint of
Little, Brown Book Group
Carmelite House
50 Victoria Embankment
London EC4Y 0DZ

The authorised representative
in the EEA is
Hachette Ireland
8 Castlecourt Centre
Dublin 15, D15 XTP3, Ireland
(email: info@hbgi.ie)

An Hachette UK Company
www.hachette.co.uk

www.littlebrown.co.uk

For my brother, Henry

Contents

1

Is it Right or Left
for England?

At 11 am on 20th March, 1930, we set out on our final hop from Saint Quentin to London on a course setting recommended by our French friend.

Wait. Why a course setting? Did they have no map? They had no map. A school atlas purchased in Marseilles, but no actual map, no aeronautical chart. Those had run out at Cairo. From Cairo, they'd just followed the coast to Homs where, as later in France, they'd been given a bearing – for Malta. Ditto Malta to Sicily. After that, it had just been a question of keeping the sea to starboard and land to port until crossing over the straits of Messina into Italy, at which point it was the other way round, sea to the left, land to the right. Making their way past Etna and Vesuvius, they had refuelled at Naples then headed north past Rome to reach Pisa where, agog at its leaning tower, they'd spent the night.

After that, easy. Round the Gulf of Genoa and along the French Riviera. At first their intention had been to stop at Toulon but, thanks to a providential change in the direction of the wind, they'd scraped into Marseilles, 'with both the sun and our petrol gauge well below the horizon'.

Who were these people? Oh, just two young fellows from India – Aspy Merwan Engineer and his friend R. N. Chawla, piloting. Their aircraft? A second-hand de Havilland Moth fitted with a 100 hp Gipsy engine.

What were they up to? As a matter of fact, they were in pursuit of the recently announced Aga Khan Trophy. Or, rather, Aspy was. There was a handsome cash prize for the first Indian national to fly solo from Karachi to London, or vice versa, in under a month. This was a proving flight. Once they'd made it to Croydon, the plan was for Aspy to fly back alone: it was his aeroplane.

But first, there was the matter of getting themselves to England.

From Marseilles they had found their way to Lyon by following the Rhone valley and then headed for Paris. But there the weather had turned and, although they caught a glimpse of the Eiffel Tower through the fog and low cloud, they could not locate the aerodrome at Le Bourget. The thing was, Chawla, who spoke no French, had been shown its position relative to Paris 'by an obliging Frenchman', who, for his part, spoke no English. Now that they were in the air – and what with the weather – finding their way proved harder than they were expecting. This is one of the odd things about aerial navigation. Once you are lost, unless you have some obvious visual reference point – such as the Eiffel Tower, although, by now, it was far behind them – it is extremely difficult to re-establish your position. Especially in poor visibility. Moreover, if you are freezing cold and tired from the constant battering of your head by a rain-bearing wind hitting you at 75 mph, if your nerves are shredded from the constant lurching of the aeroplane as it bounces around in the bluster, if your hearing is failing from the unrelenting row of an unsilenced engine such that you can barely hear, and if, on top of all this, you haven't the faintest idea how much you need to aim off course because of the wind drift, then, in such circumstances, there is every chance that once lost, you will stay that way. So it is quite understandable that RN and Aspy should have decided to put down in a field.

However, no sooner had they landed than:

a very irate farmer arrived from nowhere and proceeded to lambast us. The less we understood him, the faster he spoke. We could gather that we had done damage to his crop but it took us a long time to realise that what really made him furious was the fact that a perfectly good landing strip was located barely six fields away. All we could say in our frozen state was 'Pardon Monsieur' and with that we started the Moth and hopped over to what turned out to be St Quentin aerodrome.

St Quentin: an ex-First World War airfield close to the Somme battlefield. Approximately 80 miles north-east of Paris. Oh well, at least they were now within striking distance of England. Three hours next day should see them to Dover via Calais.

Staying at a local inn, they enjoyed 'a good meal and some excellent French wine' before turning in for the night, relaxed and ready for the last leg. Early the following morning, they were given a bearing to get them to the coast, after which it was twenty minutes over the water to the White Cliffs – they'd soon be making their way into the history books.

However, just after becoming airborne, they ran into heavy weather with low clouds and strong winds:

At last, we hit the French coast, only by then we were dazed from the cold. After circling the town twice, we were satisfied that it was Calais and England lay only a few minutes away to the west.

But:

Either due to the wind, which was very strong, or a wrong setting of a wrong course, the town was in fact Ostend in Belgium and not Calais in France.

And:

Now the weather was turning really nasty. We were completely frozen and our projected twenty minute crossing began to turn into something quite different and alarming. Instead of the green fields of England we'd heard so much about, all we could see was angry waves below. I could have sworn that it was well over 1½ hours since we last saw land.

Furthermore:

The gravity of our situation suddenly hit us like a bombshell. Here we were, out in a small aircraft, over a dark and angry sea. Instead of finding the British Isles we were flying over an exceedingly inhospitable part of the world. We discussed what could have gone wrong – everything except the very obvious. The fact was, we were far too much to the right and flying over the North Sea.

In the days before GPS, you would find out from the weather forecast the wind speed and direction along your route. You would then use your slide rule to calculate how much you needed to aim off from the bearing you had established by drawing a line on your chart, between your point of origin and your destination. Before reliable weather forecasts were available, however, this was not possible. All you had then was the wind speed and direction at take-off and, if you were able to put a telephone call through to your destination, some idea of what it was doing at the other end. All very helpful except that, before you got there, there was every chance the wind would either have backed or advanced and blown you off course. What you were left with was having simply to follow your progress closely, noting where you were at intervals along your track and, if off course, adjusting accordingly. But if you had no map – well, you really were in the lap of the gods.
So:

To my enquiry, Chawla replied that he had already made a hefty correction to port. By now, he was convinced that the compass had taken too much of the French wine the previous evening.

At least they kept their sense of humour. That was quite something in the circumstances. There being no intercom, they'd have had to have shouted at each other down the Gosport tube.

The problem was:

We had taken off at 11am from Saint Quentin and it was now getting on for 4pm and, once again, our fuel gauge was trying on its disappearing act. We had to make some decision and it had better be the correct decision or else it would be our last one.

Fortunately:

Just then, I spotted a tramp steamer directly below us. Chawla started a series of dives with me gesticulating with my arms. After the second or third attempt at attracting attention, some seamen appeared on deck and waved back to us in greeting. I tried to indicate distress, but in vain. As a final effort, for we could not afford to play this game any longer, I made the letter L for land with my two hands.

But what could this even mean? In the front cockpit of a DH60 Moth, you sit just behind the struts attaching the fuselage to the upper wing. The only way Aspy could have got his message across would have been for Chawla to throttle right back and come alongside the ship at no more than, say, 40 feet above the waves, tipping to starboard while his co-pilot dropped the side-hatch and . . . then what? Touched his elbows together with hands held wide perhaps? Then maybe shrugging his shoulders and waving his arms randomly?

Luckily:

One of the men on deck guessed our predicament and pointed out the nearest land with his right arm and leg.

Semaphore without flags?

This was good enough for us and with a parting farewell and thanks, we turned sharply to port and disappeared in the rain in the direction our unknown benefactor had indicated. Fortunately, we soon struck the coast. We did not know where we were but at least we were now over land. We kept going until again the fuel finally disappeared out of sight.

The fuel gauge on a Moth is actually just a glass tube, mounted at the rear of the tank, in which you watch the level go slowly down. From the moment it vanishes, you have about fifteen minutes of flying time before your engine stops.

So:

I left Chawla to execute the third forced landing of the flight and the fifth since buying the aircraft only a few months back.

They'd made it! Not actually to Croydon as they'd hoped but to Thetford in Norfolk – about as far from Croydon as St Quentin is from Paris, but never mind. Having been put up for the night by a local landowner, they arrived at their intended destination the next day where, rather to their surprise, the two young men found themselves given an elaborate welcome by a reception committee:

the Lord Mayor all dressed up in his striped pants, with tail coat and top hat and his insignia of office prominently displayed.

So this was it.

At last, we had reached here in one piece thanks to some good luck and not forgetting our guardian angels.

All that remained was for Chawla to make his way home by boat and for Aspy to fly back the way they had come, albeit more directly thanks to his belated acquisition of a full set of maps. This he did, duly winning the Aga Khan's trophy just as his mother had prophesied he would. As it turned out, he beat his nearest rival by a mere two and a half hours. It was a magnificent achievement – an achievement made astonishing by the fact that, on the day he landed back at Karachi, he was not yet half a year past his seventeenth birthday.

2

'You really think you know enough? To build a flying machine?'

A century and more after it first flew, the sight and sound of a de Havilland Moth drifting lazily across an English summer sky uplifts the spirit and stirs the heart. With its unmistakable biplane wing layout and the pop-popping of its Gipsy engine, this iconic aircraft puts one in mind of a kinder, gentler world – of milkmaids and their pails, of horses and carts, of bonneted spinsters cycling to evensong, of young men on the village green in striped blazers cheering good-naturedly as willow smacks leather spinning to the boundary and the squire, tweedily benevolent, looks on wreathed in port-soaked smiles.

This is completely wrong, of course. It never was like that. The aeroplane drifts slowly only because it can't go any faster. Those stampeding horses, trapped inside the motor that drags this unwieldy apparatus of wood and fabric and stainless steel about the sky, are at the limit of their powers. Down below, the milkmaid yearns for the day when those newly available milking machines come to her farm. Perhaps then she can swap the stench of cow for the scent of lavender and violets at the cosmetics counter of the department store recently built in the nearby town. As for those spinsters, they feel as doubtful about the Virgin birth as they do about their own virginity and dream instead of entanglements with the men in blazers. The squire is port-soaked all right, but his smiles are at the prospect of an assignation with the young serving girl his wife has just employed.

And yet, is this more cynical view really any closer to the truth? The first flight of Captain de Havilland's Moth, on 22 February 1925, took place hardly more than six years after the armistice ending the Great War. Fourteen years later, there was to be further conflict. But, in the interval between them, the hope for a better future, not just for the few but for the many, seemed a genuinely attainable possibility. This was true not only in Britain but throughout her empire. At home, domestic and agricultural servitude was in the process of giving way to a democracy predicated on rights for everyone. Votes for women came to those over thirty in 1918 and to the over twenty-ones ten years later. So although the catastrophe of war had shell-shocked society as a whole – and this was compounded by the economic misery that followed – by the middle of the twenties, prices had begun to fall and, while unemployment remained high, many in the emerging chemical, automotive and synthetics industries enjoyed an increasingly high standard of living. For anyone with money, the roaring twenties were a grand time to be alive. Clubs and bars, jazz, cocktails and smoky rooms provided the backdrop to what many came to see as a golden age. This was a time when the weekend country house party became a feature of the social circuit and the controversial birth control methods advocated by Marie Stopes began to find their way into polite society as young females bobbed their hair, shortened their skirts and learned to dance in unseemly ways.

One of the things that helped facilitate this social revolution was the huge upsurge in car ownership, epitomised above all by the Model T Ford. In 1920, there were just under 200,000 cars on the road in the UK. By 1923, the figure had doubled. By 1930, the number would rise to well over a million. It was only natural, therefore, that people began to wonder whether the success of the Model T could not be replicated in the air. As it turned out, that was never a realistic prospect. Although the unit cost of aircraft came within reach of middle-class salaries, they were always expensive to hangar, to maintain and to run. On top of that, learning to fly was a big commitment in terms not just of money but of time. To get the most out of private aircraft ownership, you needed plenty of leisure – not least because the weather was often lousy, making forward planning difficult, if not impossible. Aviation for the masses would have to await the technology that enabled production of large transport aircraft. Yet there was, just for a moment, a sense that light aircraft were central to a coming democracy of the air. This is an aspect of modern social history that has been largely overlooked, but the advent of the Moth, coupled with other astonishments such as Lindbergh's arrival in Europe following his transatlantic flight, induced a kind of mania for the air that lasted the best part of a decade.

Of all the aircraft in the history of powered flight, it was the de Havilland Moth that came closest to realising the impossible dream of aviation for all. Without question, it is the one in which people had the greatest adventures. And it is the de Havilland Moth that most readily symbolises a world which then seemed so full of hope and possibility – a world where the gulags and the gas chambers lay safely in the future.

The Moth's designer was the visionary son of an angry and disappointed Victorian parson. Born in 1882, Geoffrey de Havilland came into the world on the cusp of one version of it disappearing and another rising to take its place. That year was the last in which an amateur team won the FA Cup (the Old Etonians beat Blackburn Rovers) and the first in which the English cricket team lost a test match on home ground (to the Australians, inevitably). Six years before, Alexander Graham Bell had patented the first telephone. In 1886, Carl Benz patented the first motor car. Before the young Geoffrey was out of short trousers, Otto Lilienthal made the first of over five hundred controlled flights in a glider. Yet in 1961, four years before de Havilland's death, Yuri Gagarin had returned safely from his orbit of the earth. There was never an epoch like it. Even in the event that humans attain the ability to travel via teleporter, it is unlikely the psychological impact could be as great as that conferred by the dawn of mass air transportation, which, to a significant degree, was brought into being by this modest and unassuming man.

In his autobiography, GDH, as he was affectionately known by friends and colleagues, records his very first memory as the occasion when, one Guy Fawkes Night, his father let off fireworks and he witnessed 'a ball of fire going over our house'. This was, he continued, 'an achievement that seemed to me of worldwide importance'. A later memory was of the time when he and his elder brother, Ivon, witnessed the ascent, to the accompaniment of a brass band, of a passenger-carrying hot-air balloon from a local fairground:

> Fascinated, we watched it until it finally disappeared in the far distance and at a great height. Neither Ivon nor I ever forgot that balloon, and we would [often] talk about flying and the practicability of man one day conquering the air.

The de Havillands are a family of Norman descent whose ancestry can be traced back, via a Bailiff of Guernsey – and a prisoner of Napoleon – to the time of William the Conqueror. Young Geoffrey seems not to have been particularly close to either of his parents, however. His father, Charles, a Church of England vicar, who had a pronounced limb length discrepancy necessitating use of a special boot, was an otherwise fine-looking but deeply frustrated man. He had been educated at Merchant Taylors, the famous sixteenth-century public school, and then at Christchurch College, Oxford. Acknowledged as a brilliant sermoniser, the Reverend Charles de Havilland had, for all this, several unfortunate habits including a hot temper, a pathological tendency to hoarding, a misplaced certainty that he would one day write a book that would shake the world, an inadequate fortune (to his way of thinking) and complete faith in the rightness of his opinions.

'I have found out why we get so little electric light,' he once announced to his astonished family. It had, he explained, nothing to do with the decrepitude of the oil-fired generator used to power it. The problem was that 'in some rooms the light bulbs have been taken out of their sockets, and this allows the electricity to stream out of the empty lamp holders'. Alas, there was nothing anyone could do to persuade him otherwise.

On top of these unfortunate characteristics, the Reverend Charles bore a deep resentment towards his wife's family. The reason for this was the uncomfortable fact that Alice, GDH's mother, was the one with the money. Moreover, it was money that had been acquired through trade. Grandfather Jason Saunders was a keen hunting man 'of humble yeoman farmer stock', who strode about in bowler hat and breeches, wearing a stock pin mounted with a miniature horseshoe surrounding a fox's head. Although he looked like a caricature of Mr Jorrocks, the fictional Victorian hunting squire, he was nonetheless a man with a keen business sense. Building up the family fortune by founding a removal company in Oxford, he was able to expand greatly his landownership and, in due course, to acquire the imposing manor house at Medley, just over the river from Oxford city's Port Meadow. Yet, despite Charles having being bailed out frequently by Saunders, he and the rest of the de Havillands looked down on him as their social inferior. Worse, GDH recalled how his father had 'a strongly held belief that well-off people should be *glad* to lend him money and not pester him' for repayment. However, 'This made for considerable awkwardness when we were sent on errands . . . and told bluntly to pay our bills or get out.'

In spite of the snobbish animosity the de Havillands felt for Alice's father, Grandfather Saunders was evidently man enough not to allow any feelings he might have had in the matter to intrude on his relationship either with his daughter or his grandchildren, and it was of his time here, at his grandfather's house, that the young Geoffrey had his fondest childhood memories. It was here, too, that GDH developed his passion for the natural world. At one point, he became fascinated with the pike lurking in the River Thames that ran along the eastern boundary of the farm. When Ivon and his father – on a rare visit – together with Odey, the groom, brought back not one but two of the sinister creatures, young Geoffrey was beside himself with excitement. What was even more thrilling was the fact that poor Odey had been bitten on the thumb when extracting the spinner:

'Did it bleed?'

'Yes it did.' Ivon told me and, when I asked how much, he added 'About an egg-cup full.'

I looked with awe at Odey's bandaged thumb, and knew that this was the perfect end to a day's fishing. Bitten by a pike!

From that day on, the young GDH's fascination with pike turned to obsession. He read everything he could about them and listened to every exciting story he could persuade people to tell. One of these was told by a local countryman who explained the art of catching them by using a bootlace as a noose and patiently drawing it through the water without touching the fish until, at the right moment, you suddenly draw it tight and flick the creature onto the grassy bank. Using a variation of this method, Geoffrey succeeded in making several catches of his own. It was not only the aquatic life of the farm that inspired him, however. He also took delight in learning the names and calls of all the birds in the nearby woodland such that, in later life, he enjoyed nothing better than the natural history expeditions he and his wife made to Africa. He was an early convert to the concept of shooting wild game with a camera rather than a rifle, though he did on one occasion use a gun. It was an episode which he found 'so completely distasteful' that he never did it again.

The budding aircraft designer's closest relationship during his childhood and after was with Ivon. Together the two of them would build, among other things, working model steam engines and, on one memorable occasion, a homemade artillery piece. This, astonishingly, they used in mock battles against some of the local village lads. A three-foot-long gas pipe mounted on a mail-cart, loaded with saltpetre rammed down with wads of paper it 'made a terrific roar' when it went off, though their opponents 'were not much intimidated – with reason, for the danger was much greater to us than to them'. There was also an elaborate model railway that the brothers built in the garden. But of all their projects, the 'most interesting, prolonged and expensive experiments in which Ivon and I indulged were with the electrical plant at Crux Easton' – this being the house to which the family moved when he was twelve, courtesy of Jason Saunders. Clearly worried for his daughter and her young family, now increased to four children, the old man had stumped up the cash for an 'avowson' (an ecclesiastical appointment) near Newbury for his improvident son-in-law. Several early attempts to modernise the electrical system brought only modest improvements. Success was eventually achieved with a Crossley oil engine 'which worked faultlessly, gave us constant electric light and required little attention'. Although it had been, he admitted, quite appallingly expensive, 'we had at least gained a great deal of pleasure and practical experience' that would stand them both in good stead in later years.

Unfortunately, the family's move did little to improve the

fraught situation at home and Alice, driven frantic by the permanent embarrassment and frustration caused by her husband's recklessness with money, rowed often with Charles, suffering, as a result, recurrent bouts of depression and illness. One might have thought that, in light of this unhappiness, Geoffrey might have found respite in his time at St Edward's School in Oxford where he was sent to board at the age of thirteen. He had enjoyed his prep school – where he won a modest reputation as a slow bowler – but Teddies (as it is still known) he hated.

Despite his obvious bent for engineering, when at seventeen GDH left school – without passing a single exam – he was sent by his father to study with a clergyman in the adjacent county of Gloucestershire, with a view to his entering the church. But there followed an event that was to change the course of his life. He learned that the owners of a local bicycle dealership had acquired two 3½ hp Mercedes Benz motor cars and that these were available for hire with a driver. Together with a friend, he saved enough money for a visit home. 'It was an epic trip, sustaining speeds on level stretches at anything up to 15 mph . . . ' he later wrote, tongue-in-cheek. But after 'that short drive I knew that my future life lay in the world of mechanical travel. The fascination of independently powered and swift transportation from place to place gained a hold which was never to relax through all my working life.'

The church's loss was aviation's gain, though to begin with the young man set his sights on the car industry. Thanks again to the generosity of Grandfather Saunders, GDH and his brother were able to buy, second-hand, a two-cylinder, 6 horsepower Panhard-Levassor. This had solid rear wheels of large diameter and smaller front wheels with pneumatic tyres, which kept bursting, and an antediluvian – not to say potentially lethal – starting mechanism that required a pair of tubes to be heated until red hot by means of a Bunsen burner. Physically resembling a sort of conservatory on wheels, the car was already long out of date. But, as with the house electrical system, the vehicle's main importance was as a test bed for the brothers' experiments. Because of its marked tendency to topple over given the slightest turn on the steering wheel, they began by lengthening the chassis. Next, they installed magneto ignition. It wasn't long, however, before it was replaced with a pony trap on account of an incident involving the local coachbuilder, Mr Hamilton:

With his finely chiselled features and long black beard, [Mr Hamilton] looked like one of the Apostles. He certainly needed saintly patience as far as the Panhard and the de Havillands were concerned. I was driving him back to Highclere one day when something went wrong and the car set off at a tangent towards the ditch. I was quite unable to correct the swerve and jammed on the brakes as we struck the verge. Hamilton himself disappeared from the passenger seat beside me and the next I saw of him he was sitting in the hedge facing me.[1]

By this time, GDH had enrolled as a trainee at the Crystal Palace School of Engineering, while Ivon was a student apprentice at Brush Electrical Engineering in Loughborough. The two brothers now embarked on a project to build a steampowered racing car. Working in their spare time and holidays, and 'with the headlong exuberance of youth and inexperience', they turned the stable block into a workshop fitted with two lathes, a planing machine, drilling equipment and a separate oil generator for power. Alas, despite backing from a wealthy enthusiast, their money ran out before the car could be completed and they were forced to attend the event they had been convinced they were going to win – the 1903 Gordon Bennett Cup – as mere spectators.

Next, GDH set about designing and building a motorcycle engine in the workshop at the Crystal Palace school. Bringing it home to Crux Easton, he fitted his engine to a frame and added a petrol tank. Unfortunately, the leather belt drive he had ordered was slow in coming and impatience got the better of him. Installing a piece of tarred rope in its place, he wheeled the contraption to the top of the hill and set off down it. First the rope fell off. Then the brakes failed. The rider was left to choose between a wall at the bottom and the jagged flint of the 'road' itself. Choosing the latter, GDH was rewarded with deep gashes to his knees and hands. Undeterred, he continued to develop the motorcycle engine in his free time, eventually selling the drawings and patterns for the princely sum of £5. It became the basis of the Blackburne motorcycle range.

His first salaried job was with a company that manufactured steam engines but it did not take de Havilland long to realise that neither his nor *the* future lay in steam. After two years, he left to join the Wolseley Tool and Motor Car Company in Birmingham as a thirty-shilling-a-week draughtsman. He found the work, under 'harsh orders and a harsh régime' dull and uninspiring and resigned after only a year with 'no idea where I would go or exactly what I would do. All I knew for certain was that I had to be my own master and do exciting creative work. Whatever it was, I was sure I could make a success of it.'

At the time, it still looked as if the young man would remain within the car industry. Ivon was by now working for Iris and had designed their entry for the second ever British Motor Show in 1905. Featuring a shaft drive and an aesthetically pleasing diamond-shaped radiator, the car boasted many novel features, including a cleverly sprung chassis. It was with immense pride that GDH stood in for his older brother on the trade stand when Ivon was forced to miss the show due to a bout of ill health. Pride turned to grief, however, when Ivon took a turn for the worse. A bad cold developed into pneumonia and, this being long before the advent of penicillin, he died before the year was out.

It was a cruel loss, not just because the two young men were so close but also because it was clear they were destined to do great things together. They had recently developed a mutual interest in aviation and it seems likely that they would quickly have become rivals to the Wright brothers. As it was, GDH went to work for another automotive company – a bus manufacturer in Walthamstow – for two more years before he finally determined to go cap in hand to Grandfather Saunders and ask for a sum to enable him to design and build an aeroplane.

'It was in the evening and he was in the sitting-room, wearing his usual smoking jacket. He had a long cigar alight, and beside him there was a whisky decanter and a glass on a silver tray.' They began by talking about buses and old Saunders ventured his opinion that they would surely soon be coming to Oxford:

> 'They'll have to come to Oxford one day,' I said in agreement and, taking this as my cue, went on rapidly. 'But I've now got a far greater interest than buses. It's flying. That's what I'm

keen to get into now. In fact, I'm so keen to design and build one, I'm trying to find someone to put up the money . . . '

My grandfather looked at me in silence for some seconds. At last he asked me, 'You really think you know enough about it to build a flying machine?'

'Yes, I'm certain I do.'

There was another silence while my grandfather gave un-divided attention to the length of ash hanging precariously at the end of his cigar. 'I intended leaving you a thousand pounds,' he said to me at last. 'But if you prefer to have it now, you can.'

This was beyond the young man's wildest expectations.

I hardly knew what to say. But I did manage to thank him, probably quite inadequately, before I left – my mind already hard at work dreaming and planning the future.

To get an idea of the value of £1,000 in 1908 in comparison with its value today, it is no use simply adjusting for inflation. Instead, you have to ask yourself what it would cost to buy today what it could back then. In GDH's case, he was able to pay an engineering assistant, his friend Frank Hearle (later, both company managing director and his brother-in-law; Hearle married GDH's sister, Ione, a fiery socialist), a living wage. In addition, his grandfather's money allowed him to pay himself a modest salary – needed because he was by now courting and in 1909 married Louie (née Thomas, his younger brother's governess) – to run a car and to buy the machinery necessary to fit out a workshop, together with materials for not one but two prototypes (including an engine of his own design built for him by Iris, his late brother's firm, for £250), to rent a drawing office and a workshop (the latter in Fulham – he was still living in London at the time) and, the following year, to take on an apprentice and then buy a hangar and workshop near his father's house from the future Lord Brabazon (himself an early aviator). This was at Seven Barrows, an area of gently sloping downland adjacent to the modern A34 (where a blue plaque on the verge honours de Havilland). The start-up costs of such an enterprise today would run far into seven figures – not including the funds required for negotiating with the Civil Aviation Authority and its engineers and inspectors.[2]

Fortunately for de Havilland, the demands of bureaucracy were then non-existent and he was able to proceed purely according to the dictates of his own judgement. Almost at once, he co-opted Louie into the workforce. She was put in charge of the fabric, which, using an ordinary hand-turned Singer sewing machine, she stitched together ready for covering the flying surfaces. Once in place, it would be painted with dope – a liquid cellulose substance that, when dry, shrinks the fabric drum-tight. By December 1909, the very first de Havilland aircraft began its taxying trials, during which seemingly endless snags and disappointments manifested themselves. A gearbox disintegrated, the propshaft bent, the carburettor needed replacing. Working 'day after day and often late into the night', GDH and Hearle began to wonder whether they would ever get their creation airborne. When at last they were ready to try for an actual take-off, they found the weather against them. Eventually, though, they did manage some actual trial runs when the wind was just right and everything seemed set. Unfortunately, the aeroplane resolutely refused to leave the ground. Naturally, the two men refused to give up. They would simply have to find a means of going faster. This they did by going further and further uphill to begin the take-off run.

At last, on a date later in December 1909 which GDH did not record, with Hearle, his father and his surviving brother, Hereward, as witnesses, on a perfect winter's day – a light breeze barely ruffled the handkerchief held in his outstretched hand – the twenty-eight-year-old designer started his engine, climbed into the crude basket that passed for a cockpit and began his fateful journey. At this time, only a handful of controlled flights had been successfully completed on British soil. In April of that year, the future Lord Brabazon had become the first ever Englishman to fly a heavier-than-air machine, completing a distance of all of 450 feet. In July, Alliott Verdun Roe flew the first aeroplane of British design (the Americans and French were at this time ahead of the field) for just a hundred feet. During that summer, the first attempt to fly the Channel was made, though engine trouble brought it to a watery end. In the intervening short period, much progress had been made, but if de Havilland was successful, his would be only the second aircraft of British design and manufacture to accomplish humankind's oldest dream.

Turning the flimsy contraption round, with Hearle guiding the wing-tip, GDH eased the throttle forward until it was fully open and he was hurtling downhill, faster than he ever had before. This was the moment! Hauling back hard on the control column, the aircraft leapt almost vertically into the air and—

Disaster. The piano-wire rigging wires ripped out of their fittings, the woodwork snapped, the main-spar splintered, the wing fabric tore as the whole contraption folded and fell heavily to the ground.

Stunned and rising unsteadily to his feet to climb out, de Havilland was struck on the arm by a still-rotating propeller blade just as his father retreated from the scene, speechless with shock.

At once realising his mistake – in his determination to get airborne he had pulled back too hard, causing an overload of the structure – GDH wasted no time in arranging transport of all reusable parts (luckily this included the engine) back to the Fulham workshop. He and Hearle were completely certain that they would soon be back and that next time they would be successful.

Marvellous to relate, even at this late stage, de Havilland had yet to see an actual aeroplane in flight. It was not until April 1910 that he did so. Arriving at 5 a.m., he was just in time to watch the rather uncertain take-off of Claude Grahame-White in his attempt on the *Daily Mail*'s astonishing £10,000 prize for the first flight between London and Manchester – to be completed within twenty-four hours and with no more than two landings. Alas for Grahame-White, on the final leg of the journey, with fewer than 70 miles to go, engine trouble forced him down and, though the problem was put right, and repairs made to his undercarriage, high winds prevented onward travel and he was forced to abandon the attempt.

As GDH was later to recall, watching the intrepid aviator take off for his distant objective was a 'thrilling sight'. Unfortunately, it did not yield 'any practical hints on how to get an aircraft into the air' and it was almost three months before he was satisfied with the second iteration of his own design. One major modification was the reconfiguration of the engine which now sat in-line driving a single propeller in place of two. Other developments included the use of a pair of bicycle wheels and a tailskid for the undercarriage, while the overall structure was made 'simpler, lighter and more robust'.

By the summer of 1910, they were ready to begin taxy trials again. Making minor adjustments after almost every run as he tried out each of the controls, within three weeks GDH was confident enough to make another concerted attempt at becoming airborne. This time, he was content to ease the machine off the ground just a matter of inches – which he succeeded in doing over a distance of about twenty yards. It was hardly Icarus redux. Yet de Havilland counted this among his greatest triumphs. He knew that if he could sustain flight at six inches above ground, 'there was no reason why, with equal ease, I should not rise to six hundred feet – so long as I took things slowly and carefully'.

Caution was doubly well-advised. Not only did de Havilland wish to keep himself out of hospital, but Grandfather Saunders' funds were getting worryingly low. If he crashed again, that would be the end of his career even if he himself survived.

It was, however, not very many days before he daringly took the craft right up into the air, to 'an appalling height' from which he could no longer land straight ahead, and making his first gentle turn, landed back in the field from which he had set out. This was the moment of real triumph. Thereafter, progress came in ever more confident stages – to the point where heights of a hundred feet and figure of eight turns became commonplace.

Meanwhile Louie, despite her work at the sewing machine, remained somewhat hesitant about the project. Fortunately, GDH managed to persuade her to come down from London to lodge with his parents in the country. It was there that she bore their first child, also named Geoffrey, and it was where, just eight weeks later, that, babe in arms, she climbed gamely

aboard for a first flight – only the second British female to
take to the air and her baby, at that time, almost certainly the
youngest passenger in the world.

Throughout the spring and summer of 1911, de Havilland
continued to fly and modify his aircraft. But, by now, he really
was out of cash. What was he to do? His achievement was
highly impressive but no one at the time seriously thought that
powered flight had much practical use. The government of the
day thought the proven concept of lighter-than-air craft a more
promising avenue for research. Although Louis Blériot had by
this time achieved the first Channel crossing, of much greater
interest and concern to the War Office was the recent ten-hour
flight, over 240 miles, of a Zeppelin airship in Germany.

It was by chance that GDH met with an old colleague at
that year's Motor Show. When he explained that he was at a bit
of a loss, the friend, who was now working at the government's
Army Balloon Factory in Farnborough, said that he would have
a word with his new boss who was much more sympathetic to
the aeroplane than his predecessor had been. The upshot was
that following a promising interview and a nail-biting wait of
several weeks, de Havilland was the recipient of a cheque of
£400 for his aeroplane and the offer of a job for both himself
and Frank Hearle ('I could not leave him out').

With what pride he wrote to his grandfather offering to pay
back part of the original gift, we can only guess.

'You keep it, my boy,' the old man replied. 'You'll need it
later.' He was right, of course. There were to be several times
during the next decade and a half when de Havilland found
himself on the brink again.

Although the job was a godsend, GDH now found himself
part of a typically dysfunctional government agency. He and

Hearle with their newfangled contraptions were regarded as upstarts who would presumably soon go the way of the previous in-house designer, the aristocratic J. W. Dunne, who disappeared as a result of budget cuts. According to de Havilland, Dunne deserved better. His swept-wing design for the Factory did, in fact, enjoy some success as a float-plane operated by the American army and his experiments with aircraft stability yielded valuable research data. At a demonstration, Orville Wright himself was astonished to see Dunne take his hands off the controls and write notes while actually in flight. Unfortunately, ill health precluded Dunne's continued career in aviation and he retired to write books. His first, *Sunshine and the Dry Fly*, is regarded as a classic by trout fishers, while his second, *An Experiment with Time*, which the more down to earth de Havilland described as a 'curious and puzzling work', to this day retains cult status with students of the supernatural.

The Army Balloon Factory's experiments with lighter-than-air craft continued alongside de Havilland's re-established heavier-than-air research department. Unfortunately, they were not notably successful. One airship suffered an accident in its shed before it could be flown. When eventually it did take to the air, its main spar broke and it took on a V-shape as it floated gently and ignominiously to the ground. On another occasion, having made some unsteady circuits of the testing ground, the wind speed rose, the pilot lost control and it ended up draped over a private house.

Following these embarrassments, it did not take long from the initial axeing – eighteen months, to be exact – to restoration of the heavier-than-air budget and, with it, a change of name. The Army Balloon Factory became the Royal Aircraft Factory. In the meantime, de Havilland wasted no time in designing a follow-up to his 'Number Two' aeroplane, as he called it. This was another pusher (that is to say, the engine was mounted behind the cockpit such that the propeller pushed the aircraft along), officially designated the FE2, in which he successfully demonstrated a one-hundred-mile round trip culminating in a 'dead-stick' (that is, an engine-off) landing, gliding down from 2,000 feet.

Unfortunately, the name change to the Royal Aircraft Factory was soon rendered a misnomer. Vested interests within private industry ensured – on grounds of unfair competition – that the government was not permitted actually to manufacture aircraft, only to repair and restore them. It was thus under increasingly awkward conditions that de Havilland continued his work for the government. In spite of this, he did manage to create, test-fly and develop what proved to be, for its time, an outstanding aircraft, the BE2. With its tractor engine (in front of the pilot, pulling the aeroplane along), it had a performance superior to its competitors and, with de Havilland himself at the controls, set an altitude record of over 10,500 feet, which stood for almost two years. First flown in February 1912, the aircraft is a clear progenitor of the Moth with its braced biplane structure and the graceful de Havilland tail. Altogether, 3,500 of the type were produced – in five different variants, ranging from 'A' to 'E' – reflecting its employment in a number of different roles, including as an artillery spotter, as reconnaissance aircraft, as a trainer and even as a fighter forming the backbone of the Royal Flying Corps (RFC) during the first year of the war. Unfortunately, when, in early 1915, the Fokker Eindecker appeared with an engine-synchronised interrupter gear that enabled its machine gun to be fired 'through' the propeller, the BE2, like the RFC itself, found itself hopelessly outgunned.

Another (very attractive) design produced by de Havilland just before the war and intended as a 'scout' or single-seat fighter aircraft, was his SE series. Although he crashed the SE1, breaking his jaw in the process, with a modified elevator and rudder the aeroplane impressed the RFC and saw service at the outbreak of war when, for a time, it was able to outpace anything the enemy had to offer. The SE1's one drawback was, of course, its inability to fire its armament forward.

As war loomed, de Havilland's work at the Royal Aircraft Factory was increasingly resented by others working in the fledgling field of aircraft design and development. Whereas he had a large budget, a ready-made and highly skilled workforce to call on and whatever materials he required, the privateers had to raise their own funds, train their workforce and pay for everything themselves. The most vocal opponent of state-subsidised research and development was Noel Pemberton Billing, at one time a professional boxer, who had made a £500 bet with Frederick Handley Page, the industrialist and designer of the first successful long-range bomber, that he could learn to fly within twenty-four hours. Having won the bet, Pemberton Billing founded his own aircraft company. At once, he began to lobby against the Royal Aircraft Factory in a campaign that, with surprising ease, succeeded in ousting the then superintendent of the Factory, eventually causing it to be abolished altogether.

Pemberton Billing was subsequently rewarded for his de-fence of free enterprise when he sold his company for a good sum, even though none of its products were notably successful. Using the proceeds to propel him into politics, he also founded his own magazine, *The Imperialist*, in which to disseminate his decidedly idiosyncratic theories. He then won a seat at the

1916 general election and was soon distinguishing himself by challenging a fellow MP to a fight in the boxing ring. This was in 1917. A year later, he was ejected from the House, feet-first, following a dispute over parliamentary procedure. But it was his magazine that caused the greatest controversy.

A century later, the libel case in which he became involved looks eerily reminiscent of the American QAnon conspiracy movement. In various articles, Pemberton Billing alleged that German agents, mainly Jews, were blackmailing '47,000 highly-placed British perverts' to 'propagate evils which all decent men thought had perished in Sodom and Lesbia'. Worse, the Kaiser knew the name of a vast number of high-ranking homosexuals who were listed in the so-called *Berlin Black Book* of the Mbret (king) of Albania. This supposed document was alleged to give details of how these agents planned to exterminate 'the manhood of Britain' by luring them into unnatural acts through the 'defloration of children' and other obscenities. As if this were not enough, Pemberton Billing also put his name to an article entitled 'The Cult of the Clitoris' which insinuated that the popular actress, Maud Allan, was in league with the conspirators. Allan sued, naturally enough, but, such was the temper of the age, she lost.

GDH's description of Pemberton Billing as 'an eccentric and unreliable person' was mild in the extreme. Yet it is clear that the better man was not given to resentment. Instead of wanting to settle scores, GDH was far more concerned with getting on with the business of developing aircraft which could take on the German air force. However, as a result of Pemberton Billing's campaign, just weeks before the outbreak of war, Geoffrey de Havilland found himself without a job.

3

Captain

Fortunately, both for the war effort and for the man himself, as soon as word got out that he was available, Geoffrey de Havilland was offered the job of chief designer at the recently founded Aircraft Manufacturing Company (or Airco as it was more generally known). Headed by George Holt Thomas, Airco was to become, by the end of the war, the largest aircraft producer in the world. 'Brilliantly clever as well as kind and likeable', according to GDH, Holt Thomas 'possessed a knowledge of business only equalled by his ignorance of engineering'.[1] It was the ideal partnership. Holt Thomas had been quick to recognise the enormous potential of heavier-than-air craft and had sponsored the eventual winning entry of the *Daily Mail*'s London to Manchester air race (Claude Grahame-White whom GDH had seen take-off was, in the end, beaten by Louis Paulhan), and it seems likely that Holt had had his eye on de Havilland for a long time. In any case, it was an inspired move. De Havilland's design genius was responsible for four of the most successful of the war years and, at its end, almost a quarter of the 20,890 in the RAF's inventory were de Havilland progeny – not to mention the thousands more within those of allied air forces – all of them built by Airco and its subsidiaries. Personally, Holt Thomas made out like the proverbial bandit.

For a moment, however, it looked as though war service would intervene. Although too old to fight, as he was already on the Royal Flying Corps reserve, GDH was immediately ordered into uniform and, within a week of Britain declaring war, found himself posted to Montrose on the east coast of Scotland. For the next fortnight, he flew a Blériot monoplane on submarine patrols along the coast down to the Firth of Forth – despite the fact that he and his co-spotters had only the haziest idea how to distinguish between an allied and an enemy vessel. Moreover, the fact was, without a radio – a wireless apparatus one should say – the soonest he could report any sighting would be when he landed back at base, by which time, of course, the sub could have got up to all manner of no good. Fortunately, this pointless squandering of de Havilland's talents was quickly recognised and, before the end of the month, he had returned to Farnborough.

Back at his desk, the first de Havilland creation for Airco, was the DH1, a two-seat armed reconnaissance machine of pusher configuration. The pilot sat in the rear while the observer/gunner sat in a nacelle at the front. Frustratingly, development of the type was hindered by lack of availability of the 120 hp Beardmore engine that it was designed to use. In the meantime, it had to get along with just the 70 hp provided by the default motor (a Renault V8 which was itself the progenitor of the de Havilland Gipsy series). His next design was the first effective counter to the Fokker Scourge, the DH2.*

Like its predecessor – which, by dint of working round the clock was rushed into service in July 1915 – the DH2 was a pusher. But rather than have a crew of two, this was a single-seat, high-speed 'scout'. Again, the pilot sat in a nacelle forward of both wings and engine. This gave him an unrestricted field of fire to his front, though operating the gun with its swivel mounting while at the same time flying the aeroplane proved demanding, to say the least. But the aeroplane was fast, manoeuvrable and had an outstanding rate of climb – even if it was in turn soon outclassed by German aircraft such as the Albatros. That said, even against the Albatros it was capable of holding its own. On one famous occasion, the Germans' leading ace of the day, Oswald Boelcke – author of the first ever manual of air combat tactics, the *Dicta Boelcke* – was pressing an attack on a DH2 from 24 Squadron when the undercarriage of his best friend and fellow ace, Erwin Boehme, caught him a glancing blow. This caused a tear in the fabric of one of the upper wings of his aircraft. Within seconds, the whole surface was denuded of its covering, rendering the Albatros uncontrollable and resulting in a fatal crash. Meanwhile, the DH2 escaped – as did that of another member of the squadron attacked by Manfred von Richthofen in the same encounter.

Certainly the most important of de Havilland's war designs

---

* Here, it should be noted that all de Havilland's designs – even, when he had his own company and was not the lead designer, as occasionally happened – were given a project number prefixed, for the obvious reason, by the letters D and H. By the time of his death almost half a century later, the number had risen to more than 120 distinct projects, albeit that fewer than half actually left the drawing board.

was his DH4 day bomber. Writing to GDH in October 1916 when the aeroplane was still in early development, the future Lord Trenchard, noted how 'it is very quick in turns, with very sensitive fore and aft controls ... I think it will be a first rate machine'. With a performance far superior to that of any other single aircraft of the time, the DH4 was capable of speeds of up to 140 mph and had a matchless climb performance. Highly effective in its role as a bomber, it was also widely used for reconnaissance. Nothing the enemy had could touch it.

Although de Havilland would have liked to do all the test-flying himself, by this time he had to delegate responsibility for this work to a third party, engaging the well-known B. C. Hucks to fulfil the role. Hucks was the first Englishman to have looped the loop. He was also – more soberly – the first to have received a radio message while airborne (in 1911). Aside from his piloting skills, Hucks was also responsible for designing and developing a mechanical starter for larger aero-engines which could not be hand-swung. This remained in wide use until the 1930s when self-starters became standard.

A shy and retiring man on the ground, Hucks had a reputation for being both careful and fearless. Added to this, he had extraordinary ability in the air. Flying the DH4, he could get it to do 'evolutions never seen before'.[2] Unfortunately, this was not always appreciated. When he took up Airco's chief engine man on one occasion, GDH and his design team watched with satisfaction as Hucks put the aeroplane through his usual spectacular routine and noted the waving passenger's obvious delight. Alas, it turned out that the poor man had been trying to signal his distress and when they landed was found to be huddled in the front seat 'in a state of near collapse'.

On another occasion, GDH, together with a different

colleague went up with Hucks on a proving flight in one of the later designs. Climbing all the way to 18,000 feet, ground observers watched as the aeroplane went into a steep spiral over the airfield, pulling out only just in time. Hucks, realising that a crash was imminent, had taken control of the aircraft. Turning to de Havilland, he yelled at his boss over the roar of the engine, 'I thought you were supposed to be flying it!' To which de Havilland replied, 'I thought YOU were supposed to be flying it!'

With respect to the DH4 itself, pilots were unanimous in praise both of its performance and its docility. It was really only vulnerable to attack in the climb and in the descent, and it was greatly respected by friend and foe alike. Its one drawback was the position of its fuel tank which sat between the front and rear cockpits. This meant that the crew, having to rely on a Gosport tube for communication, often had difficulty responding quickly enough to enemy threats. What was worse, if hit, the crew would almost invariably be incinerated, earning it the unfortunate nickname 'the flaming coffin'. Nonetheless, so successful was the DH4 that it became a staple not just of the newly founded Royal Air Force, but of the United States Army Air Service, too, with over 3,500 examples built – many of which remained in service until the late twenties, with civilianised versions continuing far into the thirties.

Another highly successful de Havilland design of the war years was the DH6 trainer. The urgent need for an aeroplane that could meet the demand for a rapidly expanding RFC and was cheap to buy, easy to build, somewhat demanding to fly, yet viceless when flown properly, saw GDH come up with his most strictly utilitarian machine. Sacrificing form to function, its uniformly straight-sided components robbed the aeroplane of any aesthetic appeal. But with interchangeable upper and lower wings and similarly interchangeable tailplanes and control surfaces, it was as easy to repair as it was quick to build. It did, however, earn a number of unflattering nicknames such as the 'Dung Hunter' – albeit the reasoning behind this one is obscure. There is no record of it being particularly prone to nosing over – any tailwheel aeroplane will do just that if you let the speed get too low on touchdown. In all, some 2,282 DH6s were built and it was the mainstay of the training fleet until superseded by the Avro 504.

The other significant de Havilland design of the war years was the DH9, a long-range light bomber intended to replace the DH4. Ordered in large numbers by the RFC, at first it proved to be underpowered and, in fact, not even equal to the DH4. The problem was engine availability. It was not until the advent of the DH9A, fitted with the 400 hp Liberty water-cooled V12, that it reached its full potential as the outstanding strategic bomber of the war. The first squadron to be equipped with them was No. 110 Squadron – bestowed, remarkably, as a gift to the RFC from the Nizam of Hyderabad. The Indian prince was at that time reputed to be the seventh richest man in the world thanks to the presence of the Golconda diamond mines within his realm. In turn, his DH9As gifted ten and a half tons of high explosives to Germany's industrial centres, unloading them in a succession of daring daylight raids. By this time – autumn 1918 – the Germans were exhausted and the raids helped exacerbate their acute shortage of munitions, which led directly to their unconditional surrender a few months later.

The DH9 remained the lynchpin of the RAF's bomber force until the last ones were withdrawn from service in 1930.

It was also used extensively in policing the increasingly restless outposts of the Empire, notably those territories of the Middle East that had come under British control following the collapse of the Ottoman Empire. Its most unlikely use was by Soviet Russia. Initially flown in support of the anti-revolutionary White Russian forces against Lenin's Bolsheviks during the 1919 Russian civil war, later the type was illegally copied and produced in large numbers by the Communists. It became the standard bomber for the Soviet air force and saw action, among other places, in China in support of Chiang Kai-shek's Nationalists.

Altogether, de Havilland designs went on to account for 30 per cent of all trainers, fighters and bombers deployed by the British and American air forces during the course of the war. It was an extraordinary achievement.

As for the man himself, gazetted Captain in the spring of 1916, the rank he was invariably known by until he was knighted three decades later, de Havilland ended the war one of the most respected and successful aircraft designers in the world. To have gone from amateur enthusiast to progenitor of some of the most successful aircraft of the First World War in fewer than ten years is remarkable enough. Yet, when one considers that at the time of those first uncertain circuits of Seven Barrows, aviation seemed to most to be destined to be nothing more than a curiosity – a rich man's diversion – it looks almost fantastical.

Of course, there were some others in the same position: Tommy Sopwith being one obvious example, Anton Fokker another. But the achievement of these pioneers – especially when considered in terms of the relatively short history of human civilisation – in taking the aeroplane from trembling

cat's cradle of wooden stringers and piano wire with their
stuttering engines to screaming dogfighters and ocean-crossing
troop transporters in less than a decade, verges on the miraculous. What was more, GDH's employer, Airco, was now
the world's largest aircraft manufacturer and he himself was
the prosperous (though by no means rich) father of four children. Brimful of ideas for the future of aviation in peacetime,
Captain de Havilland seemed set fair for a glittering career. But
then, just weeks before the war ended, all was put in jeopardy
as those short, sharp years of unparalleled intensity caught up
with him in an instant and, unable so much as to raise himself
from his bed, he suffered a catastrophic nervous breakdown
which put him out of work for the best part of a year.

4

The de Havilland Aircraft Company

Following the armistice, the general consensus within the aeronautical industry was that, as soon as everyone had settled down a bit, the aeroplane would come into its own. Released from the bondage of war, people would be wanting to go places and the airways would take them there – at unprecedented speed. Of course, there would be a short period of adjustment first and, in the meantime, everyone would have to diversify. Airco's 4,500 strong workforce was put to manufacturing everything from motorcycles and car bodies, to bicycles and household furniture, even to milk churns. At the same time, some of the stock of aircraft was repurposed. By widening the fuselage of the DH9A to provide accommodation for four – two pairs of seats facing one another in a glazed cabin – a new design, the DH16 was swiftly brought into being. This formed the basis of Holt Thomas' latest venture, Aircraft Transport and Travel Ltd, which, he was convinced, would quickly grow to absorb a large part of Airco's production capacity. Competitors would doubtless come into being but they would be buying Airco's products too, so it was a win-win as far as the company was concerned.

The inaugural flight of Holt Thomas' airline took place on 25 August 1919, the first of a daily schedule between London (Hounslow) and Paris (Le Bourget) at £20 per passenger and 5 shillings for a letter. At the same time, sales teams were sent to the furthest reaches of the Empire and beyond carrying glossy brochures of the DH17, GDH's 1918 design for a large, twin-engine biplane capable of carrying a crew of two and sixteen passengers, with innovative features such as a semi-retractable undercarriage. Sadly, they came back empty-handed. Not a single order was placed and the aeroplane never left the drawing board.

Geoffrey de Havilland meanwhile spent most of the first half of 1919 convalescing. He came back towards the middle of the year when he began work on the last of his designs for Airco, the DH18. This was a more modest affair than the DH17, with a single engine and accommodation for eight plus one. It was revolutionary in one important respect, however. By paying utmost attention to the structure and weight of the airframe, the operating cost of the DH18 was drastically lower than that of the competition, all of them modified military types designed with no thought for economy. Offering a ton-mile operating cost of just 2 shillings and 8 pence, operators could make money from the aeroplane even if not every seat was sold.

Unfortunately, it was barely six months after the aeroplane's first flight that Airco folded, its assets bought by

BSA, the small arms to motorcycles to car manufacturer (it owned the Daimler brand). Wanting only Airco's manufacturing plant, BSA immediately closed down aircraft production. The boom envisaged by Holt Thomas had failed to materialise.

Although at first it did not look that way, Airco's demise was a blessing in disguise for GDH. Concluding that there was just enough work available to make it worthwhile setting up on his own if he could raise sufficient capital, the Airco design team began by pooling their resources (in GDH's case, £3,000). With outside investment coming from, among others, a clergyman who invested £1,000, it looked as though they might just have enough capital. Holt Thomas himself, though badly affected by Airco's demise, offered a further £10,000 in staged payments. On this assurance, the company was registered in September 1920 'with a working capital of £1,875 and perhaps an unwarranted degree of optimism', opening its doors – not much more than those of a wooden shack in the case of the design office – at Stag Lane Aerodrome, Edgware.

Immediately taking on the two DH18s that were in the final stages of development when Airco went under, the de Havilland Aircraft Company set about readying them for service with Holt Thomas' airline which, fortunately, had survived the collapse of its parent company. Within a year of its first flight, the DH18 was flying passengers from Croydon to Paris, Brussels and Cologne – not, it has to be said, in very great comfort. You had to be an above averagely intrepid traveller even to sit in the back of the aircraft of the day. They were extremely noisy (zero soundproofing), bumpy in flight (because of the low wing-loading the slightest variation in wind speed caused a lurch or drop) slow (your bladder had better be empty), shuddering (due to engine vibration) and, very often, bitterly cold. Every thousand feet in altitude causes a decrease in temperature of one degree so that, except in the summer months, passengers would be muffled to the eyeballs and wrapped in layers of blankets. And, of course, there was no such thing as inflight service. As for entertainment – well, that was hardly needed. The experience itself was entertainment enough. Indeed, what these early commercial aircraft lacked in comfort, they more than made up for with the sheer amazement of being able to cover distances at hitherto unimaginable speed. Think of it. In theory at least, you could leave the Ritz in London after breakfast and be at the Ritz in Paris in time for lunch, for heaven's sake!*

Thanks to the comparative success of the DH18, of which they built another four, de Havilland's fledgling company found itself in very reasonable shape at the end of its first year of trading. By now, work on a successor, the DH34 was well underway and when, in early 1921, Daimler Airways placed a start-up order for six, the future looked almost rosy. Precisely for this reason, the owners of Stag Lane Aerodrome, where the company was headquartered, chose this moment to announce that they wished to sell the property. De Havilland could either find £20,000 or clear off. Despite having a full order book, this sum far exceeded the company's immediate resources. For the

---

* This assumes breakfast at 7.15 a.m.; departure at 7.45 a.m. Motor to Croydon (12½ miles), 35 minutes, arriving 8.20 a.m.; airborne 8.50 a.m., just under two hours' flight time; arrive at Paris Le Bourget 15 minutes before noon (GMT +1 hour); 20 minutes to disembark and clear customs (your carriage awaits you, madam); motor to Place Vendôme (again, 12½ miles), 35 minutes, arriving at 12.40 p.m.; 20 minutes to spruce up; luncheon at 1 p.m. Just about doable.

second time in two years, GDH and his team faced the ignominy of the dole queue.

It was at this moment of looming disaster that there occurred one of those serendipitous meetings that only a smiling
angel could contrive. An enquiry came from out of the blue
from one Alan S. Butler. Could the company build him an
aeroplane in which he and a companion might take a comfortable and reliable private tour of the Continent? This was so
unexpected, and so unlikely to come to anything, that GDH
and his team decided the only possible response was to name
a price ludicrous enough to give them breathing space while
they sought more funds and to scare off anyone but the most
determined punter. Yes, they replied, but such a machine
(employing all the very latest technical advances) would not
cost less than £3,500.

The proposal was accepted at once.

Thus began an association that quickly developed into friendship and was to last until the end of GDH's life. The customer,
it turned out, was already an enthusiastic private pilot – one of
only a handful in the entire country. The son of a prosperous
Bristol merchant, Eton-educated and a former Guards officer,
twenty-three-year-old Alan Butler, having just missed the war,
had learned to fly during the year of the great flu pandemic.
With his freshly minted certificate, he had settled briefly in
Canada where he had met his future wife, Lois. Buying a civilianised Bristol Fighter on his return to England at the end
of 1920, he used this to compete in two of the earliest air races.
But while the aeroplane was a good performer, its limited range
and utilitarian construction made it an unsatisfactory tourer.
What he wanted from de Havilland was something that would
combine the performance of a scout with the long-range ability

of a bomber, but with comfortable cockpits and the possibility of carrying a second passenger.

The resulting design was the DH37, a conventional braced biplane with a 275 hp Rolls-Royce Falcon engine turning a four-bladed propeller and set off by its magnificent red and gold livery. Giving a comfortable cruising speed of just under 115 mph, it exceeded expectations and was entered by Butler in the 1922 Aerial Derby at Croydon. Unfortunately, magneto trouble on the day caused a delayed start and eventual retirement. But a month later, Butler came fifth in the round-Britain King's Cup air race – the winner being another de Havilland design (a modified DH4 bomber with a considerably larger engine). The bespoke DH37 gained widespread acclaim when, in October that year, following an urgent request put to de Havilland by the government, Butler loaned his aeroplane to fly a senior military official to Constantinople. With A. J. Cobham at the helm, the flight was accomplished in a single day; a remarkable achievement which did much to enhance the company's growing reputation. The success of the DH37 was not, by itself, sufficient to ensure the company's future, however. What it did do was to persuade Butler of the excellence of the team behind it. In a discussion with GDH about the future of private flying, he wondered whether the company could do with a capital injection? If so, he would be interested in investing £10,000. It was in that moment that the company, which still faced a very uncertain future, was saved. They were able to buy the freehold of the aerodrome at Stag Lane.

As for the matter of private aviation, it was a subject that, as well as being of great interest to both Alan Butler and Geoffrey de Havilland, also interested the British government.

Under the energetic direction of the Minister for Air, Sir Sefton Brancker, a committee had recently been set up to explore the future role of civilian aviation. Brancker's enthusiasm for flight can be traced to the occasion when, in 1910, he went up in a Bristol Boxkite at Aurangabad in India, on what may have been the first time an aircraft had been used successfully in a war setting. Heading off in pursuit of some insurgents, Brancker and his pilot spotted the enemy and he was able to report their position within ninety minutes of take-off, leading to their successful destruction. It is true that the subsequent mission was not so successful. The aeroplane was lost in a crash from which Brancker was lucky to escape alive. On his return to England, however, he learned to fly as soon as he the opportunity presented itself.[1] He subsequently became Director of Military Aeronautics before being appointed Minister for Civil Aviation in 1922. He was later killed in the R101 airship disaster in 1930, when Britain's answer to the Zeppelin went down in flames.

Although the postwar boom in non-military aviation had failed to materialise, Brancker was clear that aeroplanes were destined eventually to play a major role in the future of the world. What was more, it was clear that, in the event of another war, the country would need a pool of trained pilots on which it could draw. One way of achieving this would be by encouraging the emergence of private flying. The first of several initiatives of his that had this end in view were the gliding trials announced by the Royal Aero Club to be held in East Sussex in the autumn of 1922. With prize money donated by the *Daily Mail* (£1,000 to the winner), the intention was to stimulate interest in gliding as an amateur sport which, through advances in aerodynamics, could have spin-offs useful to the aviation sector generally. There was also the fact that the Air Ministry, which had close ties to the Club, had been stung by a recent German gliding record of sixty-six minutes aloft. It was outrageous that the country which had been defeated at such cost should show signs of resurgence so soon and Britain wanted redress.

A design by Geoffrey de Havilland was among those entered for the competition. His machine, a pretty little shoulder-wing monoplane nicknamed *Sybilla*, betrayed a concern with aesthetics that many rival designers clearly lacked. With a gracefully curving fuselage and tail fin, the glider boasted a fifty-foot wing span. As such, it was one of the few competitors to employ the high aspect ratio seen on modern gliders. De Havilland had understood correctly that this configuration – simply put, a long, thin wing – gives the best lift versus drag coefficient. Shorter wings create more drag, even if the actual wing area, and thus the wing loading (pounds per square foot) are identical.

Following successful initial trials, one important modification called for reconfiguration of the undercarriage. The conventional frame that attached the wheels to the fuselage was abandoned in favour of wheels tucked right below where the pilot sat both as a means of saving weight and of reducing drag. Being without the encumbrance of external undercarriage would also help during the launch phase. At that time, the aerial towing and winch launching of gliders both lay in the future. Instead, they were heaved into the air by the simple expedient of getting teams of men pulling elasticated ropes to race downhill as fast as they could, dragging the craft behind them. With luck, this, combined with an updraft of wind, would suffice to get the glider aloft, at which point the pilot would pull a toggle to release the rope as he fought to stabilise his machine.

With their glider suitably modified, the de Havilland team took up residence in Itford, a small village nestled at the foot of the South Downs, where it took its place in a line-up of entrants from all over Europe. Anton Fokker, the Flying Dutchman whose Eindecker design had caused such devastation to the RFC during the first year of the recent war, put in an appearance with a new design, as did the Australian Bert Hinkler, subsequently the first person to fly solo from England to the Antipodes. Amazingly, some excellent film footage of the event survives and, in flickering black and white, we catch a sense of the occasion as we watch one rather ungainly looking biplane rise twenty feet or so before tipping forward and flopping back to earth, the crowd surging forward, unrestrained by barrier or fence of any kind. Another aircraft gets considerably higher before doing the same thing and one is relieved to see the subtitles saying that the pilot had a 'lucky escape'. Other attempts are more successful and, after agonising seconds, the craft are brought under control.

There is also footage of one of the de Havilland gliders being launched – they fielded two of the same design. It stayed aloft for two minutes and thirty-eight seconds, though the flight ended with the machine in a hedge, considerably damaged. In a bid to improve lateral control but without increasing weight, the ailerons of both de Havilland gliders were then replaced with a system of control that relied on wing warping. This works by increasing and decreasing the camber of the wing, whereby an increase in camber increases lift (as well as drag, of course) and vice versa. The method was successfully used by the old Blériot monoplane but had the disadvantage of increasing the torsion loads on the wing. The dangers of this were shown vividly on the little glider's next outing when, at the very moment that the tow rope was released, the wings failed. Though the incident is not included in the film, a remarkable photograph captures the moment of catastrophe, following which the craft dropped 30 feet, like a discarded package; a jumble of wood, fabric and wire. Fortunately, it landed erect and there was no injury to the pilot.

On a happier note, there is footage of Monsieur Maneyrolle, the eventual winner of the competition. His entry, a late arrival from France, drew guffaws and derision for its appearance. With its parallel wings and short, stubby fuselage, many doubted it would even get off the ground. But he sits in the cockpit smiling endearingly behind a moustache almost as outrageous as his wing plan, a smile that gives way to a shy laugh, as if he is in possession of some tremendous secret. So it proved. When dusk came, the little craft was still aloft. The German record was smashed. The British record set earlier in the day followed. Then night fell and still Alexandre Maneyrolle soared the ridge wave. When, eventually, his strange-looking contraption came into land, having been aloft for a then astonishing three hours and twenty-one minutes, it landed in the modest glow of an assemblage of car headlamps.

The affair of de Havilland's foray into unpowered flight is not mentioned in GDH's autobiography and we can safely assume that, for him, the demise of the *Morgon* (as the second of the two was called) was an embarrassment best forgotten. As for the trials themselves, most considered they had done little or nothing to advance the cause of general aviation. The following year, the Royal Aero Club, again with encouragement from the Air Ministry, organised a similar trial, but this time for powered craft. With an emphasis on fuel economy and practicality, the rules stipulated that the engine capacity should be of no more than 750 cc, while each entry should also be able to pass through a standard five-bar gate and require no more than two men to push it along a mile of country lane. This, of course, meant that the wings must fold or detach. De Havilland's entry for this competition was the tiny DH53 Humming Bird, a single-seater with a modified motorcycle engine. It turned out to be a reasonable performer given the size of its engine and even won orders from the RAF, though it did not win any of the various prizes on offer. Nor did it endear itself to many of those who flew it. Alan Cobham famously found himself overtaken by a goods train while on a return flight from Brussels in the freezing cold of the following winter. The lesson in this case was that aeroplanes like the Humming Bird were just too small and underpowered to be of general use. If private flying was to catch on, it would require aircraft capable of cruising at a worthwhile speed and carrying a pilot and passenger over a reasonable distance – ideally at a price that more than just the very rich could afford.

During this period, government-led discussions about introducing a network of state-subsidised flying clubs across the country began in earnest. Unfortunately, the plan that emerged was hampered by the fact that, in its admirable enthusiasm to open sport flying to the Everyman, the Air Ministry persisted with its interest in what, today, we would call microlights. As a result, the 1924 Light Aircraft Trials, again organised by the Royal Aero Club with government backing, called for entries with a specification not much different from the previous year, although this time two-seaters were encouraged. But, given that the engine size was restricted to 1100cc, it was inevitable that the resulting aircraft should be, at best, marginal performers. For his part, Geoffrey de Havilland did not bother to submit an entry. He saw correctly that there was no future in the class. Instead, he was by now convinced that, given a more generous specification, it should be possible to come up with a design that would indeed do for aircraft what Ford's Model T had done for the motor car.

The Captain's first attempt at building such an aeroplane for the man in the street, the DH51, was a failure. The aim was to produce something along the lines of Alan Butler's aeroplane, but with a cheap, low-powered war-surplus engine giving 90 hp. While satisfactory in terms of flying characteristics, the DH51 was found to be still too low powered to be of much practical use. With its large, slow-turning, four-bladed propeller, it had a reasonable rate of climb, but its straight-line performance was underwhelming and, though of much lower power than the Rolls-Royce Falcon engine fitted to Butler's machine, it was not especially economical. Most seriously from de Havilland's point of view, it had only single ignition – that is, only one magneto – whereas the Air Ministry now specified two magnetos for civilian aircraft. If the company wanted to certify the aeroplane, they would have to put it through a more thorough engine testing programme in order to obtain an exemption to the rule. Rather than go through the agony, de Havilland decided simply to replace the engine with the newly available and rather jauntily named Airdisco engine, producing 120 hp. At once, performance was dramatically enhanced – but so were the running costs. And not only was it expensive to operate in the air but, having a 37-foot wing span and, without folding wings, it required considerable hangar space, making it expensive on the ground, too.

The major obstacle to success, GDH saw, was the non-existence of an engine powerful enough to do the job and yet small enough, light enough and cheap enough to be installed in an airframe that lay somewhere between the DH51 and the Humming Bird in size. But, in this regard, the Captain had an idea.

5

Design Number 60

The Holy Grail, de Havilland realised, was an engine producing something like 60 hp but weighing fewer than 350 lbs, so that the maximum all-up weight of the aeroplane could be kept below 1,200 lbs. This would give a wing loading of around 20 lbs per horsepower. Unfortunately, the cost of designing and developing an engine from scratch – should such a thing even be possible – lay beyond the company's means.

But what about this? The 120 hp Airdisco had been developed, by a brilliant young engineer called Frank Halford, from a war-surplus Renault engine – the very one that had, in an earlier form, powered the DH6 and was now selling at a mere 25 shillings a pop. A keen car and motorcycle racing enthusiast (he rode in the 1922 Isle of Man TT), Halford went on to design one of the world's most powerful piston engines ever, the 24-cylinder Sabre used to power the Hawker Tempest and Typhoon fighters that emerged, with devastating effect, towards the end of the Second World War. In the meantime, thanks to the inspiration and backing of de Havilland, he would also be responsible for one of the most successful light aero engines of all time.

The Airdisco motor, a V8 (eight cylinders arranged in a V above the crankshaft), was double the weight and produced twice the power that de Havilland was looking for. What, GDH wanted to know, sitting the younger man down at a table on which he had placed a stripped-down engine, if it was simply halved? Was there any reason it could not be built as a straight four to give half the capacity and half the power for half the weight? At first unconvinced that 50 per cent of an Airdisco engine could make a satisfactory whole, Halford quickly rose to the challenge and massively surpassed not only his own but also de Havilland's expectations.

The Cirrus engine that he came up with, in late 1924, produced 65 hp for a weight of just 286 lbs. Should it prove as reliable as was hoped, it would be the answer to GDH's prayer. There was nothing on either side of the Atlantic that could offer a comparable power to weight ratio. Indeed, as de Havilland wrote in his autobiography, the success of the Cirrus engine was an 'event of far greater significance than we realised at the time'. This was on account of the engine's miraculous development potential. Within a year, its power output had been upped to 85 hp and, by 1928, to 90 but with a *decrease* in weight of more than 20 per cent. This startling increase in the power to weight ratio was largely down to the fact that, while the cylinders, pistons, conrods and gearing were all lifted straight from the Renault engine, the crankshaft, crankcase and valve gear were all newly designed by Halford. Even in its first incarnation, the little engine was a revelation. Its relatively large capacity meant that maximum power was produced at under 2,000 rpm, making for a smooth delivery that minimised vibration and ensured low stress. One of the disadvantages of most contemporary engines was that they relied on high revs to produce their power – hence their marked proneness to failure.

As soon as news of Halford's breakthrough on the bench came through, de Havilland set to work building an airframe of proportionate light weight and strength. This was achieved by creating a forward fuselage that consisted, in essence, of a plywood box built around four square-section spruce longerons, stiffened by vertical and horizontal cross members that were first glued then screwed together, before being enveloped in a plywood skin and surmounted by symmetrical wings. These were braced in the conventional manner with four interplane struts. The overall brief was to create an aeroplane that any amateur could operate safely, leading GDH to specify duplication of the elevator and rudder cables – in spite of the weight penalty. If, for any reason, one failed, there was a backup. On the other hand, a high degree of inherent stability meant that there would be no need to duplicate the cables for lateral control. Also, by giving the lower wings three and a half degrees of dihedral – that is to say, by positioning the wing tip higher up, relative to the ground, than the wing root – the aircraft could, with care, be brought back to base even without functioning ailerons. Stability is, however, the enemy of manoeuvrability and, because GDH also saw the aeroplane as a potential trainer, it must not to be too stable, so the upper wings were given slightly less.

The aeroplane's unsuccessful predecessor, the DH51, did have one innovative feature that the new aeroplane inherited. This took the form of its differential ailerons, the brainchild of one of GDH's co-designers, Arthur Hagg. As a member of the team that developed the DH4 high-speed bomber, Hagg was later to lead, on behalf of Heston Aircraft Company, the design team responsible for the ill-fated Napier-Heston racer which, it was hoped, would take the world airspeed record. Alas, it crashed soon after take-off, happily without injury to its pilot. But Hagg's crowning achievement was to have designed the world's first system for combatting aileron drag – a system standard on all subsequent de Havilland designs and, in due course, on many other types. Indeed, some mechanism of differential is now standard on all aircraft.

Arthur Hagg's insight was to realise that both the yaw induced by banking and, incidentally, the drag on the wing could be mitigated if the aileron on the inside of the turn (i.e. the aileron that goes up) did so to a greater degree than the one on the outside. The effect of doing this is to increase the drag on the inside wing, creating a force that counteracts the yaw effect of banking, thereby reducing the overall drag on the wing. To bring about this happy state of affairs, Hagg devised a simple system which moved the ailerons in such a way that their deflection was not equal and opposite but, rather, unequal. This was genius. Beginner pilots tend not just to be ham-fisted but ham-footed too, and failure to balance your turns with rudder is one of many royal roads to disaster.

Apart from its differential ailerons, one other important novelty was found in the DH60's undercarriage. Anticipating that, in the hands of private owners and beginners, it would be subject to plenty of hard landings, the de Havilland design team fitted a telescopic system sprung with rubber blocks to which were attached wide diameter wheels clad in pneumatic rubber tyres, while the third component of the undercarriage consisted of a simple rigid and non-steering tail skid.

Aside from these innovations, the layout of the DH60 was

entirely conventional. The occupants sat directly behind one another, with the pilot in the rear. This was out of consideration for the centre of gravity, which was placed in such a way that the front cockpit could be flown empty or occupied without need for adjustment. The fuel tank, slightly forward and above the front cockpit, lay between the two upper wings and had a capacity of 17 gallons – sufficient to give a still-air range of around 300 miles at the normal cruise speed of 75 mph.

Design work on the new aeroplane had begun in early 1924 and, by the middle of the year, its prototype was taking shape in the workshop. Although the general layout and structure had been finalised, with only the detailed parts still to be decided, there remained one important consideration. As this was to be an aeroplane for Everyman, GDH realised that the public needed something more than simply a design number by which to know the new machine. Up until then, only a minority of de Havilland designs had names. In many cases, the only way to identify a de Havilland aeroplane was by its design number. Recounting the story many years later, GDH noted that 'a great many names were put forward before my enthusiasm for natural history ... led me to seek the solution in entomology ... It suddenly struck me that the name Moth was just right. It had the right sound, was appropriate, easy to remember and might well lead to a series of Moths, all named after British insects.' History shows him to have been correct.

When, at last, the great day of the new aeroplane's first flight arrived – 22 February 1925 – it was cold and wintry, with leaden skies. This can only have increased the feelings that GDH admitted to later. Having awarded himself the privilege of undertaking the sortie, the prospect aroused in him 'a mixture of concentrated interest, some excitement and a little apprehension'. This apprehension was mainly connected to the question of whether the angle of incidence of the tailplane had been correctly set (that is, its angle relative to the airflow). The problem was that 'if set at too great an angle, it might result in the pilot not being able to hold the nose up, and if at too negative an angle, in not being able to hold it down'. Fortunately, the design team's judgement had been correct and after 'five minutes in the air, I knew my hopes for the new aeroplane were justified'. It flew beautifully.

Given her then still unpainted fuselage and, at the time, clear doped wings, G-EBKT (Kilo Tango for short) does not show up terribly well in the ground-to-air black and white photographs taken on this historic occasion. But there is one shot taken later in the day that says it all: GDH stands, dressed smartly in suit and tie, a Fedora on his head (less formal than a Homburg), with hands on hips and wearing a look of supreme confidence, sure in the knowledge that 'we had produced something outstanding in light aeroplanes'.

From then on, most of the test flying was undertaken by the de Havilland company test pilot, Hubert Broad. This was not the only piece of good fortune Broad enjoyed in his life. As a young officer in the Royal Naval Air Service during the war, he had found himself in a dogfight with one of Germany's most famous air aces, Adolf Ritter von Tutschek. Realising he was being pursued, Broad glanced back, only to be met with a hail of bullets – one of which entered his opened mouth. By an incredible stroke of luck, the angle was such that it came out through his cheek and he was able to put his aircraft into a deliberate spin, recovering just in time to make a safe landing.

As the weather improved, the Moth began a full schedule of testing to determine its characteristics in every phase of flight. Importantly, the stall proved to be benign, coming in at around 35 mph, albeit that the wing would drop quite smartly in the developed phase. Cruising speed was a little more than double this figure and, though not of much practical use since it caused fuel consumption almost to double from around three gallons per hour to almost six, it could reach a maximum speed of almost 90 mph. By early March, the company was ready to show off its new baby to the press. 'It can be said at once that the Moth is the most promising contribution yet made to the difficult problem of getting the youth of the nation into the air,' reported *The Times* rather pompously.

By the end of April, the Moth had logged forty hours' flying in a total of sixty sorties and the company was confident enough in its new product to advertise it in the aeronautical press in French, Spanish and German as well as English. More daringly, one early photograph of the prototype shows it being towed, wings folded, behind a car in which the actress Estelle Brody is a passenger. This was a brilliant publicity coup on the part of de Havilland's PR team. Brody herself was on the brink of stardom playing the female lead in the romantic and, for its day, rather racy *Mademoiselle from Armantieres*, the most successful film of 1926.

The one significant modification to the prototype demanded by Broad was to the rudder. The amount of force required to bring about an effect was higher than desirable: you needed a boot-full rather than just a dab on the pedals. The way they overcame this was by providing a horn balance, whereby a portion of the control surface was placed in front of the hinge line. Doing this has the effect of causing the airflow to assist in the operation of the control. The dodge itself was well understood. Borrowed from a boat-building practice pioneered by Isambard

Kingdom Brunel, it had been in use on aircraft since the First World War. The one drawback was that, if overdone, the control surface could take on a life of its own and become, in fact, *un*controllable. And even when well judged, it was already known to lead to flutter in certain situations. This dangerous phenomenon consists in the uncontrollable vibration of a control surface that develops when an elastic structure (elastic in the sense that it bends to some degree under pressure) meets with a certain threshold of aerodynamic force. Just such a tendency beset the first examples of the DH80a Puss Moth, a monoplane successor to the DH60 first flown in 1929. Aileron input coupled with insufficient rudder was found, under certain conditions, to cause uncontrollable vibration in the port wing. Nine aircraft were lost as a result before a survivor of one of the crashes, working with the design team, determined the cause. No such tendency has ever been reported in connection with the DH60, however.

In May 1925, the prototype Moth was reported to have flown more than 5,000 miles. This was a good start. But what really made people sit up was when Alan Cobham, having breakfasted before dawn, set off from Croydon at 5 a.m., arrived in Zurich (almost exactly 500 miles distant), took off again after a forty-five-minute turnaround to reach Croydon at 7.30 p.m. that evening. This caused a sensation in the aeronautical press. At a stroke, the Moth had shown its potential as a world-beater.

6

'The most practical and successful light aircraft the world has ever seen'

A second prototype of the DH60, G-EBKU, flew at Stag Lane on 13 June 1925 and both it and the original prototype were entered for the forthcoming King's Cup air race. This event, established in 1922 by George V himself (no doubt with the encouragement of Sefton Brancker), was intended to encourage civilian aviation, the first winner being a modified DH4. The 1925 race followed a course of approximately 820 miles, running from Croydon to Glasgow and back. Given that it was handi-capped, the de Havilland team considered itself to have a decent chance of success, despite having to compete against several much larger and faster machines. The way the handicap system worked was by awarding a time penalty based on the aeroplane's declared top speed. If, at the end of the race, it came in any more than 1 per cent faster than this, it was automatically disqualified.

Unfortunately, bad weather on the day caused both Moths to abandon the race and only three of the fourteen starters finished. Nonetheless, the advent of the aeroplane caused intense excitement at Sefton Brancker's new flying clubs. Subsidised by the government and set up in the hope of encouraging both aircraft development and the emergence of a cohort of civilian pilots ready to exploit the technology as it advanced, the first of these clubs to place an order for a Moth was not, as might have been expected, the London Aero Club, but the Lancashire Aero Club. When the London Aero Club did open a few months later, it did so with much fanfare thanks to the presence of Sir Philip Sassoon, Under Secretary for Air (and therefore Sefton Brancker's deputy), a man reputed to be not much less rich than Croesus himself. The minister having made his speech, a ballot for the first use of the club's Moth was held. When his name was called out, David Kittel, the winner, gallantly passed the opportunity on to Mrs Eliott-Lynn, or Sophie Elluva-Din as she came to be known. She put the gesture to good use by becoming the London Aero Club's first pupil to qualify for a pilot's licence and the first person to learn to fly a Moth *ab initio*. While on her qualifying flight, which took place in rapidly deteriorating weather conditions, she became disorientated and was compelled to make no fewer than three forced landings before abandoning the Moth near Slough. Although this did not qualify her for her ticket, all agreed that it was a splendid performance.

As might be guessed, Sophie Eliott-Lynn was a woman of remarkable determination. Whether this came about because of, or in spite of, her tragic childhood is hard to say. Before she was a year old, her father, Jackie Peirce-Evans, who lived with his family on their small estate in a fine Georgian house, bludgeoned her mother (his former house-keeper) to death. The body was found with Sophie, wrapped in a blanket and sleeping beside it. Subsequently declared to be criminally insane, her father was institutionalised for the rest of his life. Sophie, meanwhile, grew up in the care of her grandfather and a pair of disapproving maiden aunts. In spite of all this, the six-foot-tall Sophie excelled both in the classroom and on the athletics field. Later enrolling as one of few women students at the Royal College of Science in Dublin, she proved a popular and promising student, winning academic prizes and distinguishing herself on the hockey pitch. In 1916, interrupting her studies at the behest of her aunts, she married an army officer twenty-one years older than herself. Almost immediately thereafter, she volunteered as a motorcycle despatch rider for the Women's Auxiliary Army Corps, serving close to the front in France throughout 1917. After the war, Sophie went back to college, passing out top in her class. During this time, her husband had moved to Kenya, where she joined him for as long as she could bear it – which was just long enough to publish a book of poems, before moving to Aberdeen University where she undertook postgraduate work in zoology. Having gone down to London in 1922, she filed for divorce soon after on the familiar but somewhat improbable (given the little time they spent together) grounds that Major Eliott-Lynn regularly beat her.

Now aged twenty-six and having recently become ob-sessed with athletics, Sophie threw herself into the world of sport, becoming a founder member of the Women's Amateur Athletics Association. In 1923, she represented

Britain at the Women's Olympiad at Monte Carlo, coming third in the javelin, third in the pentathlon and again third in the high jump. She did even better at the following year's Olympiad, held in London, when she won both the long jump and the javelin events, setting a record for the longest two-handed throw of 52.78 metres. Cultivating a high profile, she undertook frequent public-speaking engagements and, in 1925, published a coaching manual, *Athletics for Women and Girls*, the preface to which she read on BBC radio. The following year, she again represented Britain at the Women's World Games in Sweden, where she came fourth in the javelin.

Following her first flight in an aeroplane, Sophie largely dropped athletics in favour of aviation. Having attained her A licence before the year was out, she now set her sights on the commercial, or B licence, which would enable her to take paying passengers. At the time, this was not open to women but she successfully petitioned the authorities, though they insisted on her submitting to a fitness test while menstruating. In March, Sophie Eliott-Lynn bought the Moth prototype from de Havilland, the aircraft having by this time completed its testing programme.

Almost immediately after buying the Moth, Sophie Eliott-Lynn acquired a war-surplus SE5a fighter as well. With its 200 hp engine, it was substantially faster than the Moth and was her preferred mount for competitions. Becoming an enthusiastic member of the burgeoning air-racing scene, she continued her pursuit of the B licence, finally meeting the requirements – which included a night flight – in June 1926. Besides becoming the first British woman to obtain a commercial pilot's licence, she was also the first female in the country to make a parachute jump (her landing interrupted a football match but it seems she was forgiven).*

Sophie Eliott-Lynn's greatest air-racing success came a year later when she won the Grosvenor Cup in her Moth. Later that summer, she made a well-publicised tour of the country, making an exhausting seventy-nine landings in a single day. In the meantime, her former husband, who presumably funded her flying, was found drowned in the Thames. Following this, and having, it is said, drawn up a list of the twenty richest bachelors then on the market, Sophie set her sights on Sir James Heath, a man very nearly forty-five years older than she was, but a wealthy baronet and retired Member of Parliament for all that.

Becoming the third wife of Sir James and adopting her middle name, Mary, the new Lady Heath sold her Moth and gave up on the SE5a (it is recorded as having been withdrawn from use), acquiring in its place an Avro Avian which she had boxed up and sent out by ship to South Africa where the couple would be honeymooning. Having demonstrated this aeroplane at several local flying clubs, she announced her intention of flying it from Cape Town back to England. Setting off in January 1928, she expected the journey to take three weeks. It ended up taking three months, during which time she was laid up for several weeks suffering the effects of sunstroke.

---

* Without wishing to take anything away from Sophie, it is worth noting that this was considerably later than the first female jumper in the United States, where Georgia 'Tiny' Borwick made her first jumps from a balloon aged fifteen in 1908 (by which time, having married at twelve, she had a daughter of two) and from an aircraft in 1912. Remarkably, Tiny (who lived to be eighty-five) made her last of more than a thousand jumps before Sophie had even made her first.

Finally arriving back at Croydon on 18 May 1928, she stepped out of her plane wearing not flying clothes but a fur coat and elegant hat declaring, somewhat disingenuously, that 'Really it was not hard. When my powder blew off I simply clamped the joystick between my knees, held my mirror with one hand, and powdered with the other', something she claimed to have done 'many a time with a lion, a giraffe, or a herd of elephants gazing up at me'.[1] In fact, she had made several forced landings en route and been shot at as she crossed the Libyan desert. It was, nevertheless, an epic achievement and, as a result, she became, if briefly, one of the most famous women in the world and the toast of London society.

A promiscuous owner of aeroplanes, Mary Heath subsequently sold the Avian to Amelia Earhart when the American aviatrix visited Britain following her crossing of the Atlantic (as a passenger) in 1928, and replaced it with the third of an eventual seven Moths. It was in this aeroplane that she claimed a world altitude record for a light aeroplane which, unfortunately, turned out not to have been properly recorded and was therefore discredited. Already considered to be a self-seeker, this severely damaged her reputation. The following year, she moved to America with the intention of settling there, Sir James having regrettably tired of writing cheques on behalf of a spouse he complained of never seeing. He announced publicly that he would no longer be paying creditors who sold goods or services to his wife, filing for divorce at the same time. Amazingly, he went on to marry once more, this time to a woman forty-seven years his junior.

In America, Mary, lecturing extensively on her aviation exploits, enjoyed rapturous popularity. She also acted as sales representative of Cirrus engines. Unfortunately, this happy state of affairs did not last long as she found herself up against George Putnam, the ruthless publicist who had masterminded Charles Lindbergh's recent lecture tour and media. He was now seeking to repeat the trick with Amelia Earhart – whom he would eventually marry and to whom Sophie had sold her Avian. While Mary regarded Amelia as a friend, Putnam saw her as a rival. Even though as Lady Heath she had actually flown solo from one end of Africa to the other and Amelia Earhart had merely been a passenger on her recent transatlantic flight, it was imperative for him that the one did not upstage the other. This led to Mary being humiliated on turning up for what she understood to be her place on the inaugural commercial flight to Cuba and finding that Amelia Earhart had taken her seat on the flight deck. She nonetheless found herself a sponsor for the forthcoming National Air Races at Cleveland, Ohio. It was there, while practising for the event that, tragically, she clipped a chimney while practising for the race. Although she survived the ensuing crash through a factory roof, she had to have a metal plate inserted into her skull and was unable to fly for the next two years.

Mary married a third time, in 1933 – to a West Indian aviator, Reginald Williams, son of a prominent Trinidadian – and returned to Dublin where the pair set up an unsuccessful air service and aircraft hire company operating several Gipsy Moths among other aircraft. Depressed at her lack of continued success, Mary became increasingly dependent on alcohol. When both her marriage and her company failed, she moved back to London to live in obscurity, save for intermittent appearances in court on charges of being drunk and disorderly having been picked up off the street. She died in 1939 following a fall in a double-decker bus in which she hit her head on the ticket machine. The autopsy showed no alcohol in her system, however, and death was thought likely to have been due to the impact on an old clot on her brain – probably a result of the Ohio crash. It was a grievous end to a life begun in tragedy and yet was one in which this extraordinary woman, now largely forgotten, had contributed so much – above all, to expanding the notion of what the so-called weaker sex was capable of.

Following the Moth's instant success, not just with the London Aero Club of which the future Lady Heath was a member, but with each of the regional clubs too, orders began to roll in steadily – and not just from domestic customers. Before the year was over, a production aircraft was sent to Australia where it was exhibited at that year's Melbourne motor show, garnering much interest. This was largely thanks to its wing-folding feature which proved a great hit with the crowd. On Christmas Eve, the company announced an order for six aircraft, to be delivered as soon as possible, the Moth having been selected as standard equipment for the aero clubs of the Dominion of Australia – a most welcome seasonal gift for GDH and his team. This came on top of an order for four further aeroplanes by the Royal Aero Club, another four from the regional clubs, for one aeroplane from the Chilean military and several from private owners in the UK. By the year's end, fifteen examples of the type had been sold.

In a further publicity coup, a Moth was flown, just before the year's end, from Stag Lane to Dublin by one of the period's most celebrated private pilots, Colonel – later the Master (it being a Scottish baronial title) – of Sempill. This brought an order for four aircraft from the Irish government. A decorated former RFC pilot, Sempill later converted variously to Roman Catholicism, druidism and the Cornish bardic tradition and was a furious anti-Semite who subsequently became notorious for his pro-Nazi sympathies. What was not known about him until right at the end of the twentieth century, when the records were released, was that, during the Second World War, Sempill – who set several aviation records, including one in a de Havilland Puss Moth – became a spy for the Japanese government.

In 1921, he had led an official British military mission to Japan and in 1926 took the emperor's brother for a demonstration flight in a DH60 Moth. Never formally charged, Sempill's wartime treachery quickly became known to Churchill. The Master was one of only two people who had access to a set of notes from the prime minister's personal agenda when he met with President Roosevelt aboard ship in August 1941 (four months before the attack on Pearl Harbor) to discuss the Japanese military threat. The content of these notes was subsequently discovered, by the codebreakers at Bletchley, to have been transmitted to Tokyo from the Japanese embassy in London. The reason the Master was not formally charged was, of course, the fact that it was imperative that the Enigma codebreaking project be kept secret. Instead, and following a raid on his office shortly before Pearl Harbor, he was forced to retire from public service.*

----

* Unexpectedly, Sempill's successor to the baronetcy was his younger sister Elizabeth, who became one of Britain's first trans-men. Presenting at court as a debutante in 1929 and as a man following various treatments in Germany over the next decade, Elizabeth changed name to Ewan by deed poll in 1952, marrying his housekeeper of the past five years shortly afterwards. It was not until 1965, however, that, following a complex lawsuit he finally inherited the family baronetcy. By now a qualified medical doctor, Sir Ewan served first as senior casualty officer at the Aberdeen Royal Infirmary and then as a popular rural GP outside the city, before retiring to manage his estate at Brux Castle, in which role he adopted the broad Doric accent he had learned as a child, and becoming a respected member of his local kirk in Kildrummy.

Sempill's 1925 flight to Dublin entailed a crossing of 70 miles across water on the way out. On the way back, he took a shorter route across the sea, departing from Belfast and landing at Stranraer in Galloway, where he refuelled from cans carried on the passenger seat. This was not his only significant flight in a Moth, however. During the Whitsun holiday of May 1926, Sempill undertook an 800-mile tour of Wales and the West Country with his wife, beginning at Stag Lane, 'landing where and when I wished and never going near an aerodrome or aeroplane hangar' and, on two occasions, putting down on sandy beaches, his aeroplane spending most nights with its wings folded in the barns of local farmers.

The first set-back de Havilland faced was when the Air Ministry, having put the aircraft through its paces reported that 'The aircraft is very easy to fly and, in respect of handling qualities, is very suitable for instructional purposes. It is, however, underpowered and the take-off run is too long, and the rate of climb off the ground is too slow.' As a result, the hoped-for large order from the RAF did not materialise – for the time being. Meanwhile, work on getting more power out of the Cirrus engine was underway.

Shortly after Sempill's Whitsun wanderings, Sir John Rhodes undertook a tour of similar length round the East Midlands and along the south coast. At the end of this, Rhodes calculated his total running costs at just under six-pence (2½p) per mile, a figure comparable to that of running a luxury car. Later that same year, 'Billy' Sempill became – again in a Moth – the first person to fly directly from Land's End to John O' Groats. In order to achieve this, the Moth was fitted with a special long-range tank in the front cockpit, giving twelve hours' endurance. The flight was intended to be non-stop, beginning from a field near the Land's End Hotel, of which he did a circuit, but carburettor trouble caused a brief diversion en route. Nonetheless, the ensuing publicity was extremely welcome – as was the news that the 67-year-old Duchess of Bedford had taken to the skies in a Moth. Having been extremely active all her life, she was now very hard of hearing, suffering terribly with tinnitus, and found flying not only an agreeable way of getting around but also, thanks to the engine noise, a distraction from the ringing in her ears. From now on, she hired Moths to take her to engagements whenever possible. One such was luncheon with friends on the south coast. Having flown down from her home at Woburn Abbey, she diverted via Southampton to view the recently refitted *Mauritania*, the 45,000-ton ocean liner, before landing on the golf course at Lyndhurst. After lunch, she made sure to wave to Mr Ogilvie, the senior surgeon at Woburn Hospital, on his yacht at a local regatta. It was not long after this that Her Grace ordered a Moth of her own, for delivery in 1927.

In the meantime, a further publicity stunt presented itself during the General Strike of 1926 when a number of Moths were employed in dropping newspapers, printed in Paris, onto towns and villages throughout the country, as a means of countering the rumours that inevitably sprang up in the absence of reliable news.

All the time this was going on, the company was making small adjustments to the aeroplane. The fuel cock was moved, a longer exhaust was fitted, the storage space was given outside access, an auxiliary 'windy' airspeed indicator was added to one of the wing struts – all of which became standard on the new 'X' model, which also had a redesigned undercarriage. Another development put in hand was a floatplane version of the Moth, thought likely to appeal to enough people to make its introduction worthwhile. This first flew in November 1926.

In the meantime, the longed-for win in the King's Cup came in midsummer when Hubert Broad, piloting one of five Moths entered, took first place – though, personally, GDH was somewhat disappointed with the result. He was flying a specially prepared machine fitted with the prototype of the Cirrus II engine, which was Frank Halford's riposte to the Air Ministry. It gave a full twenty horsepower more than the original version and was slated to be offered as an alternative powerplant from now on. Unfortunately, GDH was forced out of the race when he came down near Chelmsford with a fractured oil pipe. In spite of this mishap, however, the engine itself quickly proved its worth and soon became standard for the type.

As well as being a year of significant progress for the Moth, 1926 was also the year of the long-distance flight in a DH50 to Australia and back by Alan Cobham which electrified the public imagination. When he landed his aeroplane – specially fitted with floats for the purpose – on the river outside the Houses of Parliament, a crowd of over a hundred thousand gathered to greet him. It was thus a major coup on the part of de Havilland when the freshly ennobled Sir Alan was engaged to take the Moth floatplane prototype on a tour of the east coast of America.

Arriving on board ship within a short distance of Ellis Island on 25 November 1926, the plan was to lower the Moth into the sea, when he and his wife would take the aeroplane up the Hudson River to Newark, where its floats would be exchanged for a conventional wheeled undercarriage. He would then take it on, in due course, to Washington, DC. Unfortunately, the water on that day was extremely choppy and Cobham was unable to get airborne. His (pregnant) wife disembarked, along with her luggage to lighten the load, but still the aeroplane would not unstick. As a result, it had to be towed into New York Harbor. Unsurprisingly, Cobham felt humiliated. When he discovered that de Havilland themselves had only ever tested the floats in benign conditions and were aware that the Moth might not unstick in anything more than a flat calm, annoyance turned to anger and his association with the company came to an abrupt and acrimonious end.

It was to be a further two years before any more Moths arrived from England in America, although the type became familiar thanks to visits from a number of Canadian Moths. This encouraged intense interest in the aeroplane and, following negotiations between chairman Alan Butler and a number of local businessmen, the Moth Aircraft Corporation, a wholly independent entity was established in Delaware in late 1928. Shortly thereafter, two examples of the type arrived from Stag Lane. The first of these was registered to a private owner, the other became a test bed for modifications. This test-bed aircraft subsequently came into the possession of Laura Ingalls, after Amelia Earhart one of America's most celebrated aviatrices. In it, she broke the existing record for a woman by flying 344 consecutive loops. Not content with this, three weeks later she broke her own record with a run of 980. It is interesting to speculate on what prevented her from reaching the full pony. Did her Moth run out of fuel? Did she herself run out of energy? Did she miscount? Or did she lose the will to live as any sane person might, in the circumstances? We only know that she was not minded to repeat the exercise, though she did go on to establish a record for the highest number of barrel rolls ever performed in one go, executing an amazing 714 in her Moth one day in August 1930. In the same year, Laura Ingalls flew her aeroplane to third place in the Women's Dixie Derby, which began in Washington and toured the southern states before finishing in Chicago. As if that were not enough for the year, again in her Moth, she established a coast-to-coast record with a total time of just under fifty-six hours – a record she broke again in 1934 when, flying a Lockheed Orion Special (fitted with a 525 hp radial as opposed to her Moth's 85 hp Cirrus II), she flew the distance in just one third of the time. Probably her greatest achievement, though, was her 17,000-mile solo flight around South America made in the same aircraft later that year.[2]

Unfortunately, it is not just for her aerial feats that Ingalls is remembered. Twice during the Second World War she was imprisoned for pro-Nazi activities. Regrettably, this did not alter her views. She supported Hitler on the ground that he fought for 'independence for Europe – for independence from the Jews. Bravo!' It is pleasing to know that her two applications for clemency after the war were firmly rejected.

The exact number of Moths eventually built in America is unknown. Production was actually carried out at Lowell, Massachusetts, where it seems that around two hundred aircraft were built. Partly as a result of the Great Depression, but also in part because of competition from American-designed aircraft, the Moth Aircraft Corporation ceased operations after only two years. One big advantage the US companies had was that fuel in America was much less heavily taxed than in Britain. This meant that the higher fuel consumption of more powerful engines than the Gipsy was less off-putting to owners. It is also a fact that there existed a presumption against foreign aircraft. Though built in America, the Moth was unable to overcome this bias and, as soon as an effective competition emerged in aircraft like the Air Travel Trainer, the Moth type was quickly overshadowed.

All this lay in the future, however. Setting aside the embarrassment of the floatplane's failure in America (easy enough to do before the advent of instant communications), enough good things had been reported of the Moth for the company to be able to proclaim with confidence that this was 'the most practical and successful light aircraft the world has ever seen'. When Selfridges put a Moth in one of its display windows in the run-up to Christmas of 1926, the notion that here was an aeroplane that was as much a practical proposition as a motor car began to take hold.

7

Far Horizons

If there was one moment that demonstrated conclusively that aviation had, by 1927, come of age, it was the sudden and dramatic appearance of Charles Lindbergh in Paris during the night of 21 May, following his solo transatlantic flight. With respect to aviation the public imagination was galvanised in a way that no single event had done before and none have since. Not even the moon landing forty-two years later provoked such astonished delight. Lindbergh was, as one commentator wrote, an archangel, come to deliver a prophecy. When news of his sighting over England was broadcast in France, people began to flock to Le Bourget airfield outside Paris in anticipation of his arrival. It is estimated that 150,000 were present when he landed. A further 35,000 jammed the square in front of the Hôtel de Ville in the city centre for a reception given him by the French government five days later. Anywhere between 500,000 and a million lined the Champs-Élysées as he passed along it in an open-top car. A similar thing happened when he visited Brussels two days later. When, at the end of the month, he flew into Croydon, it took police ten minutes to clear the runway of the hundred-thousand-strong crowd that awaited him.

Following a meeting with the prime minister, Lindbergh was received in audience by King George V who awarded him the British Air Force Cross. When he returned to America, he was accorded arguably the most lavish homecoming of any single human being in all history. Did even the great Oriental despots, Chairman Mao, Pol Pot or one of the Kims enjoy such adulation? It is doubtful. A vast array of naval ships, several dirigibles and squadrons of aircraft escorted the vessel carrying Lindbergh as it steamed into Chesapeake Bay and he was greeted by the thunderous salute of its gun battery. A few days later, around four million people jammed the streets of New York to toss an estimated eighteen tons of confetti in his direction. As one wit said, it was as if Lindbergh had not crossed the water but walked on it. There was a prevailing sense that, in some not quite definable way, the world had changed for ever.

For the next decade at least, people became obsessed with flight. In Britain, the aero clubs were immediately oversubscribed – Amy Johnson herself had to wait more than six months before she could join the London Aero Club. Films were made, bestselling books written (Lindbergh's autobiographical account of his flight, published a scant four weeks after his return to the States was a runaway success), poems, music and opera were composed and pictures painted. Some of the most striking art of the period features aircraft and views of the earth from the cockpit of aircraft. The prophecy that Lindbergh had delivered was that humanity had entered on a new age, one in which it was destined to rule the skies. And here, with the Moth now at a reduced price of £650, thanks to economies of scale in production, was the means for any resourceful person to travel the world as it had never been travelled before.

There was a looming difficulty for the company, however. Thanks to the Moth's sudden success, by the end of 1926 around fifty had been sold worldwide. By the end of 1927, a further 117 and for 1928, production was increased to thirty a month. Almost all these aircraft were fitted with the Cirrus engine (a few specialist aerobatic machines for the RAF had the Genet radial). But other light aircraft manufacturers had entered the fray (among them Avro, who were developing the Moth's nearest competitor, the Avian, and Westland who were developing their parasol monoplane, the Widgeon) and all had adopted the Cirrus engine. It was clear that, at this rate, the supply of the war-surplus Renault engines would soon dry up – a problem recognised both by GDH and his team, and by the manufacturers of the Cirrus engine themselves. The latter decided that they must build the engines from scratch. The de Havilland team decided to go a step further and design and build their own engine. GDH did not wish for his company to be beholden to another for such an indispensable component and now that Halford had moved from Cirrus to set up on his own, there was no reason why they should not get him to lead the project.

The specification for the new powerplant – named the de Havilland Gipsy – agreed as early as October 1926, was for it to weigh no more than 300 lbs and yet be capable of producing 135 hp – more than double that of the original Cirrus. In order to give a wide margin of safety, as well as the longest possible time between overhaul, the production engine would then be derated to 100 hp – still a full 15 per cent more than the

Cirrus II. It was hoped that the new powerplant could be ready for bench testing within six months or so, with a view to trialling it in a racing aeroplane, the DH71, which de Havilland would campaign in some of that year's air races – the King's Cup being the most important of them.

The DH71, of which two prototypes were built, was less successful than its engine. Although it proved to be faster even than most of the RAF's fighters, its handling characteristics made it challenging both on the ground and in the air. The prototype in which Broad competed in the King's Cup was so badly behaved that he withdrew from the race early on, with the result that a standard DH60 Moth again won. Thereafter, he made an attempt on the world altitude record for a single-engine aeroplane. Unfortunately, although the DH71 (its official designation was Tiger Moth but is not to be confused with the production aircraft of the same name) was still climbing strongly at over 19,000 feet, its absolute ceiling was never established due to the fact that the machine carried no oxygen and Broad, beginning to feel the effects of deprivation, wisely decided to abort the mission. The type did, however, set a world speed record in its class at just over 186 mph. At this point the project was mothballed for several years until one of the two examples built was shipped to Australia for a high-profile event. Unfortunately, it crashed, killing its pilot. But by then, the aeroplane had done its work. It had shown that the Gipsy powerplant was indeed capable of producing the power output claimed and at the weight specified.

The final test of Frank Halford's new Gipsy engine before it entered series production took place during the summer of 1928. Aboard a DH60X Moth fitted with an extra eighty gallons worth of fuel tankage and – as for most aircraft making very long-distance flights – a vent with an angled pipe (to avoid blowback) inserted beneath the seat cushion to facilitate waste disposal, company test pilot Hubert Broad took off at 5.30 p.m. on 16 August. Equipped with flasks of coffee, one of cocoa, a stash of sandwiches, several boiled eggs and a pile of novels, he proceeded to fly the aeroplane in a meandering circuit north as far as Lincolnshire and round much of the south of England, staying aloft throughout the night and for all of the following day until, having read three books and managed to keep awake throughout, a Very light at 5.30 p.m. in the evening of 17 August told him he was clear to land, having been airborne continuously for twenty-four hours. Throttled back, the engine had given a fuel consumption of just over three gallons per hour.[1] It was an astonishing achievement on all counts.

The engine went into full-scale production immediately thereafter, with the first Gipsy-powered Moth aircraft being delivered at the beginning of 1929. In the meantime, Moth mania became increasingly widespread as news began to roll in of ever more wonderful adventures.

Actually, the DH60's potential for long-distance travel had been recognised long since. As early as the summer of 1926, two young enthusiasts had begun to plan a flight heading east. One of them, Neville Stack had originally been a drummer in the orchestra at London's Kit Kat Club. Having learned to fly during the war, he had recently been recruited as chief flying instructor at the Lancashire Aero Club. The other, Bernard Leete, had also learned to fly in the RAF. Both were now reservists. They wondered if de Havilland could be persuaded to supply two aircraft at no cost on the basis that their flight, which they would continue all the way to Australia if all went well, would garner huge publicity for the company? The company could only say no. Unsurprisingly, given the economic climate of the day, that was precisely what they did say. But it did agree to providing two second-hand aircraft, both refurbished and fitted with long-range tanks, on easy terms.

Sensibly, not wanting to raise expectations too high, it was only shortly before taking off from Croydon on 16 November 1926 that the two men let it be known that their intended destination was Cairo and, if all went well, Karachi – though they kept alive the thought of ultimately getting to Australia. Surviving relentless bad weather, Stack and Leete's journey saw the two Moths become the first civilian aircraft to cross the Syrian desert and reach Baghdad, a major achievement for both planes and pilots. There, on 19 December, Stack, a renowned aerobatic pilot, was persuaded to put on a display of 'trick flying' for the Baghdad (horse) races which left an 'outstanding impression'.[2]

Thus far, the only mechanical trouble either aircraft suffered was when a magneto seized on one of them. This was rectified by RAF mechanics in Iraq. Flying along the treacherous coast of the Persian Gulf, however, Leete was forced down when his plugs oiled up. Having cleaned them, he took off again and joined Stack, who had been watching from above, the pair of them continuing to Bushire. There, they discovered that one of Stack's cylinder heads was cracked, necessitating a running repair to get them to India. When they subsequently landed in Karachi on 8 January, having covered over 5,500 miles without serious mishap, the pair of Moths was met by crowds said to have been the largest ever seen in the city. For several days afterwards, the two aeroplanes put on public displays which proved so popular that the local authorities sponsored trains to bring in people from miles around.

Following their triumph, Stack and Leete were awarded the Air Force Cross for their contribution to British prestige and to the arousal of 'air-mindedness' among the masses, both British and Indian. This 'air-mindedness' was, from the mid-twenties (when the term first began to appear) until the beginning of the Second World War, regarded as an important civic virtue, much as today we think of, for example, 'sustainability'. It seemed an obvious good borne out of an awareness of the harm likely to arise in its absence. In the case of aviation, the worry was that other countries might get ahead in the field.

Unfortunately for Stack and Leete, de Havilland themselves, though delighted at the pair's success, did not go so far as to commit funds to enable them to continue their flight on to Australia. Perhaps the company felt that getting the Moths safely to Karachi was triumph enough. The bad publicity following a crash might just undo it. Indeed, Leete, who stayed in India for the time being, did indeed write off one of the aircraft not long afterwards.

Although news of the company's refusal was disappointing for both, their achievement, accomplished without the fanfare in Britain accorded to many of their successors, nonetheless provided the inspiration for increasingly ambitious flights by privateers in their Moths.

The first of these, also to Karachi, was undertaken by Dennis Rooke – allegedly for a £10,000 bet, though with whom is unknown. He, too, had Australia, his homeland, as his intended final destination.

Setting out in April 1927 to achieve what Stack and Leete had failed to do, he took off quietly from Croydon, dressed in a grey lounge suit and overcoat. According to *Time* magazine, apart from a long-range tank, his equipment consisted of only a few spare parts and, somewhat optimistically, a collapsible canvas bath. Unfortunately, on reaching the Libyan desert, he was forced down with engine trouble. Having – even more optimistically – failed to take any emergency supplies with him, Rooke was compelled to endure three days without either food or water while he carefully packed his pistons with strips torn from his shorts. Thereafter he made it safely to Cairo. The venture finally came to end in Karachi on 20 June when, following a 1,200-mile leg from Basra, he was forced to land in darkness. Misled by the lights shining from a nearby barracks, he mistook a cricket pitch for the actual runway. Realising his mistake just too late to go around, Rooke hit a bank and damaged his machine, necessitating repairs that, he calculated, would last a week. Blaming the red tape he had encountered at his previous stop, Rooke announced that he was abandoning his journey. The imminent monsoon meant that he could not hope to get across the subcontinent within the time he had available.

Another epic but even more low-key early flight in a Moth was that of Dick Bentley, who took off from Croydon on 1 September 1927, bound for Cape Town. Without encountering a single mechanical problem en route and suffering only minimally from bad weather, Bentley's journey was as unremarkable as the man himself. If he did have one outstanding characteristic, it was his modesty.

Born at Richmond-on-Thames in 1898, Bentley joined the RFC in 1916 and began his career flying the R.E.8 in its role as artillery spotter. This entailed scrambling to watch the fall of shot from the British guns, noting this in relation to the target and marking it on a map. The intelligence gathered would then be dropped in a weighted bag on the gun emplacement carrying out the barrage. Often, bad weather meant that these sorties were conducted at very low level, making the aircraft highly vulnerable to rifle fire from the ground. With a cloud base of no more than 150 feet during the Battle of Cambrai in November 1917, Bentley's job was to fly up and down the line as the troops crossed into enemy territory, reporting back with hastily scribbled messages every fifteen minutes or so in order that the commanders would know which elements of their plan were working, and which not. All the time, the British howitzers were in action behind him and he narrowly missed being shot down by his own side on several occasions. Yet, despite the extraordinary risks he took in providing these reports, there is no trace of awe or even much self-reflection in the account Bentley gave of his wartime exploits late in life. He had a job to do and he did it, that was all.

Demobbed from the services and with few prospects at home, Bentley sought a life for himself in Africa, spending three years working on the railways, much of the time in the wagon repair yard at Devil's Cataract near to Victoria Falls. Chancing to see an advert in the Johannesburg *Times* requesting applications for the newly formed South African air force, he eventually returned to flying, serving four more years. With his tour of duty almost completed, Bentley read about the Moth in the aviation press and 'instantly had the idea *Why don't I fly one from London to Cape Town?*'[3]

Bentley's problem, as it was for Stack and Leete – and as it would be for many future record-breakers – was lack of money. Even when de Havilland agreed to sell an aeroplane at cost, the £400 asking price was too much for him. Accordingly, he went to the chairman of the Johannesburg Light Aircraft Club and asked whether, should he succeed in flying a Moth

out from London, they would be interested in buying it for
£600 as against the list price of £650? As it turned out, they
would. That was a promising start. Reckoning his incidental
expenses (including fuel, oil, accommodation and insurance)
at £200, Bentley then contacted the *Johannesburg Star* asking
if they would provide funding in return for exclusive publicity
and the promise to pay them back on sale of the aircraft. He
heard nothing, but a few days later was called on to provide
an aerobatic demonstration for some visiting dignitaries in one
of the air force's SE5as, an advanced fighter during the war
but now obsolete, though still capable, in the right hands, of
putting up a good show. Pulling out all the stops, he was just
walking away from the aircraft afterwards when the editor of
the newspaper came up and announced that, given his outstanding performance, he would have no hesitation in backing
his proposed trip.

With this assurance, Bentley took a third-class cabin in a
steamer bound for the Old Country at the end of June 1927,
arriving at Stag Lane in the middle of August. His aeroplane
would be ready at the end of the month, giving him time to
acquire maps, the necessary permissions and to arrange for fuel
and oil at each of his intended stops.

Flying via France, Italy, Sicily and Malta, he reached the
African seaboard without difficulty. As much of the Libyan
coast lay in Italian hands at the time, Bentley availed himself
of the hospitality of the Italian air force who gave him a warm
welcome and much Chianti when he stopped for fuel at Homs,
Sirte and Benghazi. In Egypt, fascinated by the Valley of the
Kings, he flew up and down several times before continuing
to Wadi Halfa where, as a dinner guest of the district commissioner, he narrowly missed dipping his nose in the soup, so

tired was he. Fully restored the next morning, Bentley pressed on to Khartoum by following the railway line, reaching there exactly a fortnight after his departure from Croydon. There followed a precautionary landing at Jerbil, where he happened on a resthouse for white hunters and spent a day checking for the source of the slight rattle that he thought he had detected. Examining each piston and valve, he satisfied himself that there was nothing wrong and that what he heard was probably no more than the slap one sometimes gets from aluminium pistons working in cast-iron, air-cooled cylinders. The next legs took him over some decidedly remote country, including a three-hundred-mile stretch of swampland. Entering Kenya, he landed near Victoria Falls before heading on to Tabora in Tanganika (now Tanzania) then Abercorn in Northern Rhodesia (now Zambia) and Broken Hill at Livingstone, close to Lake Victoria which he admired from a height of 250 feet. He was dined by the governor before passing in easy stages via Bulawayo to Johannesburg. There he reunited with his girlfriend, Dorys. The only time Bentley's progress was interrupted by bad weather came on the final leg into Cape Town, where a small crowd waited patiently for two hours while he diverted out to the coast to avoid fog over the mountains he had intended to cross.

Bentley was subsequently accorded a reception by the mayor of Cape Town, a representative of the commander-in-chief of the South African air force and the president of the local flying club. But this was hardly Lindbergh. Nor was it even close to the excitement that later adventurers were met with. Yet perhaps it was more in keeping with the spirit of the Moth itself. This was, after all, an aeroplane intended not just for the few but for the many.

8

The Obstinacy and Determination of Forty Devils

If the history of the Moth owes much to people like Bentley, Leete and Stack, the contribution of women pilots to the type's history is out of all proportion to their numbers at the time. It was another Irish aviatrix, Lady Mary Bailey who, arguably more than anyone else, opened the public's eyes to what could be done with the aeroplane. Although it is true that Mary Heath was the first woman to fly alone from Cape Town to London, it was her compatriot who was actually the first woman to have flown between the two cities. But because Mary Bailey's flight – in a DH60X Moth – was in the opposite direction, it was less widely reported.

Born in 1890, Mary was the eldest child of D. W. W. Westenra, the future 5th Baron Rossmore. Or so it's said. Both family legend and circumstance point to another possibility.

Her parents were members of the future George V's uber-privileged social set, seeing each other frequently at the house parties put on at the various social and sporting events that made up the social season: pheasant shooting in the autumn, fox hunting over the winter months, National Hunt racing in the spring, flat racing and yachting over the summer, with intervals for grouse shooting, deer stalking, salmon fishing and, just now and then, trips to London for the theatre and important royal and society gatherings in between. There was certainly plenty of opportunity for misbehaviour. Whether the allegation that Mary was an illegitimate child of the future King is true or not, it puts her in the unlikely company of Anthony Blunt, the Soviet spy and keeper of the Queen's pictures who shares the same rumoured distinction.

That apart, Mary was a daddy's girl if ever there was one. He, the spendthrift, hard-drinking, hard-riding, short-tempered younger son who never expected to inherit the family title. She, the hard-drinking, hard-riding, equally short-tempered, chain-smoking, and hell-raising daughter. Mary was affectionate towards him until he died. But towards her mother, Mittie, not so much. Mittie Naylor had been quite the catch. Her own father was one of several candidates for the title of richest commoner in the land. A Liverpool banker (though by no means self-made: he was educated at Eton and inherited property from his mother's sister), he had recently purchased magnificent estates at Hooton Hall in Cheshire (which he furnished with a stud and its own private racecourse) and at Kelmarsh Hall in Northamptonshire (designed in the Palladian style by James Gibbs, architect of St Martin-in-the-Fields church in Trafalgar Square). He quickly came to detest his son-in-law. For the sake of Mittie, he was compelled to bail out his negligent relative on multiple occasions. The feelings old man Naylor had towards Derry cannot have been improved by the book that Rossmore published in 1911, in which he revealed himself to be the thick-headed – though hardly thick-skinned – arrogant, entitled oaf he had long suspected – someone who considered dogfighting, badger baiting and schadenfreude to be actual sports.

Not that Derry Westenra had had much of a chance himself. A long-standing rivalry with his County Monaghan neighbours, the Shirley family of Lough Fea, saw his father, the spendthrift 4th Baron, extend the family seat – Gothic-revival Rossmore Castle – for the fifth time since it was built in 1827, to the point where, when Derry inherited it following the death of his elder brother in a steeplechase, it had three towers, 117 windows and fifty-three rooms, all told. It also had five new lakes (each dug by hand, of course).

Mary, for her part, did not see a great deal of her parents as they spent much of their time in England while she remained in Ireland. They did try her at boarding school (Heathfield, just outside Ascot – convenient for the Royal Meeting), but that lasted not even a term before she ran away. For the most part, she was educated by a pair of governesses – two sisters of Franco-Russian origin. They did a reasonable job. Though never a great speller, and though her letters and journals show little evidence of wide or deep reading, her handwriting is neat and legible and she wrote fluently enough.

At fifteen, Mary bought a motorcycle; at sixteen, a car. At eighteen, mad-keen on hunting, she became master of a pack of Harrier hounds (Harriers being the kind that hunt hares, not foxes). She also rode as an amateur jockey in the local point-to-points and competed regularly in local horse shows.

A keen rod and a promising shot besides, Mary's carefree existence came to an abrupt end when, at twenty-one, she was presented at court as a debutante. This entailed being shipped to London and spending the next several months going from one grand party to another, culminating in Queen Charlotte's Ball at which the young women were presented individually to the sovereign of the day. From then on, she was considered eligible for marriage. Thus we find her next year on the Isle of Wight for Cowes week, during which she was a guest on Lord Iveagh's yacht (he another Anglo-Irish peer, the ennobled scion of the Guinness brewing dynasty), where she met, was proposed to and accepted the hand in marriage of Abe Bailey, the 46-year-old so-called Randlord; a South African politician, former grammar school boy, boxing champion, circus rider and, latterly, landowner and gold and diamond magnate.

Doubtless Abe's fabulous wealth was part of his attraction both to Mary and her parents. He was, though, an extremely able, clear-thinking and generous man (his remains the largest bequest of any single person to the South African state and he made numerous charitable gifts in his lifetime), who would have been attractive even without such a fortune. He was not without his faults, mind. He had a temper which rivalled Mary's own. On at least two occasions, he came to blows with a political adversary in parliament (here one thinks of Pemberton Billing) and one of their children recalled his parents' arguments in terms of two dinosaurs clashing in a forest.

As soon as they returned from their honeymoon, Mary obediently took up all the duties that were expected of her. This entailed running several households simultaneously: there were town houses in both London and Johannesburg and country estates in Sussex and the Northern Cape (the latter comprising

forty farms and totalling 300 square miles – more than twice
the size of the Isle of Wight). It also entailed producing, in the
fullness of time, five children (even if the business of bringing
them up was subcontracted to various nannies, housemaids
and servants). On the outbreak of the First World War, Mary
volunteered as a driver in the Royal Flying Corps. Her enthusiasm for speed – she was once fined for doing 40 mph along
Pall Mall – was no doubt an asset when, for a time, she was
posted close to the front in France. Abe, meanwhile, played
a significant role in the leadership of the British government
during the war. It was at a dinner in the Baileys' London house
that the then prime minister, H. H. Asquith, who had, by
1916, lost support in the country on account of his weak and
dithering leadership, was persuaded to stand aside in favour
of the more dynamic Lloyd George. Bailey was also the one
who successfully encouraged the new prime minister to take
his friend, Winston Churchill, into the cabinet.

After the war, Mary and the children spent time back in
Ireland while Abe stayed in South Africa. As a result, their son
James reported never having knowingly set eyes on his father
before he was six years old. Whatever trauma that caused him,
he grew up to have a keen sense of justice and became a powerful opponent of apartheid through his co-founding of the
first South African lifestyle magazine for a black readership.
Given the distance, both emotional and physical, that sprang
up between Abe and Mary, it was only a matter of time before
she threw herself into an activity that she would find more
fulfilling than the role of stay-at-home wife.

Her first flight took place on 7 June 1927, when she flew with
her compatriot Sophie Eliott-Lynn (as she then was). Just four
months later, Mary Bailey gained her A licence. After another

four months, having finally informed her husband of her new hobby, she became the proud owner of G-EBPU, an 85 hp Cirrus Moth, which she 'dromed' at Stag Lane. At once, she began to compete in races and competitions, appearing in foul weather at an aerial rally held in Norwich in late February 1927. Six weeks later, she had a narrow escape while swinging the prop of her still almost new aeroplane. As the engine caught, she slipped and fell forward, the propeller clipping the top of her head and scalping her. Geoffrey de Havilland, who happened to be present, recalled how he 'retrieved a large patch of skin and hair from the ground' which he handed back to her and which was 'subsequently cleaned and bound back in place'. Undaunted, she was soon back in the cockpit and entered her first air race six weeks later. She came third, albeit last, as there were only two other competitors (it was the ladies' race). Two days later, however, she was mixing it with the men – two of whom unfortunately collided and were killed. In July, she set a world altitude record for a two-seat aircraft by climbing her Moth (with GDH's wife, Louie, as passenger) to 17,283 feet. That same month, she won a handicap race against thirteen male competitors at the Birmingham Air Pageant, an achievement she followed by being the first woman to fly solo across the Irish Sea. This she did using a partially inflated motorcycle inner tube in lieu of a lifejacket. In August, she competed – the only woman to do so – in the King's Cup. Three months after that, she became the first woman to obtain her 'blind flying' ticket (now known as an instrument rating). By the end of 1927, she was an experienced pilot in search of a new challenge. A flight to South Africa was the obvious answer.

With a long-range tank in place of the passenger seat, the 38-year-old mother of five took off for Cape Town on 3 March

1928. It was a cold and rainy afternoon which, at her first stop
in Croydon, soon turned to snow. As anyone who has piloted a
light aircraft in such conditions will testify, this is deeply dis-
orientating. Apart from the difficulty of seeing the horizon, it
takes a certain doggedness not to be overwhelmed by the relentless swirl of white. At least she was dressed for it: Russian boots,
a leather flying helmet and a sensible tweed skirt, topped off
with goggles and gloves. Airborne again after clearing customs,
she flew via Lympne in Kent and arrived at Berck-sur-Mer in
Normandy at 4.30 p.m., following an uneventful Channel crossing. But though her intended destination that afternoon was
Lyon, she made it less than halfway – forced down by a thick
band of fog on her path. Reaching Lyon on the Sunday, she
took advantage of the Mistral – the punishing wind that blows
north to south along the Rhône valley – to reach Marseilles
later that same day after 'a tremendous buffeting'.

The navigation from Marseilles to Pisa, in Italy, her next
stop, was straightforward. To begin with, she was accompanied by a squadron of aeroplanes piloted by well-wishers,
enthralled at the pluck of this lone and tiny *anglaise* (she stood
at five foot tall exactly). Dipping her wings to the last of them,
she set out along the coast, leaving Monte Carlo to port – the
town by Mary's time well established as a resort for wealthy
gamblers (Winston Churchill prominent among them) and as
the European epicentre of the jazz age, attracting the likes of
Coco Chanel and, from America, F. Scott Fitzgerald, among
other refugees from Prohibition.

Proceeding from Pisa via Genoa and Rome, she made her
way the next day on to Naples whose airport, she noted, was
surrounded, most inconveniently, with 'high walls and trees'.
These conspired to make her departure the following day

fraught with 'some exciting moments'. Even lightly loaded, and even with the benefit of 85 horsepower, the little Moth did not have an exactly sprightly take-off performance. Bound for Catania in Sicily, and hoping to take a good look at Mount Etna en route, she encountered turbulence so severe that 'the volcano was skipping around like a young ram' as she flew past.

The distance – entirely over water – from the southern tip of Sicily to Gozo (the northernmost island of the Maltese archipelago) is around 80 miles. Absent any navigational aids apart from a compass, it is essential that this one instrument is accurate. For each degree it is off true, you will find yourself approximately three hundred yards off course after 10 miles and, therefore, ten times that amount (i.e., getting on for 2 miles) over a hundred miles. It is therefore something of a miracle that Mary Bailey landed at Gozo, shrouded in mist, some ninety-odd minutes after take-off. Realising that she had nearly missed Malta altogether, she instructed a local engineer to check the accuracy of her compass. It turned out to be twenty degrees out on some points.

Welcomed by the local garrison of the Royal Air Force, the Irish aviatrix was received with excitement and, doubtless, a high degree of patriotic fervour. This was the Empire at its proudest: a plucky privateer on an adventure that would have been inconceivable barely a generation earlier. It was only right, therefore, that three seaplanes should be sent to accompany her the next day (damn the cost!) halfway to the coast of Africa. 'It was,' she wrote, 'a pretty sight to watch from the air' as they took off from the water. When, though, her escort turned back, she 'had nothing to watch' and, with only 'the engine humming and the glare of the sun on the water' to occupy her senses, she soon drifted off into an exhausted sleep. Waking with a start, Mary found the nose of the Moth pointing vertically up in an attitude it could not have sustained for more than another second before stalling and plummeting into the sea. Swiftly pushing the nose down to resume level flight, she realised that, if her compass did not lie, she was exactly 180 degrees off course. 'As the sea looked the same as before, I felt the compass must be wrong, but I knew I must not argue with it, so turned round and continued in the opposite direction.' Finding the coast at last, she was uncertain which way to go, opting in the end to turn right and head west in what proved to be the direction of Tripoli, landing there just before lunch exactly a week since leaving Stag Lane.

So far, the distances Mary had covered were comparatively short. From now on, however, she would be using the endurance of her Moth much closer to its limit. Saturday saw her negotiate a four-hour sea crossing of the Gulf of Benghazi, where she spent the next night. On Sunday, another four hours in the air saw her as far as the Libya-Egypt border and then, having refuelled, a further four hours took her into Aboukir. From there it was a short hop south-east along the Nile to Cairo where, to her dismay, she found herself up against the might of British Empire bureaucracy. 'My Moth was put under lock and key and the authorities looked as if they heartily wished they could do the same with me.'

Their decision was that Lady Bailey could not continue across the desert without escort. In vain did she appeal to Lord Lloyd, the high commissioner for Egypt. In vain did she petition Sir John Maffey, governor general of Sudan. In vain, too, did she protest that there was no room in the front cockpit on account of her long-range tank. What, they countered, if she were to come down and be set upon by natives? Suppose she crash landed among the 'dominions of a cannibal king or a village of mysterious dwarfs'. There would only be one end of that. And what about the Dinka who lived to the north of Khartoum (where General Gordon had fallen to the Mahdi less than a half century before)? As the popular novelist H. Rider Haggard would have it, these were men of 'uncertain temper', often of 'unusually large physique who wore their hair bleached with dung to resemble a cock's comb'. Only three months previously, a district commissioner had been murdered by ungrateful tribesmen. Although to lose a mere man might be tolerable, a woman's demise would necessitate a punitive expedition and the expenditure of at least a £250,000. There could be no question of her proceeding alone.

It was Abe who solved the problem. 'She has,' confided Abe to an acquaintance in high office, 'the obstinacy and determination of forty devils.' Arguing that if his wife must be escorted, then surely it did not matter whether that escort flew in the aeroplane with her or in another aeroplane alongside her. Indeed, surely it would be better if there were another aeroplane that could send for help if needed. This having been agreed – reluctantly on Mary's part, but at least she would still be able to claim a solo flight – it became a matter of finding someone willing to undertake the task.

As luck would have it, Dick Bentley was at that very moment on a honeymoon safari with Dorys, having recently made her his wife. On reaching Victoria Falls in Rhodesia, they had decided on a whim to keep going all the way to England and were therefore obvious candidates. The Bentleys cheerfully accepted Abe's request, having just recently performed the same service for Mary's friend, the former Mrs Eliott-Lynn, who, now as Lady Heath, was at that moment heading in the opposite direction.

With the Bentleys alongside her, Mary Bailey departed Khartoum in the direction of Nimule on the southern side of the Sudanese desert. There, her new-found friends turned round and made their way slowly back to England. Mary meanwhile decided against taking the more obvious route via Nairobi. She was worried that the authorities might again try to interfere, so she kept to the east of Lake Victoria with the intention of landing at Tabora. With only the most rudimentary maps at her disposal, it is perhaps not entirely surprising that she ended up lost and, in fact, a full hundred miles from her intended destination. But, having been given directions, she took off again only for a more serious mishap to befall her. Not appreciating the effect of altitude on air density, she approached to land too slowly, stalled and came down heavily, flipping the aeroplane over on its back as a result.

The cartoon of the accident that Mary drew for her children nicely sums up her attitude to her misfortune. It was no more than the sort of scrape you get into from time to time when out hunting. Her aeroplane was beyond straightforward repair, however, and there followed twelve days of inactivity during which our intrepid aviatrix sought a replacement machine. At least she didn't need to worry about the cost.

Finally re-horsed with an example of the latest X model Moth, Mary took off in the direction of Abercorn (present day Mbala) on the southern tip of Lake Tanganyika, which she located without difficulty. The next day she flew on to the Kenya-Rhodesia border where a fever compelled her to rest twenty-four hours, before pressing on over the Victoria Falls and picking up the railway line to Bulawayo. On arrival, she was entertained by the mayor and his wife, who provided comfortable lodgings where she was finally able to shake off the fever that had been dogging her. Her next stop was to be Pretoria, but again she got lost. Seeing a railway line where she thought no railway line ought to be, she landed to ask the way. Redirected, she then ran out of fuel, forcing her down at an unknown village where the inhabitants obliged her by 'running round with buckets and jugs looking for every last drop' of fuel to see the Great White Lady on her way again.

After a stopover among a colony of anthills at Warmbaths, she finally reached Pretoria on 27 April. There she was greeted by a large crowd of well-wishers who watched her depart for Johannesburg that same afternoon. Two more stops and she would reach her destination. She got to both without difficulty, but then came the Hex River Mountains. Rising to almost seven and a half thousand feet, they represented, in the heat of a spring day, an impossible obstacle and Mary found she could make no headway, forcing her, like Bentley, to make a detour along the coast.

At last, the gallant little Moth was seen as a speck on the horizon and a great cheer went up from the thousands-strong crowd that had gathered with Abe to meet her. Fifty-two days, of which 121 hours and thirty-five minutes were spent in the air, had passed since Mary Bailey left England. At a grand dinner given some days later, Abe Bailey eulogised his wife saying she had 'fairly nailed the petticoat to the masthead' and, hailing her bravery, said that not even he could have imagined that Mary would cap her achievement with a flight still more audacious than her earlier flight to Ireland. However, merely a month later, she announced her intention of flying home up the west coast of the continent.

This was not met with unqualified enthusiasm. The director of African Airways was among those who tried to dissuade her, writing an article in the *Cape Times* that claimed that, quite apart from the danger, it might look like she was 'stunting' for the glory of it. Undeterred, Mary set off – without fanfare or publicity – on the first leg to Port Elizabeth towards the end of September.

The flight back was considerably more challenging than the flight down. Her biggest problem was a lack of accurate maps. She had nothing whatsoever to go by for the leg from Bulawayo to Salisbury (modern day Harare), so she just 'bobbed about from one [farmstead] to another', landing to ask directions whenever the need arose. But while that was not a huge problem, given that Rhodesia was then firmly part of the British Empire and she would have no problem getting help if needed, the same was not true of most of the rest of her journey. Her plan, in view of this inconvenience, was simply to 'find out from place to place about aerodromes and supplies'.

Another difficulty she faced was the minimal margin of power over the weight of her aeroplane. The Cirrus II was a brilliant engine, but its 85 hp struggled in the heat and high altitude of Africa. Mary describes in her journal how, on the occasion of her departure from Broken Hill, she had to abort her first take-off. At the second attempt, she narrowly missed an obstacle at the end of the runway and thereafter flew a good many miles in ground effect, dodging and weaving her way through the scrub until, having used up sufficient fuel and reaching an area of higher pressure density, she was at last able to climb. 'Luckily', she noted, 'the trees were somewhat sparse.'

Having finally made it up to altitude, she was, of course, completely lost. It then became a matter of guesswork and hope. The wind was blowing from the south-west, so she fixed on a more easterly heading to compensate, with the aim of picking up the railway line running north to Elizabethville. By this time, it was starting to get dark so when, eventually, she did see a pair of gleaming tracks, she turned to follow them with great rejoicing. Unfortunately, they disappeared underground; they must have been the service line of some kind of mine. Executing a 180-degree turn, Mary headed south until, at last, she saw the welcome sight of some buildings in the distance. Her next problem was where to land before it became completely dark. Nowhere looked remotely suitable. There were some places she reckoned she could get into, but not out again. Finally, she spotted a clearing and 'blessed if there was not a most suitable long strip [but] *a hangar as well!!!* In great glee I landed on it and was going to ask what place it was when suddenly I saw Mr Murdoch ...' He was a fellow Moth owner whom she had met a few months earlier on the Cape.

At Kamina, having refuelled, she was dismayed to discover there was no suitable oil available. Desperate to press on, she made do with a substitute 'which I knew I did not like the look of'. After only a matter of minutes in the air, the oil pressure gauge began to drop. As luck would have it, she was able to land at a Catholic mission station where she was besieged by 'a crowd of men, women and children of all ages, all talking, yelling and much interested and excited'. Eventually, some of the mission fathers arrived and brought the crowd under control. The following day, a French official produced a drum of Mobil oil which sufficed to get her safely on her way to Musese, where she was handed a caterpillar specimen, almost five inches long 'and with masses of legs', for identification at the School of Tropical Medicine. Merely to touch it, she was told, induced immediate fever and, on occasion, even death.

There followed lots of 'muddling in and out of low cloud' as

Mary made her way steadily north. At Loanda she stopped a fortnight to join some friends on safari. At Leopoldville, capital of Belgian Congo, she ended up staying another fortnight with blood poisoning. African mosquito bites, a curse of the continent, turn quickly to abscesses when scratched and Mary's legs were covered in suppurating sores.

Determined to 'try the Sahara', she used the time to try to obtain help from the French administrators who, rather loosely, governed much of north-west Africa at the time. But they took too long to answer, so when Mary eventually departed Leopoldville she had no assurance of meaningful assistance. Ever the optimist, she pressed on undeterred, negotiating persistent bad weather. Over Lake Chad she encountered tornados, vast expanses of angry cloud lit up by lightning in which 'you could see every conceivable colour', forcing her to veer first one way, then the other, to avoid getting caught in them. As per usual, Mary's method was one of haphazard meandering that took her over immense expanses of forest, alternating with hour after hour of marshland in the vicinity of the great rivers and, between them, empty scrub. At one point she lost the sun hat that she had pulled over her flying helmet, having forgotten in the agitation of her departure to do it up. Well aware of the danger of sunstroke, she emptied the flour bag in which she was carrying her maps, stuffed these under her seat, and pulled the bag over her head instead.

Crossing into Nigeria, her maps ran out again so she took verbal directions to Fort-Lamy (now N'Djamena, capital of Chad), which was served by two roads. Unfortunately, she missed the turn off 'as a result of admiring the scenery'. Unable to orientate herself, and being forced lower and lower because of the cloud, she eventually landed at an unknown

village whose inhabitants immediately thronged the strip she
had chosen to land on. Fortunately, she found one who spoke
a little English. He explained that 'Mr King' would arrive
shortly in his motor car and would certainly be able to help. In
the meantime, Mary became increasingly afraid that the gathered crowd would besiege her aeroplane and implored his help
to keep them away. At this, some elders, armed with whips,
came forward and proceeded vigorously to defend the Moth,
'hitting out with such huge strokes' and stepping so high that,
due to their voluminous robes, 'they nearly turned head over
heels as they hit out'. They got into a frenzy that delighted the
crowd and only added to the merriment, such that 'they didn't
mind one little bit whether they got hit or not'. When eventually the promised motor car arrived, Mr King proved to be the
village chief, usefully accompanied by two interpreters whom
she proceeded to bombard with questions as to her wherea-
bouts. It turned out she was only 40 miles from her intended
destination. Thanking her saviour, she took off again, men
women and children scattering in all directions as she went.

The weather had by this time deteriorated so much that,
although she found the town of Karo easily enough, ground
mist prevented her from identifying the airfield. She narrowly
missed putting down in the cemetery on which she had lined
up at first and it was only by chance that she found a place to
land safely. From there, she continued to Zaria and thence,
following the course of the River Niger, to Gao. It was here
that her dreams of crossing the Sahara came to an end. For
ten days she endured the most primitive conditions she had
yet encountered – a mud hut with nothing but a mat on the
floor for a bed and, for company, a large toad. A 'native' and
his consumptive son slept on the verandah outside while, from

time to time, a large bat whizzed round her room at ankle height and a small, beige-coloured rat came to watch her as she wrote up her journal. Each day, Mary sent telegrams ahead to try to organise the necessary permissions and supplies. And each day she was disappointed by the indeterminate replies she received. Meanwhile, the governor of Nigeria let it be known that he wanted her to put her aeroplane on a boat at Dakar and continue the journey by sea. Naturally, she would have nothing to do with the idea.

On the eleventh day in Gao, Mary's patience finally ran out. Taking off with a full load of fuel and an empty stomach, she made for the coast intending to land at Mopti. Lost again, she decided to put down at a village to ask the way, but was at first unable to find anywhere suitable to land. When at last she did, she misjudged the approach and, in her efforts to avoid some telegraph wires in front of her, stalled and pancaked down – fortunately without nosing over – but with the result that her Moth's axle was badly bent. Now she was really stuck. She had no idea where she was, nor how far from assistance. Eventually, a car hove into view. She was told that to get to Mopti (in present day Mali), where she might find help, she would need to walk to the nearest village and hire a horse to take her to the next village, 12 miles beyond. There she would find a post office at which she might telegraph for a car. Setting off straightaway, she found the first village and 'a jolly little horse' equipped with a 'wicked bit' that she rode to the next. By dropping her reins, she found that it relaxed and bowled along happily in a hand canter all the way. Arriving at Mopti late in the evening, she found an engineer whom she tried to persuade to come immediately. When they finally got going, however, it was well after midnight. Almost at once, the car, with its one working headlight, ran over a jackal and narrowly missed hitting the crocodile pursuing it. Come daylight, the Moth's axle was soon fixed and she was back in the air with a pair of (live) cockerels gifted by the local chieftain who had come down to watch the fun.

The cockerels she put in the locker and found them none the worse for wear on arrival in Mopti, where she ended up staying three nights; the first two of them in a bare room with nothing to eat, all the shops being shut for the weekend. The local French administrator was as unhelpful as he could possibly be and it was only when she kicked up a fuss that he eventually sent her to some American evangelists, a kindly couple who gave her the first proper meal she'd had in days, followed by a bath and a bed. Next day, she set out for Dakar – though not before recording her intense dislike of French officialdom which, she complained, did 'nothing for the natives' and behaved 'with the caprice of an old woman'.

When, shortly before Christmas, Mary finally arrived at the coast, reaching Dakar with a leaky oil pressure valve, her chartless meanderings were over. Now capital of modern-day Senegal, the city was already served by weekly mail flights linking it with Paris, just over 2,500 miles to the north via Saint-Louis, Cisneros and Cap Juby – airfields that were soon to be made famous by the great French writer Antoine de St Exupéry. Most famous for his book *The Little Prince*, a fable inspired by one of several crashes in the Saharan desert, St Exupéry was station manager at Cap Juby until literally days before Mary arrived there. Indeed, it is a minor tragedy that they did not meet. As a result, we can only guess at what they would have made of one another. Like Mary, he was an aristocrat, his family having been ennobled during the time of the early Crusades. But what to say? He was tall, she was short; he was a dreamer, a romantic, a poet, brooding and abstracted; she was none of the foregoing but instead brusque and no-nonsense. Both were accomplished and wicked caricaturists, and both were brave to the point of foolhardiness. But in her journal, Mary has nothing to say about the catastrophic loneliness of the place that St Exupéry makes a world of in his great autobiographical meditation *Wind, Sand and Stars*. Indeed, it is hard to imagine her taking to him, or him to her. On the other hand, one likes to think that they might at least have admired one another a little in their shared contempt of danger.

This was very real. Aside from that of mechanical failure bringing aircraft down in physically inhospitable terrain, there was the deadly inhospitality of the local Moorish tribes to contend with. Ever since the discovery that the white men's flying machines carried not only edible goods but other treasures besides, they had become a target for the massed rifles of the native population. Two French airmen had recently been forced down en route to Cap Juby and murdered.

But it was thanks to the French, about whom she had been so scathing before, that Mary's troubles were now largely over. Not only did they provide good charts covering the route along the coast, but they also had emergency landing fields all the way. And thanks to the mail staging posts at Cisneros and St Etienne, she could be sure of the help of skilled mechanics should it be required – which was soon enough.

The first time was on Christmas Day when, a short while after leaving Cap Juby, her engine failed. By putting the Moth in a dive, she managed to restart it, but as soon as she levelled off, it failed again. With the incredible luck that characterised her whole venture, it happened that she found herself within gliding distance of an emergency landing field. After putting down, she was assisted by its resident guard who guided her to the road along which passed the bus to Tamanar. Taking this, she telephoned on arrival to the 'Chef d'Aeroplane' at Agadir who promised to send a mechanic next day.

Finally airborne again, she proceeded up the coast via Casablanca, across the Straits of Gibraltar to Malaga, arriving back in Europe on New Year's Day. From now on, it ought to have been plain sailing, but the engine trouble that beset her after Cap Juby persisted all the way until she reached home. At first, she thought it was the magnetos playing up, then the spark plugs. But new plugs did not solve the problem. In the meantime, she continued up through Spain and into France, crossing the Pyrenees to the west of Andorra, arriving at Bordeaux, after a flight in the freezing cold – the countryside blanketed with snow – of just under five hours. The next day she was in Paris where, thanks to the weather, she ended up staying a week at the Ritz before she could continue. Intending to make England in a single hop, she hit a snowstorm at Boulogne and, unable to see across the Channel or to trust the compass which was sticking in the cold, she eventually put down on the Brittany coast, staying two days before she finally made it home, escorted by an aircraft sent by the aero club at Croydon. There was snow on the ground and only a small if enthusiastic crowd of frozen well-wishers waiting to greet her, but the press went into raptures. The *Daily Telegraph* declared it 'the most remarkable flight made by any woman of any country'. No doubt the writer had in mind the recent transatlantic flight of Amelia Earhart – in which the aviatrix, though a qualified pilot, was merely a passenger – as perhaps did the editor of *Flight* magazine, who described Mary's achievement as being 'not only the most remarkable feat achieved by a woman [move over the Mother of God], but the greatest solo flight ever made by a pilot of either sex'.

Instantly famous, Mary was in massive demand as a public speaker. For weeks after her return she gave interview after interview. Awarded the Harmon Trophy for the most meritorious flight of the year, she was made a Dame Commander of the Order of the British Empire in the King's birthday honours.

What, though, might be the verdict of history on her exploits? Did Mary Bailey do something that many other women, given a similar education and the same financial resources, could not have done? Surely there must have been thousands if not millions of women worldwide who might have done the same thing? All this is true. But what can certainly be said of Mary Bailey is that she did not do what she did out of self-aggrandisement. She was not in it for Mary Bailey. There is nothing in any of her interviews or in her journals to suggest that vainglory was her motive. And whatever we might say of Mary and her privilege, there is no doubt that it was her courage, resourcefulness and pluck that proved, beyond all possible doubt, the astonishing capability of Captain de Havilland's Moth.

9

Flying Gypsies

A lthough none come close to St Exupéry either for lyr-
icism or for philosophical insight, quite a number of
the long-distance Mothists left entertaining accounts of their
exploits. The one that seems most nearly to capture the curious juxtaposition of frivolity and reckless enterprise common
to the upper echelons of society at the time is that of Violette
de Sibour, whose book, *Flying Gypsies*, tells the story of the
'year's vagabondage' she spent in the company of her husband
and their DH60 Moth, *Safari*. The couple could have walked
from the pages of Evelyn Waugh's *Vile Bodies*, his 1930 satire on
the Bright Young Things whose flamboyant and self-indulgent
antics were as much applauded as derided by the commentariat
of the day. Of American parentage, Violette was married to an
anglicised French aristocrat, Jacques de Sibour – a Vicomte like
St Exupéry. Her father was the Michigan-born businessman,
Gordon Selfridge Snr, who having both made and married a
fortune had come to England in 1906 and set up his eponymous
department store. Famous for his insight that 'the customer

is always right', Selfridge also had a keen understanding of the importance of aviation. He put Louis Blériot's aeroplane on display in one of his windows following the Frenchman's successful crossing of the Channel in 1909. As noted already, in 1926, a Moth occupied the same space.

Establishing himself at Highcliffe Castle, the magnificent and many-turreted Gothic revival mansion in Dorset, Selfridge was no stick-in-the-mud. When his wife died during the great flu pandemic just after the war, Gordon Selfridge took on a new lease of life, discovering the joys of the roulette wheel and prosecuting affairs with a succession of chorus girls. His most celebrated liaisons were with first Rose, then Jenny Dolly, each one a half of the Dolly Sisters duo – identical twins who had come to prominence with their dancing and vaudeville act. It is said that, between them, they gambled away a million pounds of Selfridge's fortune. Despite the fact that she was having an affair with the French-American actor, writer and aviator, Max Constant, the septuagenarian Selfridge offered Jenny a $10-million marriage settlement if she would become his wife. Unfortunately for all concerned, while on a final fling with Max, she was involved with him in a catastrophic car accident that left her badly disfigured. Selfridge got to keep his money, though he was at least gallant enough to fund her medical expenses. She finally married a wealthy Chicagoan lawyer instead, though it did not bring her happiness. She hanged herself from a curtain rail in 1941 – the year of Selfridge's own ruin. He, meanwhile, ended up in a three-roomed flat in Bayswater from which he is said to have set out every day until the end of his life to stand, incredulous, outside the store that bore his name.

At the time of Jacques and Violette's marriage – at which the bride wore a dress trimmed with lace from Marie Antoinette's trousseau – the business was flourishing, as it did for another decade, and the young couple were at the heart of the wealthy group of aviators that patronised the London Aero Club. She and Jacques had met at the beginning of the war and married soon after the armistice, her husband's title endearing him to her father sufficiently to cause the old man to overlook his prospective son-in-law's lack of money. He made the same allowance for his other two daughters. The youngest, Beatrice, married Jacques' older brother while Rosalie, the eldest, married the equally straitened Bulgarian-born Count Sergei de Bolotoff, later Prince Wiazemsky (his mother being related to the Tsar). Sergei was also a keen aviator. He claimed to have been (and may actually have been) the fifth man ever to fly and attempted to be the first across the Channel, designing and building his own triplane.

As for the heir apparent, Gordon Selfridge Jnr, he was also a Moth owner and a frequent participant in the activities organised by the London Aero Club. Unfortunately for his many admirers, he had a secret family, having fallen for the young woman who ran the toy department. Knowing that his father would not approve, he kept his marriage and the existence of his children hidden.*

Violette de Sibour was eventually to divorce Jacques on the

---

* Remarkably, two of his three sons, both mathematicians and graduates of the Massachusetts Institute of Technology, went on to have stellar careers in American academia. The older of the two, Oliver, authored the classic 1959 paper, 'Pandemonium, a Paradigm for Learning', for which he is regarded as one of the founding fathers of artificial intelligence. Another son, Ralph – a 5,000-hour private pilot – was an expert in digital simulation and a professor of mathematics and computer science at the University of Florida.

grounds of his cruelty but, in the meantime, can at least be said to have had an entertaining few years in his company. No sooner had the young couple bought their first Moth, G-EBSS – a Cirrus-engined X model, nicknaming it *Jeunesse* – than they began to dream of making a world tour. It took them a year before they were able to put their plan into action and, as a preliminary, they swapped *Jeunesse* for a DH60G, which they named *Safari*, doubtless thinking that the extra 15 hp provided by its Gipsy engine might come in handy. Their X model was meanwhile acquired by the Cinque Ports Flying Club where it lasted only a matter of weeks before being written off. The pilot, at 15 stone considerably above average weight at that time, was seen performing a series of well-executed aerobatic manoeuvres when, at the top of a loop, his safety harness failed and he fell from the cockpit.

The original impetus for the de Sibours' round the world trip was a conversation between Jacques and John Carberry in Kenya. Carberry persuaded him that the shooting to be had in the Far East was even better than in Africa, and it was with the intention of bagging a tiger that, sending their guns on ahead, the de Sibours departed Stag Lane on 14 September 1928, Violette having decided after careful deliberation to fly in trousers under her leather flying coat. Between them, Jacques reckoned they could afford to take no more than 30 lbs of luggage and, since he needed his evening dress, she would need to make do with 14 lbs. In the end she took:

- 1 complete Beige sport suit consisting of skirt, sweater and sweater coat
- A sleeveless Beige summer frock, and wide brimmed felt hat

- A black lace evening dress, and black fringed shawl
- Two pairs of shoes, and one pair of silver slippers
- Two complete sets of lingerie and half a dozen pairs of silk stockings

Plus, we may surely assume, some suitable jewellery.

Apart from the safari suit he flew in, among the luggage of M. le Vicomte, there was: a dinner jacket and trousers, a pair of black patent leather shoes, three white silk shirts and 'of course, collars, socks and so forth'. With a 'still camera, a motion picture camera and a tiny red cross box', their luggage was complete: 'madness it was – but we were generally considered crazy, anyway'.[1]

Their first stop was Paris, 'to say goodbye to our small son', Jacques junior. That was thoughtful of them.

Passing through Spain, the de Sibours flew over Gibraltar and into Africa. At Tangiers they were welcomed by some of the more important locals, who gave them obsequious 'thanks monsieur et madame, for honouring us with your itinerary' – to which they replied that their hosts cannot have been more grateful than they were to have arrived safely. On hearing some of the stories their hosts told them about the uncertain temper of the locals – 'Dreadful things have happened to people coming down ... and with your wife with you, monsieur, it would be madness.'[2] – the de Sibours were persuaded to proceed inland to Fez rather than to follow the coast of North Africa. Violette wondered – with a frisson of excitement? – whether she would be put 'in one of their harems. But no one smiled.'

Fez charmed them and there they gave dinner to a French air mail crew. Jacques went with the chef from their hotel to the market to buy food while Violette stayed behind and organised some musicians to play while they ate. After their meal they drove round the city walls in the moonlight. Having bid fond farewells to their fellow aviators, the Gipsy engine began to run rough over the mountains on their next leg. 'Then, with a final flutter, the propeller stopped dead. The silence was horrible . . .' Luckily, Jacques kept his head and, seeing a plausible landing ground, put the Moth into a steep side-slip. 'Like a piece of paper, we fell through space.' Safely landed, the fault turned out not to be serious and they were able to continue after Jacques had cleaned the oil filter. Later, as they crossed Algeria, they were so cold that they put down in the desert and played leapfrog to warm themselves up. Here the country's extreme desolation caused Violette to vow that, from now on, she would take an emergency supply of food and water – even if it meant leaving behind her second pair of shoes. But then she regretted doing so. It could only delay the inevitable and prolong the agony.

At Cairo they met up with the Bentleys who were on their honeymoon trip back to England – having escorted Sophie Heath in one direction over the Sudan and Mary Bailey in the other. They also coincided with Philip Sassoon who was on his way back from Karachi, fired with enthusiasm for what he called the 'Third Route' to the East – meaning the air route, the others being the sea route and the overland route – which he was in the process of surveying, partly by flying boat and partly in a converted Handley Page bomber.

Their next major stopover was at Baghdad, to which they were escorted by the crew who had just brought Sassoon to Cairo. There, the local RAF commander, Sir Henry Brooke-Popham, extended 'every courtesy' and accommodated the de Sibours at his residence.

Following the First World War carve-up of the Middle East that had so disappointed T. E. Lawrence, Iraq was at the time a semi-independent state, ruled by King Faisal, while the RAF, under Brooke-Popham, provided the country's defence and kept it ultimately under British administration. Invited to dinner with the King, Jacques had a lengthy discussion with Faisal about the latter's plans for agriculture and for irrigating the desert. Lawrence himself was meanwhile serving in humble capacity as an airman at Miranshah near the Khyber Pass, where he had recently met with Sassoon for some amiable conversation. It is clear that Sassoon had a respectful understanding of the compulsion that drove Lawrence to seek anonymity among the rough camaraderie of the barrack block.

It was here in Iraq that Jacques de Sibour endured the least comfortable twenty-four hours of their trip. Some rebellious Bedouin being in need of chastisement, Brooke-Popham had ordered a flight of Handley Page bombers to pay them a visit. Always on the lookout for sporting adventure, de Sibour persuaded his host to let him tag along in *Safari*. Unfortunately for him, his engine lost power, he lost sight of the other aircraft (and they of him) and he was forced down in the desert. Faced with the prospect of an exceedingly unpleasant termination of his earthly existence, Jacques found that although he could not coax enough power out of his engine to take off, at least he could taxy it. He therefore set off in the direction of Baghdad, managing to cover some 35 miles over the ground before stopping for an anxious night while awaiting rescue.

An engine inspection conducted by RAF mechanics revealed a serious crack in one of the Gipsy's cylinder heads. This necessitated ordering replacement parts from England so, in the interval, they took an excursion to Tehran. Here they bought a bloodstained dagger to send home to little Jacques. When, on their return to Baghdad, the needful parts had still not arrived, Violette wired her father who arranged for a replacement engine to be sent to Karachi. The plan was to transport *Safari* to the Persian Gulf by train and then put her on a boat. On arrival, the faulty engine would be swapped out and the new one installed.

When the couple were finally able to resume their journey eastward, they proceeded across Rajasthan via Jodhpur, at whose palace they saw the gilded bas-relief prints of women whose last act before consigning themselves to the flames in sutti, following the death of their husbands, was to sink their hands in plaster. At the Taj Mahal, not far distant, Violette wondered out loud whether Jacques would build one for her:

'Humph,' he replied. 'She had fourteen children in fifteen years.'

   'Quite irrelevant,' she thought.

The following evening, they were astonished to hear the sound of an approaching aircraft. It duly landed, causing them to hasten to see who it could possibly be. It turned out to be none other than Joseph Le Brix, the celebrated French long-distance aviator who was attempting to reach Saigon from Paris in fewer than five stages. He and his crew looked 'tired and overwrought' so Violette plied them with champagne and sandwiches while their machine was refuelled. Two days later, Le Brix came down in a swamp approaching Rangoon. 'This,' she noted drily, 'was the sort of reassuring stuff we were always hearing.' Happily, all three crew members survived – in

Le Brix's own case for another two years before he was killed when his engine failed over Siberia en route to Tokyo.

Meanwhile, the de Sibours had better luck and flew on to Calcutta via Benares, where Violette was at first thrilled and then horrified by an extravagant wedding procession. It turned out that the bride-to-be was just six years old. That night at dinner with the Highland Infantry, they were serenaded with Scottish airs played on bagpipes.

From Calcutta, they flew on towards Akyab (Sittwe) in Burma (Myanmar). This terrified Violette: 'On our right was the shark-infested ocean; on our left, in the distance, towered the mountains of Malay.' Beneath, 'crocodiles'. 'Thank heaven', she wrote, that she hadn't realised that some of the islands they flew over were 'inhabited by pygmies – more animal than human, who live in trees and are known to be treacherous and, sometimes, cannibalistic'.[3] Things did not improve much when they were properly overland. It was 'hellish country' whose 'tropical forests were infested with tiger, leopard, elephant' and through which, should they be forced down, they would have to trek a hundred miles without provisions to reach safety. She wondered whether they would have the courage to use their revolver on themselves.

But they made it, and on arrival in Rangoon, where they landed on the racecourse, they took some time to go sightseeing. On their itinerary was a visit to a drug den. It was:

stuffy and dimly lighted. For some time, I watched a young girl. She could hardly have been more than 15. When her turn came, she offered the back of her neck. As the jab of the needle went in, I winced in sympathy but she merely closed her eyes and a look of ecstasy slowly spread over her coarsened features.[4]

At their next stop in Moulmein, where they were forced down in a storm, the de Sibours met 'the famous Gandhi of India' who happened also to be visiting. Alas, Violette noted only that he made a careful inspection of *Safari* and had nothing more to say about him.

Arriving in Bangkok not many days later, having faced tropical storms and almost run out of fuel, the couple met up with yet another long-distance aviator, the splendidly named twenty-two-year-old Baron Friedrich Karl Richard Paul August Koenig von und zu Warthausen. He, having left Berlin the previous August, was staking a claim to be the first person to fly solo round the world in a light aircraft. Taking a commendably leisurely approach to his flight, the baron had spent three months on the Indian subcontinent, where he had also met with Gandhi and about whom he has even less to say in his thoroughly tedious memoir, *Wings around the World*. He was a little more eloquent about the cat which the Crown Princess of Siam presented him with. It had, he said, 'the whitest and longest hair' he had ever seen on a cat and 'the bluest of eyes'. It accompanied him all the way home and eventually became a member of the household at his father's castle where it 'got along very well' with two German shepherds. The only really remarkable fact that the baron reveals in the course of his book is that the Daimler engine that powered his Klemm monoplane, produced a mere 20 hp. He claims that this gave him a top speed of 70 mph, but even if this is not an exaggeration (and, according to Klemm's own data, it is), he'd have been pushed to cruise at much above fifty, making his progress as slow as it was – undeniably – remarkable.

The de Sibours, meanwhile, reached Saigon in the spring of 1929, whereupon they embarked on their planned month-long hunting expedition, during which each bagged a tiger. Pathetically, Violette de Sibour dismisses the slaughter in a few short sentences. She is more concerned about having had to sleep in a 'native hut' with twenty other occupants, occasioning a furious row with Jacques. Fortunately for him, she wrote, 'nothing ever lasts long with me – illness, temper – or money' and she quickly regained her composure. Indeed, she continued, 'the queerest part is that, in the end, we slept excellently'.[5] When they finally left with their trophies, their jungle-dwelling hosts insisted that they join the tribe in a ceremony that involved bathing their feet in the blood of a freshly slaughtered pig, an event that appalled Violette far more than the tiger shoot.

Unlike their friend the baron, the de Sibours decided against flying in China and Japan, shipping the faithful *Safari* from Bangkok to Seattle via Yokohama. With the plane reassembled, they then flew in easy stages to New York, stopping in Chicago and at Angola, where they narrowly avoided a tornado which was reported to have uprooted forty fully grown trees in the neighbourhood. In New York, they passed 'possibly the busiest ten days of [their] lives ... amid luncheons, dinners, dances and theatres' after which, at a day's notice, they were called to Washington where they were received by President Hoover. About him, too, Violette has no more to say than she did about Mahatma Gandhi. At least she was consistent in her silences.

Safari was subsequently shipped from New York to Le Havre where they caught up with her in August, flying to Paris by following the Seine as they had no maps. Did they see their little boy while there? We are not told. And yet, one wonders whether this sort of unemotional parenting wasn't the very thing that produced the selflessness that propelled people such as Jacques Junior to volunteer when the Second World War broke out. He served first with the British, who put him in the army and gave him a commission, then with the Free French when the British wouldn't let him fly. He was killed in aerial combat in 1941.

When they finally came in to land at Stag Lane, a year and five days since their departure, Violette tells us that 'Jack's hasty sideslip' knocked the lipstick out of her hand. But oh well, she clearly forgave him as, a year later, they were on their way again – this time to Abyssinia.

10

Bad Luck Wimpey and the Moth Maniacs

I t has been said that Edward, Prince of Wales' enthusiasm for flying did more than anything else to popularise the idea of air travel in Britain and the Empire.[1] This is doubtful, though his purchase of a DH60G in 1929 certainly did much for the continuing ascendancy of the Moth. But in terms of popularising flying itself, arguably of greater importance was the contribution of the country's aviatrices – almost all of whom also flew Moths. The word aviatrix (of which aviatrices is the plural) simply means 'female pilot'. But it can also be understood as a metaphor that represented the claim for the equality of women – their equal skill, their equal daring. The aviatrix thus stood at – or, rather, she piloted her machine along – the edge of traditional femininity and enlarged the notion of what a woman could be – not just glamorous and desirable, not just a mother and caregiver, but someone who could compete on exactly the same terms as men in this most demanding of disciplines. Of course, it is true that some women used flying as a way of getting close to desirable men.* But, on the whole, flying seems to have held an attraction not unlike that of the hunting field: not every girl who rode a pony wanted to be in at the kill; not every woman who went up in an aeroplane wanted to be a pilot. But for an intrepid few, that was precisely the point of the exercise.

Besides the towering contribution of Ladies Heath and Bailey and, later, Amy Johnson, among other women who either owned or were trained on Moths, was Lois Butler, Alan Butler's Canadian-born wife, he being by now Chairman of de Havilland. A keen air racer, she had a custom-built Moth coupé in which she competed in the round-Europe race of 1928. Also an expert skier, she went on to represent her native country in the 1936 Winter Olympics. During the Second World War, she became one of the most experienced pilots in the Air Transport Auxiliary.

Another Irish aviatrix was Sicele O'Brien, one of the eight daughters of Sir Timothy O'Brien (3rd Baronet – he also had two sons, all with the same wife). Her father's batting score of 92 while an undergraduate at Oxford was pivotal in securing the university's only ever win over the Australians. He also had the unique distinction of having captained both the English and the Irish national cricket teams. Sicele, having served as a

---

* I fear that my great-aunt, Rosalind Norman, was one of them. According to her daughter, even though she owned two aeroplanes, first a Moth, then an Avian, which she used partly for business purposes – she had her own company making to-scale wooden aircraft models for the industry – and partly for touring (her parents had a house in the south of France), she was terrified of flying. But she was in love with the already secretly married Gordon Selfridge.

driver during the First World War, was forty when she took up flying but quickly made a name for herself, winning the 1926 Aerial Oaks – a ladies' race that took place in the environs of a West Country racecourse, with competitors taking off and landing in front of the grandstand.* In August 1927, she bought an early Cirrus I-engined Moth from the de Havilland School of Flying. This she operated for just over a year before writing it off on Mill Hill golf course (interrupting a four-ball match as it approached the ninth hole) while giving instruction to a friend, the Hon. Mildred Leith. Unfortunately, she had failed to ensure that the rudder bar was connected in the front cockpit with the result that when the student (presumably inadvertently) put the Moth into a spin, she could do nothing. As a result of the ensuing crash, Sicele lost one of her lower legs. Nothing daunted, she carried on flying with a prosthetic limb, once remarking that, 'It was worth it. One has to take risks for anything that is worthwhile.' History does not record whether her student took the same view.[2]

O'Brien was subsequently a founder member of the Aviation Ambulance Association and worked for the Air League of the British Empire, and was principal organiser of the 1929 Air Rally at Gleneagles. She replaced the Moth firstly with a Westland Woodpigeon and then with a Blackburn Bluebird, both considerably smaller and less capable than a Moth, if also a lot cheaper to buy and run. The Bluebird she co-owned with Enid Gordon-Gallien, also a pilot as well as an explorer who had recently won the Royal Geographical Society's prestigious

---

* Bert Hinkler gave a demonstration flight piloting his aircraft round the steeplechase course inches above the ground and jumping the fences as if on horseback.

Back Award for the expedition she led to Tanganyika in 1928–9. Sadly, they were both killed in the Bluebird on take-off from Hatfield in June 1931.

In the annals of British aviation, the names of two other lady Mothists, Pauline Gower and Dorothy Spicer are inseparable. They jointly ran an air taxi and joyriding company using a three-seater Spartan, the former as pilot, the latter as mechanic. The company was barely profitable and they subsequently joined the British Hospitals Air Pageant, operating a Gipsy Moth. During the war, both became members of the Air Transport Auxiliary (ATA) and, indeed, it was Pauline Gower who was the founder member and first commandant of the Women's Section. The ATA, of which fully 10 per cent of its personnel were female, went on to provide indispensable support to the RAF from the Battle of Britain until the end of the war, servicing, repairing and ferrying aircraft. Tragically, both women died young – Dorothy Spicer with her husband in an air crash in South America in 1946; Pauline Gower, by this time a highly respected engineer working at the Royal Aircraft Establishment at Farnborough, on giving birth to twins a year later. One of her sons wrote a book in tribute to her. Dorothy Spicer's daughter became a racing driver.

Another well-known female Moth pilot of the day was 'Connie' Leathart, whose determination in the hunting field was matched only by her enthusiasm for air racing. Educated at Cheltenham Ladies College and later also a member of the Women's ATA, serving under Pauline Gower (as did Amy Johnson), Connie Leathart learned to fly with the Newcastle Aero Club, writing her name as 'C. R. Leathart' on the application form to disguise her gender. With a substantial private income at her disposal, she featured regularly at events such as the 1930 Heston Flying Cruise to Germany, where she and other members of the group – which included three other lady pilots besides herself – were entertained to lunch on board the *Graf Zeppelin*. Together with her friend Walter (later 2nd Viscount) Runciman, she subsequently set up an aircraft repair company and designed and built her own glider. As a member of the ATA, she delivered both heavy bombers and fighters. When, reluctantly, she gave up flying in 1958, she retired to her farm in Northumberland where she looked after rescued donkeys and, needless to say, swam every day in its unheated swimming pool.

Lest it be supposed that only upper-class women were welcome as members of the Moth sisterhood, Winifred Brown gives the lie to the notion. The daughter of a Salford butcher, she was expelled from school aged fourteen for writing 'the headmistress can go to hell' on the wall of a lavatory cubicle and is said to have learned to roll her own cigarettes at the age of five. Having learned to fly on the Moths of the Lancashire Aero Club – and having had her portrait taken by Lafayette – she obtained her pilot's licence in 1927. She subsequently acquired an Avro Avian. Although by the end of 1929, 85 per cent of all aircraft in private ownership were Moths of one description or another, the Avian was its closest competitor. Though marginally faster than the Moth, it was less capable in that it could carry only a lighter load. But it was a delight to fly and had, some might argue, prettier lines. And as Winifred Brown (and Bert Hinkler) proved, in the right hands the Avian could, until the advent of a new Gipsy engine in 1930, compete with the Moth on equal terms.

When, though, Winifred Brown announced her intention of entering her aeroplane (bought for her by her father) in the

1930 King's Cup, the club tried to dissuade her on the grounds that an unfavourable result would reflect on it badly. She took part anyway and was one of the starters in the race's largest ever field. Bad weather over the Pennines hindered many competitors but it happened that she knew the area well and took the route over the Woodhead Pass, which put her in the lead, which she then held all the way back to Hanworth, becoming the first female winner of the race, just beating Alan Butler, in his specially configured racing Moth, into second place.

Winifred Brown switched from flying to sailing in 1935 and went on to make various epic sea voyages, including one to Spitzbergen in the Arctic and one up the Amazon, both adventures she wrote about in books. In retirement, she lived aboard her motor-sailer with her King's Cup trophy displayed in its aft cabin. Her son, Tony Adams, was a successful actor with a long-running role in the soap opera *Crossroads*.

Also a water sports enthusiast and similarly intrepid was the Hon. Mrs Victor Bruce (née Petre; a descendant of Sir William Petre, Secretary of State to three successive Tudor monarchs) who, at twenty-five, had an illegitimate child following an affair with a wealthy landowner. A year later, she married someone else – the son of a peer – and a year after that set out with him on a driving endurance trial that started in Monte Carlo and ended, after 8,000 miles, in England. Almost no sooner than they were back than they set off for the Arctic Circle, planting a flag 250 miles inside it – a feat not bettered until the twenty-first century. In 1929, alone this time, Mildred Bruce established a world record by driving her 4½ litre Bentley for twenty-four hours at Montlhéry autodrome at an average speed of 89 mph. She was an early member of the London Ladies Motorcycle Club and also an enthusiast of speed on the water who, again in 1929, set a speed record for the fastest crossing of the Channel in both directions in her speedboat *Mosquito*. It seems inevitable that she should have learned to fly on one of the London Aero Club Moths. She subsequently flew round the world – actually in a Blackburn Bluebird – before buying a Gipsy Moth and joining the British Hospitals Air Pageant flying circus, where, in addition to displaying the Moth, she flew a Fairey Fox, developing a manoeuvre known as the 'Fox Dive' for the benefit of extra thrill-seeking joyriders. The Fairey Fox was an ex-RAF fighter-bomber which she had bought for scrap, minus engine, for £2 10s. The engine cost a tenner. Her stunt involved sending the Fox into a vertical dive towards the crowd which she pulled out of at the last possible moment. She clearly took seriously the remark of the American barnstormer who proclaimed that 'bandages are box office'.[3] Astonishingly, Mrs Bruce died in her bed aged ninety-four.

Certainly, the most aristocratic Moth owner-operator outside the royal household was Mary, Duchess of Bedford. A daughter of the Anglican Archdeacon of Lahore, her married life was unhappy partly on account of the fact that the duke, although a devoted public servant and one of England's richest landowners, was decidedly ungenerous as a husband. Whenever Mary wanted to take out one of the twenty-one cars on the Woburn estate, she had to get a chit signed by the duke to hand to the chauffeur. Highly intelligent, she was a keen photographer, a breeder of rare cats, a knowledgeable ornithologist, a crack game shot, an expert gardener and an athlete who, at the age of thirty-five, became one of the first British woman to make a study of a Japanese martial art, writing an introduction to and featuring in the illustrations to her friend Emily Watts' book *The Fine Art of Jujitsu*, which was published in 1906. As if this were not enough, in middle age she trained to be a nurse – radiography being just one of her qualifications – as a prelude to opening and running a total of four hospitals, one of which, during the First World War, she opened for wounded servicemen in the grounds of her home at Woburn Abbey. Something of a rebel politically, she was a supporter of Emmeline Pankhurst's suffragettes and contributed to the militant Women's Tax Resistance League.

For someone who had been so active in so many areas of life, the loss of hearing that began to affect the duchess as she got older affected her deeply. Unable any longer to play an active role in her many good causes, flying became her solace. Although she did not go up on her first flight until over the age of sixty, she bought, in addition to her Moth – which she used for shorter journeys – a Fokker F.VIIA. She used this to fly to Karachi and back during the summer of 1928 with her personal pilot, Charles Barnard, at the controls, while she sat in the back, knitting. The following year, she upgraded her Moth to a G model and it was in this aeroplane that she finally obtained her own licence after thirty hours' dual instruction. Taking such a long time to solo makes the duchess sound like a very slow learner, given that average was around eight hours. But one has to remember that, by now, she was quite unable to hear anything her instructor might have wanted to tell her.

Mary Bedford continued flying throughout the 1930s. Having sold the Fokker, she replaced it with a Puss Moth for her long-distance flying (when she invariably took Barnard with her) but she continued to fly the Gipsy herself. Amassing almost two hundred hours' solo time, she met her end in the North Sea when flying her latest acquisition, a DH60 Moth Major, in March 1937. By then, she was seventy-one and now her sight was failing too. Her body was never found, but several parts of her aeroplane were subsequently washed up on shore. There has been some speculation that her disappearance was an act of suicide.

Overseas, there was a good number of female Mothists who made history. One of the most significant of these was Lotfia Elnady, who, in September 1933, against the wishes of her father but with the enthusiastic encouragement of her mother, was the only woman among thirty-four aspiring pilots to embark on a training course at Moth-equipped Cairo flying club. To help pay for her lessons, she worked as the organisation's secretary and telephone operator. When she qualified – simultaneously the first Egyptian woman, the first woman from the Arab world and the first African woman to do so – the press made enough of a fuss to persuade her father that this might not be such a bad thing for his daughter to do and, after a flight with her over the Great Pyramid, he too lent his support. Later that same year, Elnady was a competitor in the Alexandria–Cairo air race, following which a public subscription was organised by feminist leader Huda Sha'arawi to buy her an aeroplane of her own. This she operated for five years before injuring herself in a crash that damaged her spine and put a stop to her flying, though she lived to the age of ninety-three.

The aviatrix par excellence, however, the one held in highest regard for her piloting skills, was Winifred Evelyn Spooner. The fourth child and only daughter of an army veteran who died the year after she was born, Winifred Spooner attended Sherborne School for Girls where a scholarship in her name is still awarded every year to a pupil showing 'courage, generosity of mind, enterprise and independence'. After school, Winifred studied briefly at Reading University but left to take a job in a YMCA canteen in Germany, before following the lead of her immediate elder brother and learning to fly. Gaining her A licence in 1927, Wimpey, as she was universally known, immediately acquired the first of a succession of four DH60 Moths of her own and, shortly afterwards, flew to Venice to attend that year's Schneider Trophy competition.

Gaining her commercial pilot's licence in 1929, Winifred Spooner became the first female British pilot to earn her living as a professional pilot. Basing her Moth, now upgraded to a DH60G, at her brothers' farm (where, as all ex-cavalry officers should, they bred, bought, trained and sold hunters, chasers and polo ponies), she offered an air taxi service at £4 per hour, or a shilling a mile.

A keen air racer, Winifred Spooner came third in her first King's Cup in 1928 and fifth in 1929. At that time, the most important of the overseas air races was the Challenge International de Tourisme. Held over several days each year, the competition had, besides a timed rally that took in many of the Continent's major cities, a technical component where competitors were awarded – or lost – points for things like wing folding, whether or not a parachute and fire extinguisher were carried and the ease with which the competitors were able to start their engines. Fuel consumption was also an important consideration. The prize money for this competition was considerably more generous than anything to be won in Britain – 100,000 French francs (about £800) to the winner, 50,000 for second place, 25,000 for third and 7,350 for the next sixteen finishers, though even to participate was expensive and the competition was stiff. At her first attempt, Winifred came tenth behind company test-pilot Hubert Broad, who took second place in a factory-prepared Moth. The following year, Broad won and Winifred came seventh overall (while Mary Bailey came thirty-eighth).

In 1930, she came second in a round-Italy air race and was wildly cheered for her performance. A contemporary newspaper report notes that she 'shyly received the congratulations of the Italian Air Minister Signor Balbo' looking like 'a schoolgirl in disgrace, with one stocking round her ankle above a crimson slipper'.[4] That same year, Wimpey had a lucky escape when another aircraft she was flying (a Desouther, rather than a Moth) went into the water at night off the coast of Calabria in southern Italy, her co-pilot having fallen asleep while she herself was resting. Although he was injured, she was not and, fortunately, their aircraft did not sink. Wimpey was thus able to swim the 2 miles to shore where, guided by some lights, she found some fishermen whose assistance she engaged.

Wimpey subsequently became the personal pilot of Sir Lindsay Everard, Member of Parliament, brewer and philanthropist, who became president of the Leicester Aero Club – to which he donated a Moth in 1929 – and with him flew throughout Britain, Europe and the Middle East. She continued racing, however, and, in 1932, was placed fourth after the technical trials of the International Challenge de Tourisme but withdrew due to fuel contamination – possibly the result of sabotage – at the beginning of the next stage. Captain Barnard (brother of the Duchess of Bedford's personal pilot), chief instructor of the de Havilland school of flying, regarded her as the best female pilot in the world – having demonstrated a Moth to Amelia Earhart he could make a comparison with America's most celebrated aviatrix. Alas, Wimpey never won a major competition outright, hence, no doubt, the addition of

'Bad Luck' to her nickname. She suffered further cruel luck when, in January 1933, she took ill with a cold that progressed to pneumonia. Unfortunately, because of bad weather, the doctor bringing potentially life-saving oxygen became lost in the fog and he arrived too late to save her. She died on the 13th of the month.

Two other female Moth pilots who deserve to be remembered are Diana Guest, daughter of Freddie Guest MP – a cousin of Winston Churchill (who had himself been an enthusiastic if somewhat inept pilot, until persuaded by his wife, Clementine, to give up his ambition to learn to fly following a crash that injured his instructor). Diana learned to fly at the same time as her father, following which he gave her a Moth for her eighteenth birthday and, on her twenty-first, a Puss Moth. On the latter occasion, her mother, being more practical, gave her a French maid. Diana herself went on to be an accomplished stone carver whose work is found in collections around the world. At the opposite end of the spectrum is Kathleen Butler (no relation), who learned to fly on a Gipsy Moth at Dublin's Kildonan Aerodrome at the age of twenty-four. Less than a week later, she joined the Sisters of Charity and became a nun. She was later famous for being a prodigious writer of letters to the sick, the lonely and those in prison.

If the way that Captain de Havilland's Moth attracted outstanding females to the aviation cause was a lasting achievement, its snaring of the future King Edward VIII was nonetheless the one that, at the time, seemed more significant. When the company announced breathlessly in its in-house magazine, the *DH Gazette*, that, 'at the latter end of 1929 we were honoured by a command to supply a Gipsy Moth to the Prince of Wales for his personal use. Hitherto we have been banned by a pledge to observe the strictest secrecy . . .', this was the icing on the cake.

The prince himself had shown increasing interest in aviation ever since he had first flown in 1918. It was not until 1927 that King George permitted him to tour the country by air, however, and it was only with great reluctance that the monarch permitted him to use aeroplanes, and then only if the tightness of his schedule actually warranted it. This did not suit the prince at all. Just as he was a thruster in the hunting field, so did he prove to be one for pushing on in the air. On one occasion, he tried to insist on being taken from Castle Bromwich to Cardiff, in spite of a dire weather forecast. In desperation, his pilot engineered an intervention from higher authority. Led to the telephone, a puzzled prince found himself talking to Lord Trenchard, Marshal of the Royal Air Force, who pulled rank on him: 'Good morning, Group Captain [the Prince's honorary rank]. I am giving you an order. You are not to fly on to Cardiff.'[5]

By the time the prince placed his order, the Moth had attained its classic form, though there was one further engine upgrade to come with the 120 hp Gipsy II engine introduced in late 1930. In the four years since the prototype had flown, there had been a number of small but important changes. The exhaust pipe had gone from the starboard to the port side, its wingspan had increased by a foot, its all-up weight had increased by 200 lbs, the stagger between the wings had increased by almost two and a half inches while the lower wing dihedral had also increased by a half-inch and continuous testing and development ensured that further minor tweaks were introduced throughout the Moth's career. One such test involved a landing by Geoffrey de Havilland in which, at fifty feet, he closed the throttle and pulled the stick fully aft with the intention of bringing the aeroplane onto the ground in a fully developed stall in order to see whether the new split-axle undercarriage could cope. Unfortunately, the rigging was slightly out of true and the Moth dropped a wing shortly before arrival, ending up on its nose, though GDH was unharmed. The one major improvement – which, had they been fitted on this occasion, would almost certainly have saved the Captain's embarrassment – was the addition, at extra cost, of Handley Page slots. These devices, by causing the airflow over the leading edge of the outer wing to remain smooth right up to and even beyond the stall, greatly improved the handling characteristics of the aeroplane in this critical phase of flight.

While the civilian version of the aeroplane was more or less standardised by 1929, its development for specialist overseas and military use meant that for such customers there was a wealth of different options for them to choose from. Besides improved floats, there were skis in place of wheels for operation on snow. There were camera guns and reconnaissance cameras, flare and bomb racks for the military and a special version of the aeroplane, the DH60T Moth Trainer, was supplied in numbers to the Egyptian, Iraqi and Brazilian air forces. More or less standard Moths were also acquired by at least twenty-nine other countries (thirty if you include Japan, who stole some from the then Republic of China).

As for the Prince of Wales' own machine, it had a number of unique features.[6] Painted in Brigade of Guards colours – dark blue and maroon, with the royal cypher emblazoned on its polished aluminium engine cowlings – the aeroplane had seats upholstered in red leather and an extended locker to accommodate the royal hats and golf clubs. Alas, the prince was getting ahead of himself. He had bought the aeroplane with the intention of learning to fly but it was almost a year before the king permitted his heir to take lessons, a fact that annoyed his son intensely. It seems that he never actually qualified for his A licence, though he did make at least one solo sortie in secret, with only his instructor, Squadron Leader Don and a mechanic as nervous witnesses. Nonetheless, for the two years he owned the Moth, the prince's aircraft was a highly visible symbol of the type's success. If the Moth was fit for a future king, what was it not fit for?

Inevitably, the Prince of Wales' patronage of the DH60 did one thing above all and that was to make flying fashionable. Glancing through the list of Moth owners in England at the time, it certainly looks as though anyone who was anyone in society had similarly succumbed to Moth mania – at least the adventurous among them. Aside from Sir Philip Sassoon and Colonel the Master of Sempill, there were legions of lords and honourables, and several Members of Parliament in addition to those already mentioned. Among them was Hylton Murray-Philipson, son of the test cricketer of the same name, who kept his Moth in a coach house at Stobo Castle, the family house. Another was Robert Perkins, MP for Stroud and Tewkesbury and a close friend of Winifred Spooner. Speaking in the House in March 1932, he rather uncharitably claimed that he would rather fly in formation with 'a winged dragon' than go anywhere near most lady pilots who were, with some notable exceptions, 'notoriously dangerous and inefficient' in the air.[7] One wonders what he thought of the female pilots of the Air Transport Auxiliary. Among Moth fashionistas was the Bloomsbury Group writer and publisher David Garnett (a former lover of Scottish artist and textile designer Duncan Grant) who, though he did not in the end buy a Moth, learned to fly on one, and wrote an entertaining memoir of the three years and thirty-odd hours it took him to finally gain his A licence.

Of the many flying clubs that sprang up at this time, it was inevitable that the London Aero Club should be the most glamorous. Its proximity to the capital gave it the advantage over the others and its annual garden party held at Heston, attended on at least one occasion by both the Prince of Wales and the Duke of Gloucester, became an important fixture of the social season. Yet the club itself was neither overtly exclusive nor snobbish. Anyone could apply to be a member – even Yorkshire lasses who worked in solicitors' offices. Certainly, there were circles within circles but, in the main, people were united in their love of flying and help and advice was freely given between the membership, even if the barriers came firmly down the moment you stepped outside the airfield boundary. It is also true that the individuals who went on the club's rallies were among the wealthier of its membership. Amy Johnson could certainly not have afforded extended capers such as the one flutteringly reported by *The Aeroplane* in October 1933, when members flew via Paris, where they stayed at the Hotel George V, before heading to the south of France and, among other splendours, were entertained by the parents of several related members to luncheon at the Château de la Garoupe on the Cap d'Antibes. With its view from the hall looking in one direction, you can see across the bay of Nice to the Alpes-Maritimes while in the other, you look down its immaculate terraces to the sparkling sapphire of the Mediterranean beyond. En route, there was a champagne reception at Orly, cocktails at Cannes and, on the way home, debauchery in a Parisian night-club followed by still another champagne reception at Rheims. All this in addition to the excitements due to bad weather and mechanical problems. Somebody's spark plugs burned out, somebody else had to put down in a field somewhere and the de Sibours could only join for a day as they were off to China in their new DH84 Dragon, but nobody minded because wasn't it all so jolly?

If, though, there was one member outside the royal family that every member of the London Aero Club hoped to meet, it was Philip Sassoon. An invitation to any one of his three magnificent properties (Trent Park in Middlesex, Port Lympne in Kent and the 13,000 square foot No. 25 Park Lane, with its winter garden and four-storey marble staircase) was the secret hope of many. Chez Sassoon, they might bump into anyone from Lawrence of Arabia, to Noel Coward, to Winston Churchill, to the Prince of Wales himself.

Born into great riches in 1888, Sassoon was a prominent member of a Jewish clan, originally from Baghdad, that had established a vast trading empire – with a very profitable line in the supply of opium to China – covering the East and Far East. His mother was a Rothschild – he was born in her Parisian mansion – while his younger sister married the Marquess of Cholmondeley. One cousin, from a less wealthy branch of the family, was the poet Siegfried Sassoon. Unlike Siegfried, who attended Marlborough and Cambridge University, Philip was an Etonian and went on to Oxford. At the age of twenty-four, he inherited the family baronetcy and in the same year became a Conservative Member of Parliament, though both his father and grandfather had been Liberals. Throughout the First World War, Sassoon served as private secretary to Field Marshal Haig. In 1920, he became parliamentary private

secretary to the Prime Minister David Lloyd George. Writing
some time later, his friend Lady Diana Cooper wrote to
Sassoon saying that she had heard that Jesus Christ had risen
and was looking for a secretary: would he be taking the job?[8]

Although one of the first private pilots in the country – he
acquired an Avro 504K the year after the armistice, and a
DH60M Metal Moth in 1929 – and, although he was a founder
member of the Royal Auxiliary Air Force, it was not until he
was appointed Squadron Leader of 601 Squadron that Sassoon
actually learned to fly. He was a poor student. When his instructor, Dermot Boyle (subsequently Marshal of the Royal
Air Force) was asked whether he was having any success with
Sassoon, he replied that he was 'not actually teaching him to
fly ... only to land'.[9] He eventually qualified for his first solo
after more than double the average number of hours' tuition.
Part of the problem may have been Sassoon's legendary inability to sit still for a moment. On one occasion during a sortie,
Sassoon demanded that Boyle fly him over Blenheim Palace:

> 'I can't do that, sir, it's a prohibited area.'
> 'Oh, rubbish,' replied Sassoon sternly. 'Blenheim, I said.
> I have a friend who's thinking of buying the place.'

This was a preposterous claim but, when, against his better
judgement, Boyle complied, Sassoon demanded that he fly
lower than the demure 2,000 feet at which they were circling:
'Lower, Boyl-o! Lower!'

As they were climbing away, having had a good look, Sassoon
remarked that he thought it 'a very nice little place – but did you
notice that the kitchen garden looked a bit pinched?'

A keen garden enthusiast himself, Sassoon was not without

a sense of humour. When someone asked him how he had arranged for all the flowers to appear on the very day that the officers of 601 Squadron arrived at Port Lympne for their annual summer camp, he explained that it was 'perfectly easy. At twelve o'clock on the first of August each year, I give a nod to my head gardener. He rings a bell, and all the flowers pop up!'[10]

Famous as much for being an aesthete as a politician, Sassoon's tastes were a kind of modern baroque. He loved ornamentation and the interiors of his houses were legendarily opulent. It was even said that some of the door handles in his mansion at Port Lympne were studded with diamonds. What is more certain is that 'his Ballets Russes-inspired dining room with its walls of lapis lazuli, opalescent ceiling, gilt-winged chairs and jade-green cushions', the whole 'surmounted by a frieze of scantily-clad Africans' both scandalised and excited extreme envy in his contemporaries.[11] As for himself, Sassoon – who never married – was always immaculately turned out. In the evening, he would typically pair a blue silk smoking jacket with zebra hide slippers.

For those who failed to get an invitation from Sassoon, there were other social events that went a long way to satisfy the urge to see and be seen. Turning to popular society magazines such as *Tatler* and *Country Life* (both ran regular columns by their aviation correspondents), we catch a glimpse of the fashionable aerial gatherings that became popular from the late twenties until the middle of the thirties – aerial golfing meetings where people would fly in and land on the 'links', or 'aerial picnics' where society aviators would meet at country houses, much as hounds would during the winter. In July 1927, a Flying Fete and house party at Raynham Park was announced by the Marchioness of Townsend, with aircraft to land on the lawn.

And lest it be supposed that such gatherings were restricted to English society, an aerial gymkhana held by the Chilean army in 1932 was aptly advertised as a 'Gin-khana'. Entrants had to fly round a thousand-kilometre circuit, descend from a thousand metres with the prop stationary and land within a fifty-metre circle, tow their aeroplane a hundred metres then take off again, land near a football goal, pass through it with wings folded, re-erect the wings, fly two circuits of the aerodrome, land as close as possible to the control point, sign in, fly one more circuit, land over the finishing line and then – if not having done so already – drink large quantities of gin. Pink, no doubt.

While such antics coupled with the royal seal of approval clearly did much for the reputation of the Moth and, to a lesser extent, for the public reception of flying in general, it could also be argued that the upper classes' enthusiasm for flying did violence to Geoffrey de Havilland's dream of the democracy of the air. This, though, was inevitable. It was already obvious that flying was not a pastime that just anyone could afford. Even at the subsidised clubs, it was expensive. Typically, an hour under instruction cost £2 while an hour's solo came at £1 10s, this at a time when a working man's wage was under £1 per week. If you wanted to train at de Havilland's own school of flying, with your own bespoke programme and immediate access to aircraft without having to join the back of a long queue, it was more than double the amount. It is true that, for the professional classes, disposable income rose steadily from the mid-twenties onwards. It is also true that, for those unable to meet the expense of private aviation, there were other avenues, such as the flying scholarships provided both by private benefactors and by the government which enabled the enthusiastic young men who hoped for careers in the RAF to get airborne. But the cost of owning and operating an aeroplane was far beyond the reach of most people.

The nearest thing to Geoffrey de Havilland's vision of flying for all was the flourishing of the various flying circuses between the mid-twenties and the late thirties, when war in Europe broke out once more. Operating throughout the provinces, these gave joyrides at affordable prices. There was also Alan Cobham's 1929 Municipal Aerodrome Campaign, which had the aim of boosting air-mindedness among the masses, with the subsidiary goal of persuading local councils to invest in the construction of a network of regional airports. With sponsorship from Lord Wakefield's oil company, Cobham took a ten-seat DH51 Giant Moth on a tour of the country between May and October of that year. Visiting a total of 110 landing grounds, Cobham gave free flights to local dignitaries and, at Lord Wakefield's personal expense, gave more free flights to local schoolchildren, before giving as many joyrides to the paying public as time allowed. Following the success of this venture, Cobham inaugurated the 'National Aviation Day' displays during which teams of aircraft gave displays and joyrides up and down the country. What became known as Cobham's Flying Circus quickly became a feature of the British summer, as did the British Hospitals Air Pageant that took up the mantle when he disbanded his troupe following a mid-air collision over Blackpool in 1935. By then it is estimated that Cobham's aircraft had given flights to almost a million passengers.

There were also smaller regional circuses, such as the Cornwall Aviation company, which, in 1929, advertised a 'Burlesque Air Display' featuring acts such as the 'Bombing of

Charlie Chaplin', 'Simultaneous Wing Walking', 'Auntie Tries Flying' and 'The Ungrateful Passenger'. If that wasn't enough, there were 'SURPRISE FLIGHTS GIVEN AWAY EACH EVENING'. Another small outfit, Psyche's Flying Circus, advertised itself with a testimonial from the centenarian Mrs Sissons:

> Over the ground and up you go!
> Some are afraid but why be so,
> When Mrs Sissons aged one oh one
> Goes on the wing just for the fun[12]

Although largely the preserve of the wealthy in terms of who actually competed in them, the King's Cup and other air races and rallies were also popular days out. As Winifred Brown recalled, these regularly drew crowds in excess of ten thousand to each of the staging airfields at which competitors had to call. There would be still larger numbers at the start and finish. When the Leicestershire Aero Club organised its first air race in 1926, the crowd was estimated at 15,000. It was an enthusiasm that more or less exactly coincided with the heyday of the Moth itself but, as aircraft design progressed and the machinery became more complex, much of the amateur appeal of civil aviation was lost and the races became less popular. As a result, from 1930 onwards, the history of the Moth comes to be dominated by its use in establishing records and by its adventures abroad.

11

The Empire Strikes Back

I n July 1928, with two DH60 Moths, one donated by the
British government, the other by Lord Wakefield, Karachi
Aero Club was the first flying club to be established on the
Indian subcontinent. Not that aircraft were anything new to
the people, at least those living within the vicinity of the major
cities. One of the world's very first owners of a private aircraft
was an Indian prince, the Maharaja of Patiala, Sir Bhupinder
Singh. Born in 1891, and inheriting the crown of Patiala at
nine years of age, he was educated at Aitchison College,
Lahore, an English-style public school, where he showed a
keen interest in the technical developments emerging from
Europe and America at the time. Hardly had he left school
than he commissioned a unique monorail, a sort of hybrid of
a motor car and a train, designed by the British inventor W.
J. Ewing, to transport freight and passengers around his state.
Then, in 1910, the maharaja sent his chief engineer to England
to acquire three flying machines. In due course, a Blériot
monoplane and a pair of Farman biplanes were shipped back

to Patiala where the maharaja had created a suitable airstrip. It is not clear whether any of these aircraft actually flew. It seems entirely possible that the flamboyant maharaja had by this time become more interested in cricket and polo. Or in begetting children. He had at least five wives, is said to have maintained a harem of 365 concubines and is widely attested to have fathered eighty-eight children. One anecdote told of him noted that, 'We all have different ways of beginning the day. The Englishman begins on bacon and eggs, the German on sausages, the Americans on grape nuts. His Highness prefers to start his day with a virgin.'

Not that the maharaja was without genuine talent. A useful batsman, he captained the all-Indian cricket team that visited Britain in 1911, but it is true that, at least outside of Patiala itself, Sir Bhupinder's reputation today rests more on his fecundity and his extravagance than on any particular achievement. On one occasion in 1927, he 'arrived at Boucheron [the famous Parisian jeweller] accompanied by a retinue of forty servants all wearing pink turbans, his twenty favourite dancing girls and, most important of all, six caskets filled with 7571 diamonds, 1432 emeralds, and hundreds more sapphires, rubies and pearls of incomparable beauty'. These he ordered to be set in contemporary Art Deco style. A year later, he was back in Paris, this time at Cartier, where 'he provided the Parisian jewel house with 2930 diamonds, rare Burmese rubies and the 234-carat De Beers diamond (the seventh largest in the world) and commissioned a platinum chain festoon necklace set with this king's ransom of gemstones'.[1] For all this, his contribution to the development of aviation in India should not be overlooked. In 1929, on being informed that a young engineering student at Bristol University, a Sikh like the maharaja himself, had hopes of taking up the Aga Khan's recently announced challenge for the first Indian national to fly between London and Karachi, or vice versa, within one month, the exchequer duly provided a Gipsy Moth to the young hopeful, one Man Mohan Singh.

This Aga Khan Trophy contestant is not to be confused – though he sometimes is – with another notable Sikh aviation pioneer, also called Mohan Singh.[2] The other Mohan Singh had gone to America during the early years of the twentieth century. Learning to fly in 1912, he became the first person of Indian origin known to have obtained his pilot's licence. Under the leadership of one of the great pioneers of aviation in America, Glenn Curtiss, he subsequently became a member of a select band of pilots travelling the country and performing stunts to an astonished public, a calling he followed until 1916, when, for reasons that are unclear, he gave up flying and went to work in Los Angeles. There, he embarked on an ultimately unsuccessful attempt to become naturalised. At the time, this was open only to immigrants of Caucasian origin and while at first he was granted citizenship, this was revoked in 1924. It was shortly after this that Mohan Singh concluded that his future lay not in the air but even further afield. Renaming himself Yogi Hari Rama, the erstwhile aviator became a highly successful guru to some of the more gullible among the American chattering classes, amassing a fortune within the matter of a few years and founding the largest yoga community in America – even though the techniques he sold were merely plagiarised and repackaged versions of the teachings of genuinely qualified practitioners. Having burst onto the New Age scene in a blaze of self-generated publicity – nowhere mentioning his past as a pilot – Hari Rama, aka Mohan Singh, disappeared just as suddenly, having gone back to India. One cannot help wonder whether this was not a rather brilliant exercise in revenge-taking.

Before considering the exploits of Man Mohan Singh, the Aga Khan Trophy competitor, mention should also be made of another remarkable Sikh aviator, Hardit Singh Malik, as he was in large part instrumental in persuading the British government to accept Indian candidates at Cranwell, the RAF's officer training establishment where Aspy Engineer was ultimately trained. Hardit Singh himself was educated at Eastbourne College in Sussex before going up to Magdalen College, Oxford to read history, where he won a golfing blue. When the First World War broke out, not having yet finished at Oxford, he volunteered at the American hospital in Neuilly-sur-Seine during the long vacation. On graduating, he immediately applied to join the RFC but was turned down. Disappointed, he served as a volunteer ambulance driver for the French Red Cross in 1916 and was subsequently accepted for flying training by the French air force. When, however, 'Sligger' Urquhart, his tutor at Oxford, heard of this, he personally recommended Hardit Singh to the RFC commander, General Henderson. The young Indian was immediately accepted as a cadet in 1917. Transferred to 28 Squadron, he served on the Western Front flying the Sopwith Camel, meeting the infamous Red Baron in combat more than once and eventually claiming a total of six victories. On one occasion, he was wounded by two successive shots to his right leg in a dogfight 40 miles behind enemy lines. Having succeeded in shooting down his opponent, he found himself unable to climb due to the damage his machine had suffered. In a desperate race to get behind the allied lines, he was forced to fly at tree-top level, initially pursued by three enemy aircraft and then shot at by ground forces the rest of the way home. When eventually he made it back and crash landed, his aircraft was found to have taken more than four hundred hits. It was Hardit Singh's immense prestige that persuaded the RAF it would be making a huge mistake if it did not open its doors to Indian pilots.

That this was the right move was corroborated by all three contestants for the Aga Khan Trophy. The first of them, Man Mohan Singh, the son of a doctor, was born in 1906 in present-day Pakistan. After attending Gordon College in Rawalpindi, he travelled to England in 1917 to take up a place at Bristol University, where he studied civil engineering. He subsequently added aeronautical engineering on receiving a scholarship from the Indian government. At the same time, he began to take flying lessons at the Bristol and Wessex Aero Club on the club Moth, receiving his licence in September 1928. It was just over a year later that the Aga Khan announced a prize (of £500) for the first Indian national to complete a solo flight from Croydon to Karachi in under a month.

By this time a well-known and popular fixture on the flying club scene, there was a degree of scepticism when Man Mohan declared for the race. He was, as he himself freely admitted, notoriously poor at navigation. When his Moth was christened *Miss India* in a ceremony at Croydon by Indira Devi, the Maharani of Cooch Behar – who was in London at the time, where she was rumoured to be having an affair with the Prince of Wales – the editor of *The Aeroplane* commented somewhat sarcastically, that 'Mr Man Mohan Singh has called his aeroplane *Miss India* and he is likely to' if his navigation skills did not improve.

Setting off on 11 January 1930, Man Mohan Singh was the

first of the competitors to depart. He got only as far as northern France before tipping the aeroplane onto its nose and breaking its propeller. Returning to England, he set off a second time, on this occasion reaching almost as far as the toe of Italy before thick fog brought him down on a mountain road in Calabria. This time, his machine was damaged beyond repair. Fortunately, the maharaja provided a replacement and he was able to begin a third attempt on 8 April. Happily, Man Mohan Singh enjoyed better luck on his third attempt, although he suffered a forced landing near Marseilles which, according to him, was what eventually cost him victory in the race. There might have been another reason, however. According to one of the other competitors, J. R. D. Tata, Man Mohan's enthusiasm for *shikar* – that is to say the chase – was such that he could not resist coming down low and, using his Colt revolver, taking pot shots at any game he saw. There is even a suspicion that he actually landed in the Syrian desert to pursue a flock of gazelles he had seen from above.[3]

Meanwhile, the second contestant, young Aspy Engineer, was busy making final preparations for his own bid. Born in Lahore in December 1912, Aspy Engineer was one of eight children, six boys and two girls. The name 'Engineer' was, in fact, a nickname given to his father, who worked as a manager on the railways, but which he adopted as his actual name in place of Irani. Perhaps 'Engineer' sounded more modern and less obviously an immigrant name. The family had originally fled Iran during one of that country's periodic persecutions of its Zoroastrian minority in the late nineteenth century – Zoroastrianism being the pre-Islamic religion of the region. Once in India, the family settled with other members of the Parsi community (as Zoroastrians are known by Indians) in

Poona, where they became respected and successful merchants. Asfandiar Irani, who left his homeland as a young man, remains a source of wonder to his descendants even today. Family lore has it that he produced a new set of teeth at the age of 102, and that when, soon after, he developed diabetes he self-medicated by consuming whole trays of crystal sugar, washing them down with a special concoction of jungle plant juice. Though unorthodox, the treatment worked well enough: he lived to the astonishing age of 116.

For his education, Aspy Engineer was initially sent, together with his immediate elder brother, Homi, to a local convent school run by Catholic nuns. On day one, the two boys encountered the school bully who promptly knocked them both down. An early lesson in life came when, some time later, Aspy returned the compliment to the boy, who immediately went wailing to one of the nuns, earning Aspy an unanticipated reprimand.

At the age of seven, the future winner of the Aga Khan Trophy had his first sight of an aeroplane when a Vickers Vimy, similar to the one in which Messrs Alcock and Brown had recently crossed the Atlantic, arrived in India en route to Australia. As he wrote later in life, 'I dreamt of nothing thereafter but of aircraft landing on the rooftop of our spacious bungalow.' Realising as he grew older that perhaps a housetop was not really a viable landing strip, he switched to dreaming about landing on the flat top of the Panchgani Mountains that rose above the town – a feat he would eventually accomplish. In the meantime, Aspy spent much of his spare time tinkering, first with his father's motorcycle then with his Straker-Squire motor car, which sported 'carbide gas headlamps, crank handle and bulb horn'.

The family was not rich, though it might easily have been. In those days, there were ample opportunities for graft and, indeed, it was expected that those responsible for large government contracts should take what opportunity they could to enrich themselves. But Mr Engineer chose instead the moral life. When, on one occasion, a local businessman sent a large basket of fruit and the young Aspy remonstrated with his father that he could at least accept this, the older man instructed his son to upend the basket. At the bottom of it lay an envelope containing a large sum of money: an intended bribe. It was, therefore, a massive commitment on the part of Aspy's father when, wishing to encourage his son's enthusiasm for aviation, he allowed him to enrol as a member of the Karachi flying club and to start taking flying lessons from the resident instructor 'Red Hot' Jones. It was a commitment that deepened when, in order for his son to be able to get to the airport, he was compelled to invest in a second car, a two-seat Peugeot. This did not entirely solve the problem. At just sixteen years of age, Aspy was too young to take a driving test. A modus operandi was found when a fellow student, the twenty-six year-old R. N. Chawla, who did have a licence, took charge of the situation. In exchange for doing the driving, he got a free lift to the flying school.

It was Chawla who drew Aspy's attention to the announcement of the Aga Khan's challenge. The competition would be open to entries from 1 January 1930 and would remain open for a year or until claimed. There was something in this news that moved the Engineer family deeply. The reason for this was an earlier connection with the Aga Khan. Although educated at Eton and subsequently at Cambridge University, the leader of the world's Ismaeli sect had in fact been tutored in Persian by

Aspy's grandfather. Like the Parsis, the Ismaelis were an often persecuted minority in Iran though, unlike the Parsis, the Ismaelis are Muslims. The main point of disagreement with the majority is that the Ismaelis claim direct descent from the Prophet Mohammed, which others contest. They are also associated with a more liberal theology that seeks dialogue with the modern world, characterised, for example, by fewer restrictions on women than those imposed by the conservative majority – hence the successive Aga Khans' outward-facing engagement with the world, which, in the case of the incumbent at that time, extended to taking three successive European wives, becoming a noted racehorse owner and breeder and taking an interest in aviation. The declared motive for his challenge was his desire to further 'air-mindedness' in India.

At the end of his service to the young Aga Khan (the term means 'Commander in Chief'), Aspy's grandfather was, as customary, offered a generous gift. He proudly refused it. Astonished, but not wanting to embarrass the old man, the young prince replied with a prophecy: 'Master sahib! Perhaps you will not accept what is mine today but some day, if not you, then a descendant of yours will accept my money on your behalf.' Profoundly touched by these words, the old man replied with the solemn words: 'If he is worthy of it, then my soul will be happy.'

The teacher's daughter was Aspy's mother, Manekbai. Devoutly religious, it was in fact she who, rather surprisingly, encouraged her son's race entry for the Aga Khan Trophy. Even though attitudes towards health and safety had not, in those days, the cultic status they enjoy today, it seems unlikely that many mothers would have looked on the newfangled flying machinery as anything but a menace. However, Manekbai's faith was such that, according to all who knew her, she had privileged access to the future. Her predictions of how things would turn out were so accurate that no family member could ignore her. She was adamant that her son would win the race.

In the meantime, there were a few technical problems to overcome. The first entailed successful completion of the course of instruction ending in the grant of an A licence. This, Aspy achieved a few days after his seventeenth birthday. The second was acquisition of an aeroplane: a Gipsy-engined Moth, registration VT-AAZ (construction number 1161), but that, too, was accomplished when his father boldly cashed in his pension.

The idea was that Aspy and Chawla would fly to England together and that Aspy would then turn round and fly back. By way of preparation for the trip, the lads decided on a training flight to Delhi. Though successful in the end, it saw them, inauspiciously enough, forced to land due to lack of fuel before they reached their first intended stop. On arrival in the capital, they made a personal application to the director general of civil aviation for financial assistance to defray the expenses of their planned flight. Though without any concrete assurance, the official promised to do what he could to obtain a government bounty should they succeed in their attempt to get to England. The pair then flew up to visit Chawla's parents in Khanpur. Unfortunately, the local population was so over-excited about their impending arrival that when the youngsters flew overhead, they were dismayed to see the landing ground overrun by a large crowd of enthusiastic well-wishers. When they came down to try to clear an area in which to land by gesticulating for them to get out of the way, the crowd merely responded by waving and cheering. The problem was solved when they put down in a field some distance away from the official landing strip. The crowd responded at once by streaming towards them, enabling the two youngsters to hop over to the now vacated runway.

Back in Karachi, the young hopefuls occupied themselves by ordering up fuel and applying for the permits necessary to their forthcoming adventure. They also needed maps and charts. Unfortunately, these turned out to be in limited supply and there were none available for their route beyond Cairo. They were compelled to trust in providence that they would be able to acquire some when they reached Egypt. There was no question of waiting for them to be sent by post as news had already reached them of Man Mohan Singh's second attempt on the prize. One additional piece of preparation, at the insistence of Aspy's mother, was the painting of a Ferohar on either side of the fuselage – a Ferohar being a symbol of the guardian angel Zoroastrians believe accompany the individual throughout life.

The youngsters' plan was to fly the same route as that taken by the Imperial Airways flight, which had been operating a weekly service since March of the previous year, using the de Havilland DH66 Hercules trimotor between Karachi (soon extended to Delhi) and Cairo. Should the boys come down, there was a chance they would hear the airliner's approach and be able to send up a flare to alert its crew to their need of rescue.

They left at 7.45 one morning in early March, into the teeth of a 40 mph headwind, their first refuelling stop being Gwadar, which they reached after 'meandering along the coast' in a westerly direction. Although a part of Baluchistan and therefore an Indian province, Gwadar had the curious distinction of being administered by the Sultanate of Oman, though this had little practical effect as Oman was itself bound by treaty to the British Empire. Successfully refuelled, the youngsters proceeded to Jask on the edge of the Straits of Hormuz, arriving at 4.30 p.m. Writing of a visit there two years earlier, the British diplomat Sir Samuel Hoare had noted how 'Jask is a corner of the world [where even] the flies die of heat in summer'.

The second day saw them struggle to find the airfield at Lingeh as it had recently been washed away by rain. When eventually they did locate it, they landed to find the place abandoned, a solitary dog the only sign of life. As Hoare described it, this was a place where a seemingly endless expanse of marshland marked the 'dying efforts of the Tigris and the Euphrates to free themselves from the desert'.

Eventually refuelled, Aspy and Chawla continued their way up the Persian Gulf then along the banks of the Euphrates to Baghdad, where they had their first decent meal and night's rest since departure. Another long stretch of desolate country, following an oil pipeline, saw the two boys reach Amman at the end of the fourth day. It was not until the next leg, which took them via the Dead Sea to Gaza, that they experienced any mechanical trouble. A serious case of rough running in the vicinity of Jerusalem reminded them that they were in hostile territory. It might be the Holy Land for Jews and Christians, but for Zoroastrians and Hindus, this was terra incognita and they both recited prayers for protection. This, coupled with some gentle coaxing of the engine, saw them to their destination where removal and cleaning of the fuel filter revealed a serious miscalculation on their part. Mistakenly supposing that, because the airfield at Amman was an RAF base, they had no need to use the chamois leather-lined funnel that they normally did when refuelling, 'there was enough dirt and grit in them to put to shame most rivers supplying drinking water

GDH aboard Aeroplane Number 2

Demise of the *Morgon* at the 1922 Itford glider trials

Rigging the prototype for flight: company test pilot Hubert Broad
pulling, with actress Estelle Brody pushing

Sophie 'Elluva-Din

Lady Mary Bailey

A Moth up a tree

Violette and Jacques de Sibour

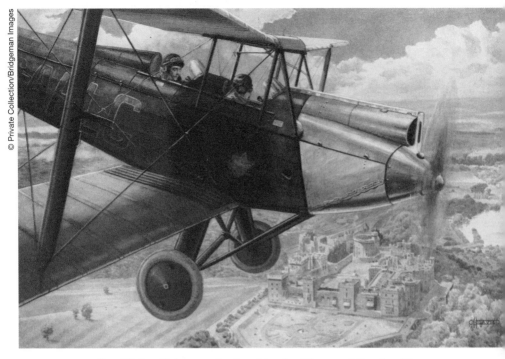

Our Flying Prince as depicted in the *Illustrated London News*

Sir Philip Sassoon, Squadron Leader of 601, the so-called Millionaires' Squadron

Aspy Engineer in
schoolboy shorts

Bad Luck Wimpey

A confident-looking Hubert Fauntleroy Julian

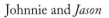

Johnnie and *Jason*

C. W. A. Scott, boxer, pianist, pilot:
the first of the record-breakers

Francis Chichester aboard *Madame Elijah*

Lotfia Elnady, the first woman from the Arab world to gain her pilot's licence

John Evans-Freke, 10th Baron Carbery (JC to his friends) leaning against the tail of his Morane-Saulnier at the Schneider Trophy races, 1914

Beryl Markham

Dressed for work: Dr Clyde Fenton

Maurice Wilson bidding a fond farewell to Jean Batten

before filtration came to modern cities'. The float chamber revealed similar levels of contamination.

Their next stop was Cairo where the youngsters were dismayed to find that there was a chart-dearth as severe as in Delhi. They were compelled to make do with a school atlas. This did not present a huge problem until they came to plot their course from Homs to Malta. In the meantime, it was simply a matter of following the North African coastline via Sollum, where, overnighting, they were attacked by bed bugs in the local fort (used primarily as a prison). When this proved too much, though tortured by the thought of the desert scorpions that were said to be in frightful abundance, they decided to camp instead under their wings in the desert.

Arriving in the vicinity of Homs next day, dangerously low on fuel, they were again unable to find the airfield so chose a deserted spot to land. Chawla then went off in search of assistance while Aspy stayed to clean the spark plugs and do other bits of routine maintenance and guard the plane. As darkness fell, with still no sign of Chawla, the young Parsi found himself the object of unwelcome attention. A band of unfriendly locals approached and surrounded the aeroplane, now bathed in the light of a full moon. His limited French availing him nothing, Aspy shone his torch in their direction. This precipitated a retreat and a regrouping that might have ended badly if not for the timely arrival of Chawla in the company of a group of Italian soldiers. It turned out that Aspy's visitors were on their 'wanted' list.

From Homs, the distance to landfall on Malta is 227 miles. In still wind conditions, this translates into three hours' flying over water. But while the skies looked benign to begin with, it was not long before the Moth was forced down almost to wave height and, such was the wind, both boys were compelled to hold the control column. As Aspy wrote later, 'the hours seemed days as we battled each gust of wind and now the rain was pelting into our cockpits and trickling down our necks'. For the first time in his life, he experienced what it meant to be truly cold.

Having only a single compass, it was down to Chawla to hold a steady course but, as they were completely unsure of the drift, it was more by good luck than good judgement that they caught sight of land far to the west. When, however, they turned towards it, they found themselves almost stationary only a short distance above the waves and, by the time they reached the shore, the fuel gauge was showing empty. With the wind gusts reaching over 60 mph, the next problem was to make a safe landing – possible only by flying on the back of the power curve using full power and getting into the right attitude, in the hope that they were not too far from the ground if the wind dropped. Fortunately, the RAF was alert to their plight and a dozen men ran out to help them down and to stay down.

Luckily for the travellers, there was at least one mechanic familiar with the DH60 and he was able to tighten the flying wires and reset the angle of incidence of the main planes, expressing surprise that the wings had not detached altogether. The wires had been stretched to their limit.

On their eventual arrival at Croydon, following their adventures in France and Norfolk already described in chapter one, it became a matter of Aspy doing the trip in reverse – albeit this time with a full suite of charts. Knowing that Man Mohan Singh was already en route meant that he had his work cut out. He finally departed more than a fortnight later than the Sikh. His first problem was burned out spark plugs in Egypt, his second, sandstorms in Badhdad, but otherwise it was a trouble-free flight. Nonetheless, on arriving in Karachi on 10 May, it was at first unclear as to whether he, or Man Mohan Singh or the third competitor, J. R. D. Tata, had in fact won.

A Parsi, like Aspy Engineer, JRD, as he was known universally, had only recently become an Indian citizen and thus eligible to enter the competition. Born to a French mother, he had spent his early years in France. His father, a successful businessman and partner of the eponymous Tata industrial group, was a key figure in the family's Hong Kong-based opium trade with China (which they shared with the Sassoons, among others) but, by the time of JRD's birth, had turned his attention to steel-making. JRD, having been educated at schools as far apart as France, India, Britain and Japan, had hopes of studying engineering at Cambridge but was prevented from doing so because, then still a French citizen, he was required to undertake a year's national service. This saw him join a regiment of sepoys, light irregular cavalry recruited mainly from France's North African colonies. At the end of his tour of duty, the young JRD had proven himself sufficiently to be eligible for officer training if he were to sign on for another year. He was keen to do so as it would mean spending time at the famous cavalry school at Saumur. His father's angry insistence that, as soon as his year was up, his son should start work for the family firm saved his life. Had he returned to his unit, he would have gone with it to Morocco where, in an action against a local chieftain, the regiment was cut down and slaughtered to the last man.

Besides being an enthusiastic horseman, JRD was a keen motorist. For several years, he ran a Bugatti – a magnet for

Bombay's traffic police. But although he longed to get airborne – he had taken a joyride as a teenager – it was not until 1929 that he became a founding member of the Bombay Flying Club and began training on one of the club Moths. Turning out to be a natural pilot, JRD went solo in fewer than four hours and became the first person to hold an Indian pilot's licence. His sister, Sylla, became India's first female pilot. Concluding that it would be cheaper in the long run to own his own aircraft, Tata acquired a Gipsy Moth a few months later that year on a trip to the UK. Having spent several weeks flying it in Europe, he sent it on to Bombay by ship. The subsequent announcement of the Aga Khan's challenge was immediately appealing. Not for the money, of course. Although his father had died recently, leaving large debts necessitating the sale of most of his real estate, the twenty-six-year-old JRD had inherited a one-third interest in Tata Steel and, while he didn't own a house, he was still able to live in a suite in Bombay's most famous hotel, the Taj Mahal.

Unlike either Man Mohan Singh or Aspy Engineer, JRD would make his bid starting at Karachi and finishing at Croydon. Departing on 3 May, he was the last to enter the race – both Aspy Engineer and Man Mohan Singh were by now well under way. His extra long-range fuel tanks did, however, give him a considerable advantage over them both and he was able to make his first stop at Jask before proceeding via Hormuz, Lingeh, Bushire and Basra.

Making good progress, JRD had reached Gaza where he was surprised to note the arrival of another Moth, which put down in a 'split-arse landing with full power* and, when it

---

* 'Split arse' (RFC slang): show-offy, swanky.

turned to park alongside, missed crashing into him 'by inches'. This turned out to be none other than Man Mohan Singh. As JRD recalled many years later, 'he was certainly not short on enthusiasm'. This, at any rate, was his polite public opinion. In a private letter to Aspy Engineer, he described Singh in less flattering terms as 'that crazy fellow ... who brought discredit rather than kudos to our country by his antics and his getting lost all along the way'. This was bit unfair given that JRD himself veered substantially off course en route to Basra, causing him to retrace his steps at one point. He again drifted off course when flying over Palestine, finding himself over the Sea of Galilee rather than the Dead Sea as intended.

Aspy Engineer, having set off from Croydon on 25 April, was not far behind and in fact met JRD at Aboukir. As Tata recalled, 'When I landed, he came out to meet me. I asked him what he was doing there. He told me he was waiting for some spare plugs.' Unfortunately, Aspy had neglected to take any spares and was stranded until such time as he could obtain replacements. Tata, better organised, had a full set of eight and very sportingly handed over four of them to his competitor. Aspy, in return, insisted that Tata accept his Mae West life-jacket as, while it was now surplus to his requirements, JRD still had to negotiate the Mediterranean – not that wearing one would have been likely to prolong his life by more than a few desperate hours.

When, finally, all three men had reached their destinations, it looked for a moment as if they all had a claim on the Aga Khan's prize. Man Mohan Singh was first back, on 9 May. Aspy Engineer landed on the 11th and J. R. D. Tata on the 12th. Man Mohan Singh was the first to be disqualified. He had taken longer, by a day, even accounting for the fact that

April has only thirty days rather than the month stipulated in the rules. Although J. R. D. Tata had taken far less time to complete the journey than his fellow Parsi, he had, nevertheless, when the times were adjusted according to the Greenwich Mean, been found to have landed two and a half hours later than Aspy Engineer. The prize was for the first Indian national to complete the journey in under a month so, just as his mother had predicted, Aspy Engineer was duly proclaimed the winner.

It is perhaps not surprising that all three competitors went on to have distinguished careers in aviation. Within two years, J. R. D. Tata had acquired a Puss Moth, the first aircraft in the Tata Airlines fleet. Taking the controls himself for its inaugural commercial flight, he delivered mail from Karachi to Bombay. The company subsequently went public as Air India, before being nationalised in 1953, in which guise it continued for almost seventy years. The Tata Group then took it back into private ownership in 2021 (though it still operates as Air India).

The irrepressible Man Mohan Singh was subsequently employed by the Maharaja of Patiala as his personal pilot until the latter's death, presumably from exhaustion in 1938. A year later, on the outbreak of the Second World War, Singh immediately joined the Indian Air Force Volunteer Reserve. You can see something of the man's enthusiasm for life in a short recruiting film made at the time, in which he appears enjoying a joke along with other Indian recruits to the war effort. One of two dozen Indian pilots to be trained in England, Man Mohan Singh eventually joined Coastal Command and took charge of a Sunderland flying boat during the early part of the Battle of the Atlantic. Thereafter, he was transferred to Singapore where he was put in command of the island's Catalina force.

Following the loss of Singapore, 'the worst disaster and

largest capitulation in British history' as Churchill described it, Man Mohan Singh was relocated first to Java and then to Broome in Western Australia. It was there, on 3 March 1942, that he lost his life when a squadron of Japanese Zeros attacked the British Catalina seaplanes as they lay at anchor in the harbour, destroying them all. In fact, he survived the attack but tragically drowned on account of being unable to swim.

As for Aspy Engineer, on arrival in Karachi he was asked if he would be returning to school following his success. He replied that his dearest wish was to join the Royal Air Force 'if they give me a chance'. Thanks in large part to Hardit Singh, his wish was granted and he became one of six candidates selected to train as cadets at RAF Cranwell. These formed the first batch of pilots in the Royal Indian Air Force. Unfortunately, their number was almost immediately reduced to five when the aptly named 'Titch' Tandon, advised by his instructor to apply more rudder in a turn, replied by asking, 'How do you expect me to apply more rudder since I cannot reach it?' At once, he was transferred to the Equipment Branch – in which Aspy's co-pilot, R. N. Chawla was also to serve with distinction, attaining the rank of Wing Commander. Aspy himself stayed the course, winning both the Groves Memorial Prize and the Kinkead Trophy for being the best all-round pilot of his term. He also became a member of the Caterpillar Club on being compelled to bail out of his Siskin trainer when it caught fire during an aerobatic sequence.

Remarkably, four of Aspy's six brothers also became pilots. Even more remarkably, two of them went on to win the Distinguished Flying Cross during the war – as did Aspy himself, thus attaining for the family a record not knowingly surpassed in the history of the RAF (of which the RIAF was a branch until Indian independence in 1947). Aspy was awarded his for outstanding service in the Burma campaign, after which he had a stellar peacetime career culminating in his appointment as India's Chief of Air Staff in the rank of Air Marshal. The top job – as was surely fitting for the schoolboy who flew a Gipsy Moth from London to Karachi.

12

Moth Rastafari

Almost no sooner than they had returned to Stag Lane than the de Sibours were planning their next adventure. They had bought property in Kenya in 1925 and were keen to visit, with a view to settling there in the near future. Having sold *Safari*, they ordered a Gipsy-engined 'Metal Moth'. This turned out to be an advantageous move. The aeroplane was identical to its predecessor save for the welded steel fuselage it had in place of the wooden original. Although wood has the supreme advantage of being both immune to fatigue and easy to repair without specialist equipment, the glues and water-proofing treatments available at the time meant that in wet and humid conditions, the aeroplane would deteriorate quite rapidly.

Another feature of the de Sibours' new Moth – which they christened *Safari II* – was the fact that it was the first to be built under licence in France by Morane-Saulnier. This was one of a number of agreements entered into by de Havilland whereby the type was manufactured overseas. As well as this French one and the one in place in America, there were by this time also arrangements with subsidiaries in Canada, Australia, Norway and Finland. There was to have been one with a German company, too, but, although letters of intent were signed, the plan never came to fruition – perhaps on account of the fact that the distinguished pilot of the *Deutsche Luftstreitkraefte* who put the demonstrator through an aerobatic sequence during a test flight, lost control of it and was killed in the ensuing crash.

Two days after taking delivery of his new aeroplane in March 1930, Jacques flew it to Marseilles where, having met up with Violette, they loaded it onto a steamer bound for Algiers. On arrival, the Moth was transported by the local Shell agent to the airport at Maison Blanche, where the couple met up with it and renewed their aerial journey. They reached Alexandria after a week, having called at Tripoli, Benghazi and Tobruk en route. After a short stay at 'the Bride of the Mediterranean', as the city was popularly known, they resumed their journey, travelling south along the Nile to Port Sudan on the Red Sea. From there, their plan was to follow the coast, first to Massawa and then to Djibouti, whence they would cross the sea and make their way inland to Aden, with the intention, if permission could be obtained, of paying a visit to Yemen. Given, though, that Yemen's ruler at the time, Imam Yahya Mutawakkil, had recently received a drubbing courtesy of the RAF (on the grounds of his threatening Aden), this was somewhat optimistic of them.

Encountering violent headwinds as they made their way south, at one point the Moth's speed was reduced to the point that they made barely 50 miles in three hours' flying, forcing them to make an emergency stop for fuel. Happening on a small village in the desert, they put down in the hope of finding assistance, which came in the unexpected form of a Scottish cotton grower who replenished them sufficiently to see them to Massawa.

The Moth and its crew endured more headwinds en route to Assab and, the day after, clouds of locusts further hindered their progress. At last, having passed over the Bab-el-Mandeb – the Gates of Lamentation as the straits between the Horn of Africa and the Arabian Peninsula are known locally – they proceeded to Aden, where the station commander was a friend of theirs. On enquiring about their permit to visit Yemen, they were informed that, although the Imam had graciously given his permission for them to visit his country, this did not extend to permission to enter its airspace. This seems unsurprising in the circumstances. Disappointed, the de Sibours then sought permission to visit Addis Ababa in Ethiopia (then known as Abyssinia) instead. To their further disappointment, this was also refused. It turned out that an insurrection against the government was expected imminently and visitors were not wanted. The following day, however, the de Sibours were sur-prised to receive a cable rescinding the previous message and explaining that, should they say they were willing to sell their aircraft to the Abyssinian government, they would be given the permission they sought. On arrival, they would then have the option of explaining that they did not think the Moth was a suitable aeroplane for the government, after all.

It was not entirely clear what this strange condition por-tended but the intrepid couple accepted the offer and, as directed, flew to Dire Diwa in the north-east of Ethiopia, where they were to await further instructions. The country's ruler at the time was Ras Tafari. Believed by some to be the Second Coming of Christ and an object of worship, he ruled, to begin with, as regent (the word 'Ras' signifies a prince). Shortly after the de Sibours' subsequent departure, he was, however, raised to the dignity of emperor with the reign name of Haile Selassie. A forward-looking monarch, he had immediately grasped the significance of air power when, in 1922, he had attended an air show organised by the RAF in Aden. Insisting on being taken aloft, he proclaimed that it was 'very fitting that he, as regent should be the first Abyssinian to take flight in an aeroplane'. Safely returned to earth, he immediately set in motion plans for a force that would become known as the Regent's Angels.

When the de Sibours' next instructions arrived, they were directed to rendezvous with three French pilots in their Potez 25s at Lake Metahara, a hundred miles from the capital, as a prelude to flying the last leg together. It turned out that these three aircraft were the basis of the air force that Ras Tafari was in the process of building.

Having met up successfully with their compatriots, the de Sibours were disconcerted to find their little aeroplane at the very the limit of its powers. Situated at an elevation of almost 8,000 feet, Addis Ababa presents a distinct challenge to a heavily laden biplane with only 100 hp at its disposal. At that altitude and in that heat, the Gipsy engine is decidedly out of breath. To complicate matters further, the effect of lower air density meant that the Moth's controls were significantly less effective than at lower altitudes. Most disconcerting of all was the fact that the landing area on the racecourse, though a thousand yards long and beautifully situated, was surrounded by stands of towering eucalyptus. The Ethiopian variety of these trees being the tallest flowering plants on earth meant that the airfield was bounded by an obstacle rising to fully 200

feet. Getting in would therefore entail a steep side-slip in order
to get onto the ground in the distance available. Getting out
would also be interesting.

Safely down, the de Sibours were surprised when, within
a short time of their arrival, Ras Tafari himself turned up at
the airfield. They had been told that, although His Majesty
would be pleased to grant them an audience, he could not do so
inside three days. Yet here he was in person, the Lion of Judah!
Looking the aeroplane over, he confirmed his wish to acquire
Safari II. The French ambassador accompanying the prince
made clear to the couple that such a sale would both confer
prestige on France – it being a 'French' aeroplane after all – and
greatly oblige the regent. Violette, with frankly shameless op-
portunism, explained that the price would be £1,200 – almost
double what they had paid for it, but Ras Tafari did not demur.

That same afternoon, the regent watched a bombing
demonstration by the three Potez. The Ethiopians having
acquired some locally made munitions, he was keen to see
them in action. At the invitation of one of the pilots, Jacques
de Sibour went up to arm and release one of the devices. To
his violent consternation, he watched as it hurtled directly
towards the royal party which scattered only just in time
before it exploded, slightly damaging one of the cars in which
they had travelled. In spite of – or perhaps because of – this
moment of alarm, Ras Tafari was sufficiently impressed to
invite the de Sibours to the palace that evening. In conversation (conducted in French, which the regent had learned from
one of his tutors, a physician from Guadeloupe), he asked
Jacques whether he would be prepared to take the Moth on
a leaflet-dropping mission to a region about 300 miles to the
north-west of the capital, where the expected insurrection

against him was gathering. With commendable candour, the regent made it clear that, should Jacques come down on the way there or back, there would be no hope of rescue and, with equally commendable insouciance, Jacques agreed. Duly arriving at the airfield the next morning, de Sibour had to get his tail up while still at a standstill by running his engine up to full power against the chocks in order to give himself a reasonable chance of clearing the trees. Even so, he was compelled to abort his first attempt and barely made it out on the second. But the conditions were too much for the Moth. Standing at over 10,000 feet, his destination lay on a plateau which de Sibour very reasonably concluded was beyond the capability of his aeroplane and he turned back. The Potez continued, however, and immediately demonstrated the value of having an air force. The unheralded sight of the Regent's Angels blasting overhead caused many of the rebels to desert their leader and Ras Tafari's forces prevailed a mere four hours after battle was joined.

Following the de Sibours' departure from Ethiopia – in a lorry, as a result of having relinquished ownership of *Safari II* – and to get round the problem of the Moth's poor performance at altitude, the aeroplane was moved to Jijiga where it was operated alongside an Italian Fiat AS.1 trainer. The Fiat quickly went out of service – not having the advantage of the Moth's metal airframe, it could not cope with the enormous temperature variations of the country – leaving *Safari II* as the sole aircraft on which the two most promising cadets were trained by a French instructor. These were Mishka Babitchef, son of a Russian adventurer who had married an Ethiopian woman and gained a position at the court of Ras Tafari's predecessor, and Asfaw Ali. The plan was that they would pilot the aeroplane during a fly-past at Ras Tafari's forthcoming coronation as emperor, scheduled for 2 November 1930.

Now bearing the royal insignia, the Moth was duly returned to Addis during the autumn to allow the two young pilots to practise getting in and out of the airfield. At a rehearsal for the coronation held in Ras Tafari's presence, they delighted the monarch when, during a low pass, Ali threw a bouquet of flowers to the royal feet. The next item on the agenda pleased him still more. This took the form of a demonstration jump by the American celebrity pilot and parachutist Hubert Fauntleroy Julian – aka the Black Eagle of Harlem – who had been brought in especially for the occasion. This so impressed Ras Tafari that, no sooner had Julian landed than the regent conferred on him the Order of Menelik, the country's highest honour, and elevated him instantly to the rank of Colonel in the Royal Ethiopian Air Force. Unfortunately, the day did not end as well as it began.

Hubert Julian, the son of a Trinidadian plantation manager, grew up in a middle-class district of the British colony before moving to London, where he is said to have picked up French and Italian in the matter of a single year. The outbreak of the First World War saw him in Canada where, when peace finally returned, he took a joyride with Billy Bishop VC, the Allies' top-scoring ace, in a two-seat Sopwith Camel.[1] Instantly smitten, Julian headed south to America and teamed up with barnstormer, showman and long-distance record breaker Clarence Chamberlin. Soon to become the first person to fly a passenger across the Atlantic, Chamberlin not only taught Julian to fly but also encouraged him to take up parachuting. His first public jump under Chamberlin's tutelage came at an event headlined by Bessie

Coleman, one of the first African American women to hold a pilot's licence.

It was around this time that Julian came to know Marcus Garvey, founder and first president-general of the Universal Negro Improvement Association, champion of the Back to Africa movement and noted anti-Semite. Impressed with Julian's accomplishments, Garvey engaged Julian on several occasions during the early twenties to perform aerobatics over gatherings of his followers. Julian also made several parachute jumps over Harlem in support of Garvey's cause, on one occasion wearing a crimson jumpsuit and playing 'Running Wild' on a golden saxophone as he came down. Landing on the roof of the post office, this was the stunt that earned him the nickname of 'Black Eagle of Harlem'.

Subsequently, Julian and his mentor, Clarence Chamberlin, conceived the idea of a solo transatlantic flight in a seaplane that would fly from New York to Africa. With the help of Garvey's followers, a suitable aircraft was sourced, purchased and named *Ethiopia*. This was to be an all-Black venture. Unfortunately, no sooner had it taken off at the outset of its attempt than one of the floats detached from the fuselage and the aeroplane came crashing into the sea seconds later.

It was despite this disappointment that Julian, fortunately uninjured, had been summoned to former Abyssinia. In planning his forthcoming coronation, the soon-to-be Emperor Haile Selassie was determined to place his country on the world stage. To that end, he had invited representatives of the monarchies and governments of all the world's leading powers to attend. It was to be a magnificent occasion with guards of honour, military displays and antique pageantry such as had never been seen by Western eyes before. But lest his guests suppose that Ethiopia was stuck in the past, both the army and the air force would demonstrate their skill with the most up-to-the-minute war materiel. After this, Julian would perform a repeat of his parachute jump.

Alas, it would have been better if, on that day of the rehearsal, the Black Eagle had been content with the honours bestowed on him by Ras Tafari. Instead, wishing also to show his proficiency as a pilot, he climbed – without authorisation – aboard the royal Moth. The result was that, after a series of disorderly bounds down the runway, he succeeded only in turning the aeroplane onto its back. Doubtless his unfamiliarity with operating at high altitude was Julian's undoing. In any case, the regent was less than impressed and immediately ordered Julian to leave the country saying that 'there are more planes to crash in the United States than in Ethiopia'.

As a result of the Moth being taken off for repair, it could not feature at the coronation, though the three Potez did. According to Evelyn Waugh, who was present, just as the newly crowned emperor was leaving his pavilion adjacent to the cathedral, 'Punctually to plan, three Abyssinian aeroplanes rose to greet him. They circled round and round over the tent ... sweeping and curvetting within a few feet of the canvas roof ... Their noise was appalling.'[2]

Safari II subsequently trained several more of Ethiopia's first pilots. It is known also to have suffered at least three further accidents, one of them necessitating major repairs. On that occasion, the Moth was being flown by two of the Ethiopian trainees when it encountered an impenetrable cloud of locusts, causing the engine to stop and necessitating an emergency landing in a dry riverbed. Unfortunately, the resultant arrival put the aeroplane on its back again, though happily both pilots were unharmed.

As for Hubert Julian, he went on to earn his living variously as a barnstormer as one of William Powell's Five Blackbirds, as a rum and whiskey runner (at one time he owned a stock said to have been worth $800,000) and as personal pilot for Father Divine, the celebrated Evangelist preacher and self-proclaimed vessel of the spirit of God, before returning to Ethiopia. This followed Mussolini's pathetically self-aggrandising but brutal and, for the Ethiopians, disastrous invasion of their country. Unfortunately for Julian, Haile Selassie had already invited another African American pilot, John C. Robinson, to lead his air force against the invaders and Julian, in memory of his earlier faux pas with the Moth, found himself relegated to an infantry training role.

There are differing accounts of what happened when Julian and Robinson met in the Hotel de France in Addis, but all agree that there was a fight, following which Hubert Julian was again asked to leave the country. On arrival back in America, dressed in a 'beaverskin coat and derby hat' he declared that he had come to 'a unanimous decision that Ethiopia does not need or deserve help'. He then travelled to Italy in hopes of obtaining an interview with Mussolini, though to what end is unclear. He said afterwards that he went with the intention of assassinating the fascist leader, though his publicly stated aim was to offer his services to Il Duce. Given that, following the Second World War – during which he served briefly, and rather unexpectedly, with a Finnish air regiment and at one time publicly challenged Goering to an aerial dual to be fought above the English Channel – it is possible that he really did have an act of heroism in mind.[3] In any case, no such meeting took place.

As for Robinson, it turns out that he, too, was eventually asked to leave Ethiopia. His crime was to have knocked unconscious a Swedish mercenary pilot, Count Gustaf von Rosen, on being told that he would not fly with a Black co-pilot.[4] One might have hoped it would have been the other way round and it was the count who had been sent packing.

Alas, Ras Tafari's Moth did not survive Mussolini's invasion and was destroyed on the ground by an Italian air strike in early April 1936.[5]

13

Jason and Johnnie

If Charles Lindbergh was a prophet of the New Age of a fully interconnected world, Amy Johnson was a prophet of the New Age of Woman – an age in which females would finally be recognised as equal to men in every respect. Although Ladies Heath and Bailey had excited attention with their African exploits, it was Amy Johnson who captured universal acclaim for her solo flight to Australia. And though, almost a hundred years later, the playing field for women remains uneven, Amy Johnson deserves far more credit for advancing the cause than she is usually given.

Amy Johnson was also Britain's first true celebrity. The proverbial Yorkshire lass, she was born in Kingston upon Hull in 1903, the daughter of a prosperous fish merchant. Educated first at a local fee-paying school and, later, at Sheffield University, where, with the professed intention of becoming a teacher, she took a degree in economics. The eldest of three sisters, her childhood was as wholesome as an Enid Blyton novel. Home-made cakes and rambles with her friends in the West Riding countryside, Sunday school at the Wesleyan chapel, visits to the circus and cinema with family – hers was the ordinary life of a provincial middle-class girl. There are few indications of her being in any way out of the ordinary – she led a minor rebellion at school over the wearing of Panama hats and she was habitually late for classes – but nothing marked her out as exceptional. In a way, she wasn't.

As befit a young modern woman, while she was still at school, Amy Johnson entered a long-term relationship – and was, in fact, the instigator of it. The object of her affection was a Swiss businessman several years her senior who had been posted to nearby Bridlington by his company. Together they went hiking and camping, to dances and 'the pictures', Amy riding pillion on his motorcycle and, daringly, smoking cigarettes and even drinking a little. More than once, they went on a secret weekend tryst to a country hotel. Yet, while they were as intimate as they dared, there was no doubt at least in Amy's mind that marriage would be the outcome of their relationship. And that, no doubt, is what would have happened and someone else would have been the first female pilot to fly from England to Australia, if it wasn't for the fact that she would have had to become a Roman Catholic. Her parents were deeply unhappy at the prospect – though Amy was willing – and appalled when they discovered that, on Christmas Eve 1926, she had slipped out of the house to attend midnight mass. Hans, her boyfriend, meanwhile, showed a thoroughly modern attitude to the relationship. Often cold and distant towards Amy, he would flirt with other women in front of her, though he resented her going out with other men. Above all, he refused to make the commitment for which she was so clearly desperate; ultimately, stringing her along for a full seven years before, finally, and without warning, marrying someone else.

In the meantime, Amy Johnson had endured a brief period working on the shop floor at John Lewis in London. This being 1927, when jobs even for graduates were almost impossible to come by, it was a lot better than nothing. Fortunately, a friend from Yorkshire introduced her to the senior partner of a firm of well-known solicitors who gave her a secretarial job with a starting salary of £3 a week, rising quickly to five. A pound of this went on her lodgings, but her disposable income was such that, when, on a whim, she paid a visit to the London Aero Club and read their terms – 'Three guineas entrance fee; three guineas annual sub; two pounds an hour under instruction; thirty shillings an hour solo' – a vague notion she had been secretly nurturing moved into the realm of possibility. She would learn to fly. Her half-hour trial lesson in one of the club Moths took place on 15 September 1928.

It was not a success. Taking her aside afterwards, her instructor, Captain F. R. Matthews warned her that, really, she was wasting her money. She would be highly unlikely ever to go solo, let alone make it as a pilot. What he did not realise, and what his pupil had not realised until too late, was that her helmet was much too large for her and had blown back in the wind, with the result that, in the air, she could hear scarcely a word he was saying.

By June of the following year, Amy Johnson had accumulated fifteen hours and forty-five minutes of dual instruction when she was at last cleared to take the Moth up for a solo circuit. It was a great moment of course, but something else occurred around this time that changed her life even more dramatically. Her newly-wed younger sister, Irene, committed suicide. Besides the grief and hopelessness felt by the whole family, Irene's death had at least one important consequence. Will Johnson, her father, had been lukewarm about his eldest daughter's aspirations to become a pilot. Now, however, he embraced the project and, on the basis that Amy would train for her commercial licence, agreed that she could leave her job at the solicitors and train full time. He would provide the necessary finance.

Amy responded by going a step further. Attaching herself to the club's chief engineer, unpaid, and insisting that she be called Johnnie, she became determined to qualify as a mechanic as well. This got off to a slow start. The other members of the team clearly resented her presence and it took several weeks of persistence and showing herself willing to get her hands properly dirty before she won acceptance. By the end of the year, however, she duly became the first woman to attain the Air Ministry's ground engineer's licence.

With her total enthusiasm and commitment, it is no surprise that Johnnie soon came to the attention of similarly ambitious club members. One of them, (later Sir) James Martin, saw in her just the person he needed to partner with in developing his revolutionary design for a monoplane that, using the same engine, would both outperform the Moth and be substantially cheaper to buy. The project itself came to nothing, though Martin would later find fame as the designer of the Martin-Baker ejector seat. But one of the publicity ideas they discussed, a flight to Australia, survived. What if she could find sponsorship and become the first woman to make the journey?

With the same tenacity that she had shown in getting herself accepted in the engineering works, Johnnie, as everyone now called her, set about applying to anyone and everyone she thought might be persuaded to help. Not all members of the club appreciated this. She failed to make a good impression on the club secretary (also secretary of the Royal Aero Club). Similarly, Major Travers, the club's chief flying instructor, found her unattractively pushy. Nonetheless, the enthusiastic letter she wrote to Sir Sefton Brancker, following a talk he gave at the Royal Aeronautical Society, caught the great man's eye and he passed it along to Lord Wakefield, millionaire founder of Castrol Oil. He, in turn, contacted Travers for an expert opinion. It was a brave idea, Travers said, but the woman herself was unfit for the journey. Her navigational skills were non-existent. She would lose her way. She relied too much on luck in flying. She had no idea what such a journey entailed.[1]

There was a lot in this. Her first tentative cross-country flight was a minor disaster. She got lost and had to land in a field. It is to Wakefield's great credit that he did not drop the idea at once, instead inviting Travers to lunch the next day to discuss the matter further. The outcome was a tacit agreement between the two men that, if Travers would agree to train her properly, Wakefield would put up half the money for an aeroplane and provide fuel and oil along the way.

Jubilant, Johnnie wrote to her father who responded by immediately sending the cheque for the other half – insisting only that she wear a parachute during her journey. Within a matter of days (it being by now the end of April 1930), she became the owner of G-AAAH, a well-travelled Gipsy-powered Moth with bottle-green fuselage and silver wings, which she named *Jason*, the trade name of her father's fish-processing business. First registered in 1928, the Moth had accompanied the royal

tour of Africa where it was used by the *Daily Mirror*'s photographer. Meanwhile, her training with Travers continued.

Aware that she must cross India before the monsoon reached
the country's northern latitudes (it bursts in the south-west
usually during the early part of June and covers the whole
country by mid-July), Amy Johnson chose Monday 5 May as
her start date.

Taking delivery of *Jason*, now fitted with two long-range
tanks to give eighty gallons in total (and, therefore, potentially,
something like fifteen hours' flying time and, in still air, a
range of around 1,100 miles), Johnnie had time only to fly her
aeroplane once before setting off for Australia. Thereafter, it
was a matter of carefully stowing the Moth with her supplies:
a revolver, a pith helmet, a mosquito net, a portable stove, ra-
tions, water, a first aid kit containing various medicines suitable
for the tropics, tools, spark plugs, some other small spares and,
very wisely, a spare propeller, which was lashed to the outside
of the fuselage. A great letter writer, she did not fail to pen a
valedictory missive to her parents, signing it with 'very dearest
love from Johnnie'.

It was a cold spring morning when Johnnie lined *Jason* up
at the beginning of their epic trip. Her father and her best
friend came to wave them off, along with several pressmen. It
had been a busy week for them. The Duchess of Bedford had
returned in her Moth from a trip to Cape Town and back in
just nineteen days. She'd have done it in a day less if she hadn't
been forced down with a broken oil pump near the Bulgarian
border, necessitating that her pilot walk to the nearest railway
line, flag down the Simplon Express and cadge a lift to Sofia,
where he telephoned for a spare that arrived the next day. In
other news, the Prince of Wales had just arrived back from his

second Africa tour, flown from Southampton to Windsor in a Westland Wapiti. The *Graf Zeppelin* – at 772 feet, as long as an ocean liner – had called in to make the first landing on British soil of a German airship since the last one to be downed during the war. The English-born Marchesa Louisa Nadja Malacrida, poet, novelist and, alongside her aristocratic Italian husband, one half of a celebrity couple that renovated properties and undertook interior design and who later appeared in a national newspaper advertising campaign for Vim – 'it's no use having new ideas of decoration with old ideas of dirt' – had been announced to have attained her A licence. An annual Oxford and Cambridge balloon race had also been inaugurated. Compared to these excitements, the improbability of a mere girl making it all the way to Australia meant that this was not much of a story and reporting of the event was minimal. It was just as well. On her first attempt, *Jason* failed to become airborne. Never having flown a Moth so heavily laden, Johnnie failed to make use of the full amount of runway available and, worse, failed to get her tail up before attempting to unstick. Luckily, she had the sense to abort her take-off before reaching the far fence. Second time lucky, the Moth wallowed into the air, turned slowly, and set course for Vienna.

They arrived in good order during the early evening, following a trouble-free flight, and were ready to go again soon after dawn the next day. On startup, however, the engine ran roughly so Johnnie shut it down and removed and cleaned the plugs. Given that the airport ground staff had insisted they would take care of everything it must have been satisfying to show that, actually, this was a lady pilot who knew what she was doing.

The second leg of their journey took Johnnie and *Jason* to

Constantinople (today's Istanbul) and it was now that they encountered their first problems. The first was a leaking fuel pipe. Every stroke of the hand-operated pump that transferred petrol from the auxiliary to the main tank caused a jet of fluid, which, if she hadn't hung her head out of the cockpit, would have hit her in the face. As it was, the smell of fuel that built up inside the cockpit nauseated Johnnie to the point of despair: 'the only thing that kept me pumping was the ignominy of giving up the flight'.[2] The second problem was pelting rain that soaked her to the skin. When the Moth finally arrived in Constantinople after an 800-mile flight, it was just before sunset. Considering that the greatest distance she had travelled before setting out for Australia was only to her home town of Hull, fewer than 200 miles from Hendon, this was a stellar achievement. Unbeknownst to her, when news of her safe arrival reached Stag Lane, the place went 'mad with joy'.

At 4 a.m. the following morning, she was ready to go. Unfortunately, her papers were not. It turned out that, of the officials whose signatures she was waiting for, one was in jail, another was in the bath when called on and a third had to be extracted from his box in the theatre. At 7.30 a.m., she was led into an office and told to wait. And wait. And wait. When it became apparent that she was likely to have to go on waiting, it seemed expedient to deploy some feminine charm and baksheesh in the form of some spare passport photographs. This did the trick and eventually she was free to go.

If bureaucracy kept her late, mishandling by the Turkish ground staff might have made her later still. Picking *Jason* up roughly by the tail the night before, they had pitched the Moth onto its propeller hub. Although there was no visible damage, she would need to be attentive to vibration in case there had been any internal damage. Fortunately, there was none and she set course for Aleppo – the leg she was dreading most. It necessitated crossing the Taurus Mountains, a range not much lower than the Alps, which, the overloaded Moth being unable to fly over, she would instead have to go through, making her way along the valleys to reach the deserts of Syria that lay beyond. Although there were no downdraughts – a major hazard for light aircraft flying in mountainous areas – she had 'one very unpleasant moment when, threading my way through an exceptionally narrow gorge with the mountains rising sheer on either side of me, only a few feet from my wings and towering high above and rounding a corner, I ran straight into a bank of clouds and for an awful minute could see nothing at all'.

It was on her reaching Aleppo, only three days out, that people back in England really began to take an interest. She was already halfway to India and, if her luck held, she would be in Karachi in another three. That would be a record. Bert Hinkler, on his epic 1928 flight to Australia had taken a week. If she could keep this up, she might even break his Down Under record. But the leg from Aleppo to Baghdad was still to come and, with it, the first of several miracle escapes. All had gone well in near perfect weather when, less than an hour from the Iraqi capital, she encountered a sandstorm. Cruising happily at 7,000 feet, she entered an area of thick haze, in which she just had time to wonder whether she would be able to see enough to continue, when the Moth gave a sudden lurch and fell 2,000 feet. Hardly had she recovered from this, than the engine stuttered and *Jason* began to be tossed around by 'some force I could not understand'. Again, the aeroplane dropped uncontrollably. It was 'as though I was in a lift with the machinery broken'. Again, the Gipsy engine coughed, stuttered and threatened to stop altogether. A third time, the aircraft fell. Now flying utterly blind, she suddenly felt her wheels touch. Closing the throttle and, doing her best to keep straight and into wind, Johnnie held her breath until eventually her machine came to a grateful stop. If this doesn't count as a miracle, what does? To have put down unintentionally and in the middle of nowhere, completely unable to see ahead, on a surface that was not only smooth and obstacle free but also firm enough not to cause the aeroplane to sink in or bounce and crash – or, because you are not heading directly into wind, to ground loop – you could not do it if you practised for a year.

But there was no time for awe. Jumping out, she quickly covered up the air intake and fuel vent in the hope of keeping the sand out. The wind was so strong that, having hastily pulled her luggage from the cockpit to further chock the wheels, she sat on the tail to keep it down.

When, after three hours, the storm eventually abated, Johnnie scrambled round reloading her equipment, fearful that the respite might only be temporary. Fortunately, her engine started at the first swing of the propeller. More fortunately still, the heading she resumed took her in the direction of Baghdad rather than back into the desert. She had no idea what effect the wind had had on her. Less happily, when she finally landed at Baghdad, she came off the runway and one of her wheels sank into the sand, seriously damaging the undercarriage. According to the resident Imperial Airways engineer, spare parts would have to be sent for from Karachi, entailing a three-day delay. This was a major blow. It looked as though her dream of beating Hinkler was over.

The next morning, however, Johnnie was delighted to find her aeroplane back on its feet. The ground crew had worked through the night to effect repairs and *Jason* stood, washed and gleaming, ready for take-off. Meanwhile, back in Hull, her flight was the talk of the town. 'What a girl and what a trip!' enthused the local paper. Even in Fleet Street, the 'Lone Girl Flyer' was beginning to attract attention.

In her own account, the 825-mile leg to Bandar Abbas would have been 'quite enjoyable' but for the fact of her engine 'spluttering all the way'. The sea was 'a vivid blue, from which rose jagged mountains looking every bit like the teeth of a giant saw' and there was 'no place where an aeroplane could safely land'.[3] Unfortunately, when she finally arrived at her destination, she again damaged her undercarriage. This time, by the purest chance, the local ground engineer had a replacement for the broken bolt that attached one of the undercarriage struts to the fuselage. As for the rough running of the engine, she quickly traced this to a burned-out spark plug. Now all she needed to do was to satisfy the demands of the Persian officials, whose obstructiveness was notorious in the world of aviation. On his way to Australia, Alan Cobham had been held up here for a full forty-eight hours. In Johnson's case, a difficulty arose over her lack of a valid health certificate. And what about vaccinations? She'd had none. In that case, she would need a full suite of them before they could think of letting her go.

Logic came to her rescue. Given that she would be in India within a matter of hours, taking with her any diseases that she had collected in Persia, what would they gain, she demanded to know, by protecting the citizens of another country at considerable trouble and expense to themselves? Though she would not have got away with this line of argument during the Covid years, in this case, reason won out and, at 4 a.m., she was back at the airfield once more and ready to go.

Arriving at Karachi just six days after leaving Croydon, the Lone Girl Flyer burst onto the front pages of a hitherto sceptical press. She was now 'Plucky Miss Amy Johnson'. The *Daily Mirror* splashed the front page with 'India in six days! ... This daring pilot, the only girl to hold an Air Ministry ground engineers certificate ...' The *Yorkshire Evening Post* called her 'Queen of the Air'. For the *Exeter and Plymouth Gazette* she was the 'British Girl Lindbergh'. In those days, the regional newspapers were at least as popular as the national press and there was hardly one which failed to report her progress. Even *Flight* magazine was agog with admiration: 'That such a young and inexperienced pilot should have beaten all records for light aeroplane flights between England and India ... is a feat which we should not have believed possible if it had not happened.'

Of course, Johnnie herself was oblivious to all this. There was, however, a telegram of congratulations from Lord Thompson, Secretary of State for Air, and she was invited to stay the night at Government House. But, although she was a local celebrity and set off the following morning with an escort of Karachi Flying Club Moths that accompanied her for the first half hour, it was not until later that she became fully aware of the fervour with which her story had been taken up back in England.

The next leg was to Allahabad. Flying directly into strong headwinds, Johnnie arrived at what she hoped might be her destination, but unable to find anything resembling an airport, she put down in a field at Jhansi, where she was informed that she still had 200 miles to go. On resuming her journey, it soon became apparent that *Jason* would run out of fuel before they got there and, reluctantly – though with commendable good sense – she turned back. This time, finding what looked as though it might be an airfield, Johnnie realised too late that it was only the parade ground of a military barracks. Moments later she was 'charging at high speed towards the buildings ... twisting her way round trees, barely missing an iron telegraph post, scattering a group of men waiting to mount guard, smashing into the name board outside the regimental offices before finally coming to rest wedged between two of the barrack blocks'. To the astonishment of the onlookers, there emerged from the cockpit 'a girl – young, almost a child, furious, wearing only a shirt, an ill-fitting pair of khaki shorts, socks and shoes and a flying helmet. The skin on her face, arms and legs was burnt and blistered by the Sun, and tears were not far from her tired eyes'.[4] Amazingly, there was only minor damage to one of her wings and this was able to be repaired on the spot while, as usual, she went over the Moth, tightening nuts, bolts and screws and taking out and cleaning the spark plugs before changing the oil and refuelling.

With the parade ground cleared of obstacles, she was up and off again in the early hours of the following morning, stopping at Allahabad only briefly to fill her tanks to the brim – she'd had to skimp on fuel to be sure of getting off the ground at Jhansi – before setting out for Calcutta, which she reached without further mishap on 12 May. She was now two days ahead of Hinkler and the papers were full of it.

Again, though, she was up at dawn the following morning. Next stop was Rangoon and she had torrential rain to negotiate. This was so bad that it prevented her from going over the top of the mountain range that lay between West Bengal and the Irrawaddy, and *Jason* was forced to alter course. When finally they picked up the railway that led to her destination, it was pouring so hard that Johnnie was 'almost touching the tops of the stations, scaring the people waiting for their trains'.[5]

On reaching Rangoon, the problem was identifying the racecourse where she had been directed to land. It was beginning to get dark and the Moth was low on fuel. She could not find it and there seemed to be nowhere else safe to put down. In desperation, she landed on what proved to be the playing field of the Government Technical Institute at Insein, 5 miles to the north of her intended destination. For the second time in hardly more than twenty-four hours, Johnnie found herself dodging obstacles and ploughing through goal posts before *Jason* finally 'buried his head and came to a standstill with a loud noise and a great shudder'. 'This,' she wrote, 'was too much for me and I cried like a baby.'[6]

To repair the Moth and transport it to the racecourse cost three days. Problem was, one wing was badly damaged, with several shattered ribs, while several square feet of fabric needed replacing. Worse, she had neither linen nor dope among her spares. Instead, she was compelled to use a batch of men's shirts (which someone remembered were made of war-surplus aeroplane fabric), sewn together and doped with an approximation of the small amount she had remaining in a tin. Sending it off to the local chemist, he judged it according to smell. When at last all was ready, *Jason* had to be road hauled, wings folded, by a fire engine in tropical rain. Johnnie had by now surrendered her lead over Hinkler but there remained a slim chance that she could make up some time and beat him all the same. Unfortunately, when eventually *Jason* did get airborne, the cloud over the next mountain range was such that Johnnie had to fly blind in cloud, losing her way and adding over two hours to her flight time. This put Singapore out of reach before dark so she landed in Bangkok, where enthusiastic but inexperienced ground handlers caused her to have to return to base immediately after take-off next morning. Someone had failed to close the starboard engine cowling and Amy herself had been too tired to notice.

Her arrival in Singapore gave Amy Johnson a foretaste of the fame that was about to sweep her up. Hundreds of expats, dressed as though for a garden party, stood by the hangars variously waving their handkerchiefs and their topees. She had arrived on the fourteenth day since departing Croydon. On cabling her father, 'Cannot break record, weather dreadful', the reply came back: 'You are wonderful. Nobody worrying about record.' His was not the only telegram. She now began to receive them at each subsequent stop, first in their dozens, then in their hundreds. One concerned an offer of £500 from the *Daily Express* for ten lectures. Another was an offer of £5,000 for a tour of Australia. In the meantime, it happened that the RAF had a spare Moth wing with which they happily replaced the one damaged in Rangoon. The original turned out to have a cracked rear spar, meaning that in severe turbulence it would have been highly likely to break up entirely. Another miracle?

Hoping to cover a thousand miles to reach Surabaya in the East Indies, *Jason* and Johnnie set off from Singapore in fine weather. Over the Java Sea it began to deteriorate, however. Forced down lower and lower, Johnnie lost her bearings and was reduced to circling low over the water in hopes of spotting a break in the clouds. The rain was stupefying. Eventually, it abated enough for her to reorientate herself so that she was flying south-east by her compass. Fortunately, the target was large enough that, so long as she could keep heading more or less south-east, she would eventually hit the coastline ahead.

But, even if the navigation was not too challenging, this was an exceedingly gutsy performance. She was over water for more than ten hours, sustained by little more than a thermos of tea and a handful of glucose sweets. By the time she reached dry land, the light was failing and again she realised she could not safely reach her intended destination before nightfall. She put down instead on a patch of ground adjacent to what turned out to be a sugar processing plant. The landing was shorter than she expected because the ground had been staked out for a building plot. Unhappily, the bamboo stakes used to mark it tore holes in the underside of her wings and she was compelled to patch them up as best she could with sticking plaster before accepting the hospitality of the Dutch factory manager, who put her up for the night.

Next morning, arriving in the rain at Surabaya after a relatively short flight, Johnnie was mobbed. A local reporter recounted that there was nothing to be seen but 'flowers and laughing, enthusiastic faces' and 'nothing to be heard but cheers and compliments and hearty good wishes' as she climbed out of *Jason*. Rather than press on immediately, she took the day to supervise and assist with maintenance and another propeller change, with a view to reaching Atamboea on East Timor, still a thousand miles to the east, the following day.

Things began well and *Jason* and Johnnie followed the archipelago of islands with the weather improving all the way. But there must have been a headwind as, by the time she reached the Timor coast, it was so dark and she had so little fuel that yet again she was compelled to call on supernatural assistance and put down on a patch of open ground. This was cannibal country and, on being surrounded by a crowd of locals, she pulled her revolver. Fortunately, there was no need. The villagers received her kindly, having perhaps been taught better manners by the nearby Catholic mission, to which they took her.

In terms of theatrics, Amy Johnson's unscheduled stop among the 'grinning savages', as she described her hosts, was a masterstroke. 'FLYING GIRL MISSING' screamed billboards all over London and the provinces, and almost every paper in the land led with the fearful news. Among others, Alan Cobham gave his opinion. There were plenty of places she might have landed en route, he said, and, even if open spaces were limited, she ought to survive even a treetop landing. Many feared the worst, however, and the next twenty-four hours saw the entire country swooning with anxiety. The twenty-four seconds or so preceding her next take-off were no less anxious for Amy Johnson. What she would have liked was for a man to hold her lower wingtips, while she opened the throttle wide and got the tail off the ground, in order to maximise her chances of getting airborne before reaching the trees ahead. But, unable to make herself understood, Johnnie was restricted to an orthodox take-off run. She swore that she actually brushed their tops as she made her escape.

Finally arriving at Atamboea, in what was then the Dutch East Indies, her last stop before Australia and with Hinkler's record now unassailable, there was no need to rush. This was just as well, since the only fuel available was in some drums so badly rusted that it took almost the entire day to filter their contents into her tanks. A single speck could foul the carburettor jet and put her in the sea. It is not clear why there were no fresh supplies available but the local Shell agent did one useful thing for her, ordering a tanker to stand midway between the Timor coast and the Australian coast as a beacon to steer by. Next day, an airmail pilot departing for Darwin offered to take the lead if she would like to follow him. But the Fokker trimotor he was flying was much faster than the Moth and she soon lost him. Given that she would be over open water for seven hours, the knowledge that the tanker was waiting for her encouraged her mightily. It was just a matter of finding it. Happily, she did and, having come down to wave at the crew, she adjusted her course according to the smoke billowing from the vessel's chimney. Now it was just a matter of holding a steady course for another three hours and the job would be done. There was one last moment of terror when the Gipsy engine began to splutter. Fuel contamination! Fortunately, she managed to clear the obstruction by sharply opening and closing the throttle. Still her anxiety lingered until, to her joy, the coast of Australia hove into view and rest beckoned at last.

As did fame and fortune, too – both far beyond her wildest dreams. Seeing the huge crowd – several thousand strong – assembled to greet her, Johnnie assumed that her arrival must have coincided with an air show put on to celebrate Empire Day, which, by coincidence, it happened to be. But no, it was all for her. This surprised her not a little: she supposed her failure to beat Hinkler's record meant that the whole thing was a failure. But nobody had a thought for the record. It was the fact that a woman had done this remarkable deed that excited the imagination. If a woman could do this, what could women not do? Again, the telegrams began to pour in, more than two hundred in all. Among the first were those from Buckingham Palace and Ramsay MacDonald, the prime minister. And, of course, there was one each from Sir Sefton Brancker, the Air League, the Royal Aeronautical Society and other luminaries of the aviation establishment. Over the next days, there followed hundreds more from home and many from abroad too:

Charles Lindbergh, Louis Blériot and even the king and queen of Belgium wired to offer congratulations. Some were formal – 'The Queen and I are thankful and delighted to hear of Miss Johnson's safe arrival . . .', others brief and to the point. Blériot's read simply, 'Bravo!' Back home, people wrote to her in their thousands, and not just to her but to her mother and father too. One letter was addressed to 'The parents of the Empire's great, little woman'. Among them were no less than sixteen proposals of marriage and, unexpectedly, 'various invitations from perverted females'.[7] Six months later, the mail was still pouring in at a rate of fifty a day.

Australia, already extremely well disposed to their heroic visitor, was doubly smitten when, at a gala dinner held for her in Darwin the following day, she insisted on being called 'Johnnie – that's what they all call me back home.'

Two days later, she set off for Brisbane, this time under escort of another Moth. Stopping briefly at Toowoomba en route, she 'was literally dragged out of her machine and pulled through a surging and enthusiastic crowd'. At Brisbane, the welcome was even more tumultuous. Alas, on arrival, exhaustion and nerves got the better of her. She came in much too fast – the newsreel makes this plain – and, failing to get the aeroplane into a three-pointer, she turned a half-somersault when *Jason* collided with the boundary fence at the end of the runway. Horror turned to ecstatic relief when Johnnie extricated herself from the wreckage and, having been collected in a car, smoothed herself down and walked up to the dais to speak as if there had been nothing to be seen. 'People of Australia,' she began, 'I thank you from the bottom of my heart for the absolutely marvellous welcome you have given me. I have had splendid receptions everywhere, but this simply beats the band.'

Altogether, Amy Johnson was in Australia for just over six weeks. During that time, she visited and spoke in every major city as well as in many provincial towns. News that she had been made a Commander of the British Empire in the king's birthday honours merely served further to heighten the people's enthusiasm.* She was mobbed everywhere. At what point she realised that celebrity is double-edged is unclear. Perhaps it was when, putting up some resistance to their demands – her father had sold exclusive rights to her story to the *Daily Mail* for £10,000 – the paper's agent had stood over her in her hotel room and informed her that, 'We bought you body and soul.'

When Amy Johnson arrived back at Croydon, flown in from Southampton, yet another huge crowd awaited her. But there was more. All the way from the airport to the Park Lane Hotel, where the *Mail* had booked the Empire suite for her and her family, the road was lined with cheering people eager to catch a glimpse of this latter-day Joan of Arc.

Next day, she attended a public gathering in Hyde Park and a thirty-piece band played, 'Amy, Wonderful Amy' – the hit song of the day:

Amy, wonderful Amy,
How can you blame me for loving you?
Since you have won the praise of every nation
You have filled my heart with admiraaaation
Amy, wonderful Amy ...

---

* Many thought she ought to have been made a dame but, still only twenty-six, she was deemed too young. Mary Bailey had been forty at the time of her elevation.

She was presented with, among other things, de Havilland's latest creation, a gleaming DH80 Puss Moth painted, like *Jason*, in green and silver livery. She later attended a luncheon at the Savoy Hotel where such aeronautical grandees as Sir Philip Sassoon, Bert Hinkler, Louis Blériot and Sir Sefton Brancker were present, alongside Noël Coward, Ivor Novello, Alfred Hitchcock, Cecil Beaton and Evelyn Waugh, all of whom gathered to applaud her. Another reception saw her being photographed standing with Charlie Chaplin, Lady Astor and George Bernard Shaw. The *Daily Mail* formally bestowed its cheque for £10,000. The *Daily Sketch*, not to be outdone, ran a reader subscription and presented her with a new Gipsy Moth. William Morris, later Lord Nuffield, head of Morris Motors, arranged delivery of a top-of-the-range MG. There was also a Movietone film to publicise her forthcoming tour – there she sits, uncomfortably, her eyes darting all around, reading from an autocue with a phonetic script to make her sound like a contemporary BBC presenter. You can only feel sorry that she felt compelled to go along with the make-believe, to masquerade as something she so plainly was not: an angel dropped from heaven, a conqueror of foreign lands or some kind of secular saint. No, she was Amy Johnson. You know, the girl next door. The one who went to London and became a secretary. That one.

You get a glimpse of the original Amy in some footage of her homecoming reception. There she stands, briefly awed by the delight of the crowd as if she can't quite believe it's for her that they are cheering.

The subsequent tour of the kingdom was in one way an enormous success. She drew the crowds and was feted everywhere she went. But, both physically and emotionally, her sudden fame came at a great cost. Her flying deteriorated – it took her four attempts to land at Eastbourne – and, on another occasion, after getting lost in bad weather over the North Sea while flying up to Hull, she ended up on a beach having narrowly escaped a ditching after getting lost in bad weather. Soon enough, she came to resent being in the public eye. Like so many celebrities since, she wanted fame on her own terms. On the one hand, she connived in her own predicament – she threw herself unstintingly into the role of cheerleader for the 'youth of the nation' and for 'aviation' – and she was happy to take her fees. On the other, she resented the incessant intrusion. It turned out that the words of the *Daily Mail*'s agent in Australia had told an ugly truth. Perhaps, too, she was haunted by the fact that, after all, if she hadn't been the first woman to fly solo to Australia, another would have been soon enough. Did she also question the ultimate value of what she had done? When Margaret Williamson, wife of the British political officer for Tibet and the first Western woman to gain an audience with the Dalai Lama, told him of Johnnie's recent achievement, the Tibetan leader wondered what the hurry had been.

But all this is beside the point. What Amy Johnson really did – the revolutionary thing that people caught onto, mostly without realising it – was to show that courage and skill were more significant markers of success than sex or wealth or family background.

14

The Lonely Sea and the Sky

Today, no sane pilot would seriously contemplate a long journey without at least a 1:500,000 aeronautical chart, a radio and a detailed weather forecast. Yet the fact is, none of these were available in those early days of aviation. As Aspy Engineer said, you often just had to 'smell your way around'.

If, then, the exploits of Bailey, Engineer and Johnson in their Moths seem extraordinary to us, the achievements of Francis Chichester are of a different order altogether. Reading his autobiography, you are left slack-jawed with astonishment for page after page, wondering what sort of a man this was. Was he a genius? Was he mad? Did he have no limits at all?

Born in 1901, Francis Chichester was, like GDH himself, the second son of a clergyman. Unlike the de Havillands, though, the Chichesters were a large and wealthy family of West Country landowners. There were two major estates, one belonging to the recusant Catholic branch of the family, another that went with a baronetcy held by the Protestant side. There were numerous cousins – Francis' father was one of nine children – not to mention many uncles and aunts, maiden and otherwise. All of them took their religion extremely seriously. One aunt was famous for attending three church services every Sunday, while Francis' own father was renowned for his stern and unbending faith. When, on one occasion, he came upon one of his parishioners drunk from a day spent in the local pub, he did not hesitate to remonstrate with the man. On being told that it was 'all right for some' with wine on the table at every meal, the reverend gentleman went home and never touched another drop. The atmosphere in the house, far from homely before, became icier than ever.

While his elder brother George was a conformist, Francis was highly strung and highly energetic. As a result, he was often beaten – first at home, then at school. He was left in no doubt that he was the least favourite of his father's four children (he had two younger sisters). To make matters worse, he had no friends – he was too wild to form close relationships with people his own age – a fact that his parents seem not even to have noticed.

When, at the age of seven, Francis was packed off to prep school, he was almost immediately sent to Coventry for three weeks for some minor misdemeanour. Not even his own brother spoke a single word to him in all that time. Thereafter, he was always in trouble. Matters improved somewhat when, having at the time a rather weak constitution, his parents took him away from this school and sent him to another at Bournemouth where the sea air suited him better. But still he had no friends. Worse, he became something of a bully himself.

At Marlborough, things were no better. Still largely friend-less, he hated the place. The fact of being short-sighted and having to wear glasses all the time was the cause of added frustration. Deciding that he was never going to be as clever as the boys in the top sets, he determined to leave before his time was up and make a go of life – whatever that should turn out to mean.

There followed a lonely year spent working on a farm for 5 shillings a week, milking cows and spreading manure in Leicestershire, when he would 'dream of warm-hearted, friendly people, and comfortable living'. Unfortunately, this ended badly when he fell in love with the farmer's daughter. His employer needed no further excuse to sack him when he damaged a milk cart through racing another lad on their way back from a delivery run. With his tail between his legs, Francis Chichester returned home to face the wrath of his father, who took little persuading to fund his errant son's passage on a boat to New Zealand where a family acquaintance promised him a job if he could get himself there.

Setting sail, Chichester made a vow not to return home before he had made £20,000 – a prodigious sum for someone whose capital amounted to the ten gold sovereigns that, to his surprise, his father sent him off with. From sheep farming (for which his natural impatience served him badly) to bushwhacking (forest clearing), from gold-prospecting to coal mining, from selling newspaper subscriptions to land agency and, finally, to dealing in property, it took ten years of mostly hard physical labour, spent among often suspicious workmates – they did not know what to make of this bespectacled Englishman with his posh accent and antisocial ways – to achieve his aim. He still had trouble fitting in and, even though he got on with his eventual business partner, it seems that he never really succeeded in making many good friends.

This inability to form close relationships extended to his love life which, as he admitted freely, was characterised by short, unhappy affairs, invariably with unsuitable women – including the one he eventually married in 1926.

By his late twenties, however, Chichester had established a successful business, even if it was one of which he did not greatly approve. He and his partner began buying up large acreages of virgin land and selling off small plots with planning permission for housebuilding. His one solace as a child had been an intense love of nature and now he was collaborating in its destruction.

Using the capital that they quickly began to amass, Chichester and his partner began to diversify. One of their ventures was the Goodwin-Chichester Aviation Company. Taking on the New Zealand agency for Avro aircraft and purchasing two Avians, they quickly lost a large sum of money. Although they hired four experienced ex-air force pilots, there was an awful lot of accidents, chiefly, it seemed, due to farm fences being in the wrong place. In a year, they gave six thousand joyrides but, losing an average of 10 shillings a go, the total loss was £3,000. Stung by this, Chichester decided he needed to learn to fly himself so he could understand exactly what the problems were. He found being airborne wildly exciting, but also that he was no natural. By the end of the year, 1928, he had accumulated eighteen hours and fifty minutes of dual instruction 'and still could not fly'. Undeterred, he made up his mind that next year, following a trip home, he would pilot his own machine back.

On arrival in England, another five and a half hours' instruction saw Chichester finally go solo. At once, he bought a Gipsy Moth, though 'it was not the plane I wanted. I had

left New Zealand with the idea of buying a bigger machine.'
A sudden downturn in the New Zealand real estate business – anticipating the stock market crash that hit during the
autumn of 1929 – forced him to rein in his ambitions. This
was just as well as the DH60 'turned out to be a wonderful
little aeroplane'.

Remarkably, when he took delivery of his machine – which,
for no clear reason, he named *Madam Elijah* – it had no compass
fitted, presumably due to supply problems. Moth production
had more than doubled from 117 in 1927 to 336 in 1928, and
from there to well over 500 globally in 1929. The instrument
makers simply couldn't keep up with demand. But this did not
deter him. He would just have to navigate 'by Bradshaw'. This
was the humorous term used to describe aerial navigation by
means of the train timetables published by the company of that
name. In theory, if you were flying over a railway station and
saw a train pulling out, you could determine where it was by
checking your watch – these being the days when trains could
be assumed to run on time.

After a disappointing visit to Liverpool (to see an actress
with whom he was enamoured), Chichester flew down to
Devon to meet with his family for the first time since leaving
home ten years earlier. This visit, too, was no great success. His
parents were not impressed by the aeroplane or by his Kiwi
twang. Still less were they impressed by his fortune. Least of all
were they impressed to learn that, after three years of unhappy
marriage, he had separated from his wife. The local villagers
were more welcoming, however, and they turned out in force
to admire the Moth. Alas, having given several joyrides, an
encounter with a rabbit burrow ended in a collision with an
oak tree and a broken aeroplane.

With the help of the local carpenter, an old friend, Chichester made the necessary repairs himself. Unfortunately, on the day he chose to leave it was blowing a gale – fine for take-off, not so good for landing. Unless the wind is steady, there is every chance of coming to grief.

Chichester came to grief.

Again, he worked on this second round of repairs himself, gaining valuable experience that was to stand him in good stead. When at last everything was complete, he made a resolution to master fully the art of flying. Every day for over a month, and 'for hour after hour I practised landing into wind, across wind and down wind, and then in a confined space'. As he improved his accuracy, he began to make life difficult for himself: 'I used to plant my handkerchief ten yards inside a fence and practise touching down on it. Then I would move it 150 yards from the fence and practise ending my landing run on it . . . the hardest manoeuvre of all' due to the lack of brakes and variable wind. Then he would spend half an hour practising forced landings, followed by half an hour of aerobatics.

When his compass finally arrived after six weeks, Chichester added navigational exercises into his daily routine. He also began to analyse fuel consumption at various speeds. By November, he felt ready to undertake a long-distance flight to prove his, and his aeroplane's, readiness for his intended flight Down Under the following year.

It began badly. For the first leg to Paris, Chichester agreed to take a pilot friend with him. Thereafter, he would continue solo. Lined up on the runway, the co-pilot called out enthusiastically, 'Let's go!' and pushed the throttle wide. 'We were a long time leaving the ground,' Chichester recalled, only clearing the trees beyond the end of the runway 'by a foot or two':

'What on earth are you doing?' shouted Joe through the speaking tube.

'Nothing,' I said indignantly. 'I never touched the controls.'

'Nor did I,' said he.

It was a repeat of GDH's take-off in the DH4 during the war.

To revive themselves after this fright, they landed at Abbeville for glasses of cognac, before continuing to Paris. Having dropped off his passenger, Chichester proceeded to Nice and then via Milan to Venice, where he spent the night. Leaving la Serenissima considerably later than intended, he found himself far short of his intended destination at twilight. When fog began to spread, he realised he needed to land immediately. The result: a broken propeller and a ten-day wait for a new one to arrive. Subsequently flying above the Danube, he found himself again forced down by low cloud to the point where he was 'dodging telephone poles in the mist'.[1]

At Leipzig, he was given the opportunity to fly a small Junkers monoplane – presumably the A50 Junior – which he thought 'heavy on the controls and glided like a brick compared to the Gipsy Moth'.[2]

Returning to England just less than a month since departure, Chichester set about planning his flight to Sydney (where he would ship the aeroplane across the 1,500-mile Tasman Sea home to New Zealand – he didn't have the range to cross it). To this end, he acquired a set of maps that, glued together, extended 71 feet end to end. He then cut it up into manageable strips nine inches wide. Not all were equally useful. Those that covered his route as far as Rangoon were 16 miles to the inch;

those from Rangoon to Darwin, 64 miles to the inch; those from Darwin to Sydney, 45 miles to the inch. Nonetheless, his planning was as meticulous as his charts allowed. He carefully marked the magnetic variation over every hundred miles and at every course change. Assuming a cruising speed of 80 mph, he also marked his projected position at half-hourly intervals, after which he set about learning his route by heart.

At the same as doing this, he arranged with Shell for them to put down supplies – including a consignment in the Northern Territories of Australia to be delivered by camel – and applied for the necessary permits and clearances he would need for each country. Whether at the outset, or whether during the planning stage is unclear, but at some point Chichester fastened onto the idea of turning his trip into a record-breaking one, concluding that he ought to be able to cover a thousand miles a day. He could achieve this if he flew two six-and-a-half-hour stages per twenty-four hours. This would break Hinkler's record by a full four days – there being, he thought, no point in beating it by just a few hours. It was a punishing ambition.

Having set off on 20 December 1929, his first overnight stop, having refuelled at Lyon, was Pisa which he reached in the dark. Next day, he got as far as Homs, again arriving after dark, but there he missed the airport and landed in the adjacent salt flats, ending up on his nose with a broken propeller. He had been airborne for twenty-six of the preceding forty hours, having covered 1,900 miles, but there was no hope of a record now. It took ten days for the new propeller to reach him.

Finally on his way again, his next stop was Benghazi, where he received news of his wife's death. A quiet, pretty, homely young woman, she had borne him a son two years after they were married but they had separated less than a year afterwards. The event is covered in a single sentence in Chichester's autobiography. Reading this, and in view of his subsequent achievements, it is hard to suppress the thought that Chichester's single-mindedness, his ability to endure, his life-scorning determination to do whatever he set out to do, came at the price of a ruthlessness that did not count the bodies.

Although no longer under any time pressure, Chichester continued to drive himself absurdly hard. Making full use of a powerful tailwind, he flew from Benghazi direct to the British air base at Abu Sueir, adjacent to the Suez Canal; a distance of 917 miles. This took him nine and a quarter hours at an average speed just shy of 100 mph. On landing, he found himself too exhausted even to eat or drink. Nonetheless, the following morning he was up and ready to carry on.

Refuelling at Gaza, he discovered that the compression on his number two cylinder had fallen dangerously low and would need fixing as soon as possible. There was an Imperial Airways mechanic stationed at his next intended stop at Rutbah Wells (Ar-Rutbah in modern-day Iraq), so hopefully he could get it fixed there. It was on this leg of the journey that Chichester made his first serious navigational error, causing him to come down almost to the surface to watch the ground – 'so closely that I think I would have seen a rat on it' – for any clue as to his position. Yet, far from despairing, he was 'excited and thrilled' by his predicament. 'This,' he wrote, 'was the stuff that life was made of.'

Three days later, having crossed India, Chichester reached the southern tip of Burma, where he found himself having to side-slip violently to get onto the deck at the threshold of a runway that was supposed to be almost a mile long but which proved to be barely a hundred yards. This presented him with an even more serious problem when taking off the next day. Keeping his nose down until the very last safe moment, before yanking it up, staggered on the edge of the stall, he flew first over a fence, then over some trees. The narrowness of his escape 'ruined the day's flying'. But he made it to Singapore well and good. The next leg, to Batavia, was fearful for another reason. As he flew over the coast of Sumatra, he encountered the heaviest rain he had seen in his life and elected to turn back on himself. As he did so, he lost all visibility. With no instruments to guide him, he had to rely on the sensation of acceleration and deceleration. When he heard the wind screaming in the wires, he eased the nose up. When he felt the acceleration coming from the side, he rolled in the opposite direction. When, suddenly, the sea appeared dead ahead, he found himself on the point of diving into it.

At Java, he was again forced down almost to the ground. 'It was nervy work looking out for trees,' he wrote. Later on, out over the sea, he missed the masts of a fishing boat by inches before flying between the masts of first one, then another junk, as he came in to land on the beach. As soon as the storm abated, he was off again, finally reaching Darwin where he spent the evening drinking beer with some of the local inhabitants. But he would not rest.

It was so hot on the flight out of Darwin that he was worried his upper wing might catch fire. At first guided by a railway track and then a long line of telegraph poles, Chichester soon found himself having to follow wheel tracks at low level in thick haze and bumpy conditions. Correctly identifying a homestead, he landed but, finding no fuel there, decided to press on and use his final three hours of flying time. It was, he wrote, 'by far the most difficult country I had come across for navigating'. Although he knew the bearing he needed to fly, the landscape was so utterly desolate that there were no identifiable waypoints by which he could monitor his progress.

With his petrol gauge heading towards empty, Chichester abandoned the idea of finding Camooweal, his intended destination, and promised himself he would land at the next building he came to, whatever it was. To his great relief, he spotted a borehole with an engine shed adjacent. This would have to do. No matter that there was barely fifty yards of boulder-free ground on which to pull off a perfect landing after an astonishing eleven hours in the air, most of it spent at low level in turbulence and haze.

Happily, he succeeded. And there was water. But there were flies too: 'They crawled over my eyeballs, filled up my ears and each time I opened my mouth (which I did frequently for my tongue was swollen and stuck unpleasantly to the roof of my mouth), they flew in.' Finding himself too weak to move the Moth into the lee of the building, he lashed it down with rope as best he could. Then he lit a fire, 'dropped on the ground and rested. I was exhausted and panic struck so abjectly that I was disgusted with myself.'

With the determination given only to the religious believer or to the monomaniac, he finally got hold of himself: 'I was lost, true; I had no petrol, true; but compared with what might have been, I was well off.' His plane was intact; he was still functioning, more or less; he had shade; he had some food; he had no shortage of water. Consoled, he dragged out his rubber dinghy, half inflated it and fell into a fitful sleep. Recovered somewhat next morning, he went over the details of his flight of the day before and plotted all his movements carefully on his chart, such as it was. Concluding that he was only 10 miles west of Camooweal, he surveyed the tracks coming up to and leading away from the borehole. Most were at least several days old but, with sudden excitement, he spotted some that were completely fresh – only to realise, like Pooh in pursuit of the Heffalump, that they were his own. Despondently, he returned to the Moth. Did he really have no petrol at all? Lifting a wing, he heard a splash in the tank. Clearly, he had more than a dribble. Taking the billy in which he had boiled water the night before, he cleaned it out, climbed up and drained the remaining contents of the fuel tank into it. To his surprise, he found that he had around three gallons in hand. That should give him thirty-six minutes' flying. Fifteen minutes out, fifteen minutes back, six in hand.

Stowing his kit, he prepared for take-off. By now, he was convinced that his destination lay just a short distance east of his current position. He agreed with himself that he would turn back at exactly fifteen minutes. The prospect thrilled him: 'Every second of this flight was exciting.' At the eleven-minute mark, he was sure he saw a man. But no, it was only a horse. At fourteen and a half minutes, he came to a creek. Now he must turn back. Crossing to the other side of it, he banked steeply. As he did so, he had a shock. Surely that was the glint of sunlight off corrugated iron over there? It was. On landing, he was met by the station manager who told him where he was; just a few miles short of Camooweal to which he proceeded on his last thimbleful of fuel.

The last 1,300 miles via Longreach and Bourke to Sydney presented no problems, thanks to the railway lines connecting them. But then a strange desolation came over him: 'I was a human 22-day clock beginning to run down. I had been ticking away every day from before dawn until an hour or two after sunset.' Now that the clock was winding down, he felt only emptiness.

His desolation was mitigated somewhat on finding himself the centre of attention on finally landing at Sydney on 6 January 1930. Several aircraft came up to greet him and, on the ground, not only several thousand people but representatives of the world's press. There was even a telegram of congratulation from the Australian prime minister.

Having shipped his Moth back to New Zealand, Chichester was now in a position to offer joyrides in his aeroplane without needing to employ a professional pilot. Unfortunately, people were sceptical that an aeroplane that had flown all the way from London to Sydney could be as safe as one that hadn't and there were few takers. Chichester decided, therefore, that what he ought to do was fly back to England through Asia. He would begin by crossing the Tasman.

An immediate problem presented itself. The minimum distance across was more than 1,300 miles. As presently configured, the Gipsy Moth was good for a maximum of a thousand. Even with maximum tankage (which he could not afford anyway), there would be no margin for any sort of headwind. While mulling over this inconvenient fact, Chichester happened, one day while shaving, to notice marked on a globe standing nearby, two tiny islands in between New Zealand and Australia.

That was his answer. The distance from the northern tip of New Zealand to Norfolk Island, the first of them, was 475 miles: say six and three quarter hours' flying if you allow for a net headwind of 15 mph, while the distance from Norfolk

Island to Lord Howe Island was 560 miles – so around eight and a half hours' flying – and from Lord Howe to Australia was 375 miles, a bit under six hours. Doable.

Other problems began to emerge, however. The first was that no one had ever landed an aeroplane on either island and, on enquiry, he learned that there was nowhere he could hope to put down safely. The only solution was to convert his Moth into a floatplane, though this would slow him down by at least 5 mph. Several authorities assured Chichester that he wouldn't even be able to land a floatplane successfully due the permanent swell and lack of natural harbours. His most pressing problem, however, was that he could not afford the £500 float conversion kit for his aeroplane. There was also the small matter of how to navigate over such large distances with nothing to guide him but his P2 compass. The size of Norfolk Island, just 5 miles wide in one direction and three and a half in the other, meant that his margin for error was no more than one half of one degree. Lord Howe Island, actually one of a small archipelago of large rocks, was smaller still and the margin even narrower.

The problem of floats was solved when, for £20, he acquired some second-hand ones from the Royal New Zealand Navy. It was an economy he came to regret. As for the problem of navigation, he decided that he would have to learn to operate a sextant in flight. To gain proficiency, he ran with the instrument and practised taking sun shots. By doing this hour after hour, Chichester gradually mastered the art of manipulating the instrument while in motion. Yet nothing could have prepared him for the difficulty of replicating his success on the ground with proficiency in the air now that he had fitted the floats. Whereas before he had been able to trim the Moth so finely that he could cause it to climb or descend merely by moving his head forwards or backwards, now the aeroplane was a wallowing monster that would enter a dive as soon as he let go of the joystick. Nor was this his only problem. Once information about the sun's position relative to the horizon is known, the observer must make corrections for any error produced by the instrument itself (the index correction), as well as for atmospheric refraction and for altitude above sea level. These corrections are a matter of logarithmic calculations undertaken to five figures, for which Chichester would have to use a slide rule consisting of two coaxial tubes with, inside each, spiral scales of number sets. The whole exercise took at least twenty minutes of superhuman concentration, at the end of which he would have his latitude and longitude. These he would then plot on his chart.

The odds against achieving the needed level of accuracy under such conditions were enormous and the New Zealand air authorities did their best to discourage him. Three years earlier, two RAF pilots had been lost over the Tasman Sea and 'aviation would receive a setback if any more publicity occurred about lost airmen'. Yet, as Chichester recalled, 'I *had* to make the flight.' No matter that he had a barely four-year-old son who had just lost his mother.

Hardly a year since he landed in Sydney, Francis Chichester stowed his kit, having selected 6 a.m., 31 March 1931, as the moment he would start his engine.

His problems began almost at once. Up in a frenzy at dawn, he looked up into a blue and cloudless sky. This augured well and he breakfasted on bacon and egg. But when he had man-oeuvred his Moth onto a concrete pad in order to check his compass for error, he saw that it was already 6.15. There was only time to check for error on his heading to Norfolk Island.

No sooner than he had waved away his assistant, he remembered that he had adjusted his watch by fifteen minutes to set it to GMT. So he wasn't late – but to hell with swinging the compass all the way round. Climbing out, he broke a bottle of brandy on the propeller boss and fired up. To his consternation, he found that the engine was 40 rpm down on revs at full throttle. Odd, but he chose to ignore the problem. He was desperate to get airborne. Already, the sky had turned to grey. Next, he discovered that his radio – one which used a Morse pad, of course – was apparently dead. Another reason for delaying his departure. But no, he would not.

After a take-off run of more than a mile, he found it impossible to get airborne. A 40 rpm deficit should not prevent him from unsticking. Something must be wrong. Were his floats taking on water? He tried again. The Moth porpoised and bumped the wave tops, but refused to take flight. But by snatching at the joystick, he managed to induce a series of jumps. Finally, one of these was sufficient to get him above stalling speed before he hit the surface of the water. He was off!

Exultant as ever at the start of a new adventure, Chichester struck out across the ocean. The frenzy he had been in before take-off gave way to cool, methodical thinking. The first thing he needed to do was to work out what the wind was doing. He did this by making observations using the drift lines he had painted on each of his lower wings and by calculating it on three different headings, averaging them out; an exercise he repeated every half hour. His next problem was obtaining accurate sun shots. Exasperatingly, he found the Moth even more reluctant to settle than before. Finding that the only way to obtain the readings was to forget entirely about what the aeroplane was doing, he handed control of the Moth over to providence. Only when he felt it accelerating in a dive, with the wind screaming in the wires, did he drop his instrument and attend to the aeroplane – on one occasion only levelling out a few feet above the waves.

Eventually, Chichester had enough sun data to be confident of being able to make an accurate calculation. Having noted the time to the nearest second, all he needed now was to note his altitude. But this was strange. His state-of-the-art altimeter, recently fitted, was reading 2,500 feet yet he judged himself to be at no more than 400 feet. Diving down to the surface, he saw that the needle remained resolutely where it was. He would have to rely on the fault-prone back-up altimeter.

At around the halfway point, Chichester succeeding in acquiring five good shots of the sun. An hour later, at 3 p.m., he took another four shots. He was at last getting the hang of holding the Moth steady. But then, 'suddenly, I thought I could hear a muffled knocking in the motor'. This was unnerving and yet, although the knocking persisted, the rpm indicator was steady and the oil pressure held. He'd just have to ignore it. Next, he began to sense that, given the strength of the tailwind, he would do well to recalculate the sun's position in case he needed to make his turn sooner than his present plan suggested he should. He was using a version of 'offset' navigation, whereby you deliberately steer for a point at 90 degrees to your objective. Providing the distance is great enough, the result is that, within reason, no matter what the drift, you can be sure of hitting your target. On undertaking a new calculation, however, he was stunned. He was much closer to his turning point than he expected.

It was therefore absolutely essential he get some final sun shots. But the sky ahead was black. Looking round, he spotted a shaft of sunlight on the sea so, turning towards it, he flew at full throttle. There was only a small rent in the cloud, but, throwing the aeroplane into a steep turn which he controlled with rudder alone, he succeeded in getting four shots. Now it was a question of correcting them for the lapse of time since his earlier calculation. If they agreed, he was on the correct line. He was!

So now he must turn 90 degrees to his previous heading – a manoeuvre that he found psychologically taxing in the extreme. His instinct rose up against him. But turn he must and now fly for an hour in a completely new direction.

With one more set of sextant shots, again making use of a small tear in the clouds to confirm he was on the correct heading, Chichester began to look out for the shadow on the sea that would first indicate landfall. It should appear almost on the dot of the hour. But, holding his course steady, at eight minutes past, there was nothing. A minute later, he thought he saw something to his left but it proved only to be cloud. At twelve minutes past, again he imagined he saw something and again realised it was just cloud. A moment later, the sky began to clear and there, right in front of him, Norfolk Island rose from the sea.

How much of Chichester's success is down to sheer luck? It is true that there is luck in flying but this was pure genius. Could he, however, repeat his performance on the leg to Lord Howe Island? Things began unpromisingly when he found himself unable to get airborne the next day. Although he did not realise it at the time, one of his cut-price floats was half full of water. Next, as he swerved to avoid a rock, a rigging wire snapped. As a result, he was forced to stay another day – long enough to examine his engine. When he did so, he discovered why he was 40 rpm down. The exhaust and inlet valves of one of the cylinders had, unaccountably, been swapped round, and one of the metal seatings was in the process of vibrating itself loose. Had it done so, the valve would have stuck in one position and the engine would have blown up.

Worried now that even with his engine fixed, he might still fail to get airborne, Chichester ditched his dinghy – that would save a useful 27 lbs. He also reduced his fuel reserve. He finally got airborne but now, settled into the cruise, Chichester was dismayed to notice his Moth vibrating in a most unwholesome manner, the whole fuselage shaking and his rigging wires shivering. Yet the engine was running smoothly. It must be propeller damage. 'A few months ago, I would not have flown the plane in this condition over the safest route in the world.' But now? Too bad.

As before, he made drift calculations using three different headings every half hour and planned to take sextant readings on the hour. On calculating his drift for the second time, he found they gave him an impossible result – only to realise a moment later that he had forgotten that he was leaving Lord Howe Island to starboard and not to port. That was a bit of a shock, but it was as nothing to what he felt when he saw that his compass had vibrated loose from its bracket. Although he managed to keep it in situ by wedging paper behind it, the needle was no longer damped and it shook violently on its pivot. Worse still, his back-up altimeter also succumbed to the vibration and began moving round the dial in a succession of violent jerks. Then he realised that his onboard airspeed indicator was, for no apparent reason, not working. But there was no turning back now.

At the third hour, Chichester's calculations showed him to

be 26 miles from his expected position. If true, he really was in trouble. But then he remembered that the wing-mounted airspeed indicator over-read by 5 mph. Recalculating brought him to within a mile of his expected position. At this point, the weather began to deteriorate. He desperately needed some final sextant readings before he made his last course correction. In the end, he managed just a single shaky sun shot from which to calculate the moment to turn. It would have to do. With luck he would be able to get some more shots on the final stretch. The sky was getting increasingly dark, however. Thoroughly despondent, no sooner had he given up on the idea than a shaft of sunlight broke through a short distance away. Jamming his throttle wide and leaning forward in his seat 'like a jockey' urging on his mount, he steered towards it. This yielded three good shots but now he was so overcome with fatigue that it took him an age to work out his position. Astoundingly, his calculations put the island dead ahead of him. He put his sextant down and stowed his other instruments: compass, slide rule and log, as he slowly took in the immensity of his achievement. As it did so, his mood swung violently. First, exultation, then, noticing a sudden strengthening of the wind, dismay as he recalled the Admiralty Sailing Directions warning that, in a north-easterly wind, ships passing within a mile and half of Lord Howe Island were known to have been dismasted by the violent squalls. Looking down at the sea, with the crests of the waves torn off in showers of spray, his heart fell. Above, the sky was increasingly menacing. But, a moment later, there was the island. Bang on the nose.

Circling in search of somewhere sheltered to put down, the Moth was struck by a sudden gust: 'Cameras, sextant, protractors, pencils, chart, everything flurried round my head like a whirl of leaves.' The control column was snatched from his hand and only his lap strap kept him in the aeroplane. He closed the throttle and put the Moth into a steep dive. When, finally, he came ashore, and the Moth was secure as possible, it was completely dark. Meanwhile, the wind blew ever harder.

That night, the Moth sank.

When, with the help of some islanders, Chichester managed to get the aeroplane ashore the next day, he was astonished that it had not simply broken up after spending the night bumping up and down at the bottom of the sea. The Moth was 'a miracle of engineering' he declared; so light and yet so sturdy. Now, though, there seemed nothing to do but salvage those parts that were saleable and discard the remainder. And yet, the thought of 'creeping into Sydney in a miserable steamer' was humiliating beyond bearing. He'd rather carry on in a dinghy.

What, though, if the aeroplane proved repairable? And, if repairable, what was to stop him undertaking the work himself? For Chichester, the matter of his broken aeroplane became a technical problem to be solved, not shirked.

He began by stripping the wings of their fabric and studying their construction for hours. He would need to take out, clean and oil every single screw, bolt and nut. Undeterred, and using blueprints that he cabled to be sent over by ship from de Havilland Australia's Sydney base, Chichester, aided by a small team of local assistants, began the painstaking work of restoration.

Astonishingly, the whole exercise took a mere nine weeks. If ever there was testimony to the practicality of the Moth, this, surely, was it. With a minimum of specialist tools and only the knowledge that could be gained from looking and learning, Chichester not only rebuilt and recovered the airframe but also took apart and rebuilt the Gipsy engine, regrinding all the valves and producing, at the end, a powerplant that, at last, gave good compressions on all four cylinders. When the time came for a test flight, the Moth took to the air 'as easily as a fairy dancing off' the water. But then the engine stopped and he had to make a forced landing; it turned out there was foreign matter in the carburettor.

The problem sorted, Chichester spent a day giving joyrides to his helpers, during the course of which, unknown to him, his starboard float became increasingly waterlogged. It had a crack in it which had escaped detection during the rebuild. As a result, landings and take-offs became increasingly difficult, a fault that the Captain – as the islanders nicknamed him – put down to poor piloting skills. The same happened the next day when he gave more joyrides. But he was impatient to leave and Chichester spent the rest of the afternoon in his usual frenzy, fretting over this and that as he stowed the Moth with his gear. That evening, he prepared himself a new chart for a direct flight to Sydney – a decision which he came to regard as crazy given that it added a wholly unnecessary 85 miles over water. He could just as easily have routed via the nearest landfall at Macquarie and then flown down the coast.

As ever, he began the day manically smashing a bottle of brandy on the propeller boss. When he began his take-off run, again he found it completely impossible to unstick. Time and again he tried, but with no joy. Still not realising that his starboard float was taking on water, he began dumping gear and fuel. Finally, he staggered into the air, the Moth clinging to its slots in ground effect, only just clearing the palm trees at the end of the lagoon and clawing its way up and over the hill, before finally Chichester managed to get proper control – and for some of the water to drain out.

Setting his course, he was pleased to discover that he had a tailwind of 40 mph. But the wind was backing and at the end of an hour, he found himself 10 miles off course. No sooner had he corrected, however, than there was a loud bang from the engine. A moment of wide-eyed terror gradually gave way to calm. Testing the magnetos, he discovered that one of them was defective – the only part of the set-up that he had not repaired himself! It must have oiled up as, fortunately, it cleared itself in a couple of minutes.

At the end of the second hour, the wind had come round still further and was blowing harder, putting him over 40 miles off course. Given the size of his target, this didn't seem to matter much. What did matter was the deteriorating weather. At three hours, heavy rain stung his face and the wind drift began to alarm him. A few moments later and the deluge was such that he was flying blind with the water running off his wings in whole sheets. For a moment he was panic-struck but, as he wrote later, 'panic meant dying like a paralysed rabbit' and he caught a grip of himself. He would descend to sea level but, looking to check his airspeed on the wing-mounted indicator, he found he was unable to see it, let alone read it. He'd have to rely on his rpm indicator. If it rose, he was diving and he eased back on the stick; if it fell, he was heading for a stall and he eased it forward. When, finally, he saw a patch of sea directly ahead, he levelled off and opened the throttle. As he did so, the engine 'spluttered, broke into an uneven rattle and backfired loudly'. Would it hold? It did, though the backfiring gave way to 'an even, tearing noise'. Chichester, meanwhile, had only a small patch of sea visible – just a plane's length – before it merged with the wall of rain. He was so low the waves were licking at the bottom of his wings, only to be slashed away by the wind. Hugging the surface of the sea he rose and fell with the waves, not daring to take his eyes away even for a second to look at his compass. Instead, he relied on the wind itself, keeping the angle of drift constant as he crabbed against it.

When, finally, the storm eased and Chichester found himself with clear sky above, he was able to look at his compass again. A quick calculation showed him 55 miles off course. Another storm line lay in front of him and he could see the massive pillars of several waterspouts, which, if he got caught up in one, would smash his Moth to fragments. Slanting curtains of rain looked 'like spirits of the dead drifting from infernal regions' while the sea below was equally treacherous. The unheralded sight of a steamer nearby gave him momentary comfort. But seeing it crashing and wallowing from side to side through the combers, he realised there could be no help from that quarter.

He was tired now and a couple of sextant shots of a weak and hazy sun took him half an hour to reduce and calculate but were, in the end, not much use. At least the work was a distraction from the still backfiring engine. As was the sudden appearance of a series of bright flashes in the sky, and then, to his alarm, an airship headed directly towards him – a solid, dull grey mass but which, as it approached, disappeared just as suddenly. Curious. The area of sky in which Chichester was flying was now clear, save for a few isolated clouds. But a moment later, there it was again, about a mile away. He watched 'angrily intent' as, after a short while, it vanished again. On its third appearance, this time directly in front of him, the object – which he now understood could not be an airship – gradually diminished in size. Seconds later, 'it became its own ghost', completely transparent, before vanishing altogether. This strange event left Chichester feeling intensely lonely, a feeling that strengthened when, half an hour later, he finally spotted three warships lying at anchor. Seeing no sign of life either on board or on land, he wondered for one fearsome moment whether the world had died in his absence.

After setting down, his achievement began to sink in. He had successfully navigated across the Tasman Sea completely unsupported and using methods of his own devising, 'something which had never been done before and perhaps no one ever would in similar circumstances'.

He was right about that. No one would dare.

15

Out of Africa

The first privately owned aircraft in East Africa was a DH51a brought to Kenya by John Carberry, aka John Evans-Freke, 10th Baron Carbery (one 'r' – he added the second on renouncing his title when he moved to Africa). It was he who had persuaded Jacques de Sibour to fly east in search of tigers to shoot. The second aircraft in Kenya was a Moth, also brought in by Carberry, or JC as he was invariably known.

Though the competition was stiff, JC is one of the least attractive sounding of the White Mischief set; this being the group of (mostly) British ex-patriates whose exuberant disdain for conventional morality at once scandalised and beguiled inter-war society. Although a number of figures prominent in the group remained in Kenya right up to and even after independence, what was, in effect, a two-decade-long party came to an end in 1941 with the murder of Lord Erroll, shot in the head in his car late one night just outside Nairobi, almost certainly by fellow Muthaiga Country Club member,

Sir Jock Delves-Broughton – the Muthaiga being the hub of the community where members 'drank champagne and pink gin for breakfast, played cards, danced through the night, and generally woke up with someone else's spouse in the morning'.[1]

Born in Ireland in 1892, JC inherited his title and Castle Freke, with its crumbling parapets and forty-odd chimneys, at the age of six. It is said that, as a child, he would wander round the castle grounds armed with an air gun and, on one occasion, persuaded a gardener to let him shoot an apple off his head. This sounds implausible, though it says something about the man that the story has currency. It is also said of him that he used to take pot shots at family portraits when, forced to dine alone, he got bored. He was educated in England at Harrow and Trinity College, Cambridge, with a stint at Leipzig University in Germany for good measure. It is possible, therefore, that he was not a complete dunce. But then again ... At fourteen, he appeared, returning from nearby Cork, driving his first motor car, beginning a love affair with speed that lasted throughout his life. He later imported a pair of Bugattis to Kenya. In his pursuit of speed, JC also became an accomplished rider of the Cresta Run, the toboggan track in St Moritz where, lying head first, competitors reach speeds of up to 90 mph with their (then unprotected) faces mere inches from the ice. He was also a successful exponent of the bobsleigh, winning several races in the 1911–12 season.

Later that same year, Carberry acquired his pilot's licence from the Aéro-Club de France and became, on some accounts, the first person to fly an aeroplane in Ireland. Two years on from that, he was a competitor in the first of the Schneider Trophy races, flying a 160 hp Morane-Saulnier. Infuriatingly for him, he was forced to retire with mechanical trouble on the third lap. The outbreak of war saw him volunteer – within a week of the declaration of hostilities – for the Royal Naval Air Service (RNAS), in which he served for a mere three months before being invalided out following a crash in Antwerp. It is said that his vehement anti-English sentiments derived from this incident. He was told to take out an aeroplane that he believed to be dangerous – as it proved. That he was strongly anti-English is not in doubt. He was an outspoken supporter of Michael Collins, the Irish revolutionary and intelligence director of the IRA during the civil war of 1922.

In 1919, Carberry's first wife, José, began divorce proceedings against him. The marriage was eventually dissolved by Act of Parliament (there was no such things as a 'quickie' divorce in those days) on the grounds of his cruelty and adultery. Carberry had, in the meantime, moved to the US where an attempt to obtain citizenship was refused on the grounds of his involvement in bootlegging. As a result, the only thing he brought back from his time in the United States was a faux American accent, which he took with him to Kenya where he settled in 1920. There, he grew coffee, produced cheap gin, imitation Jamaican rum, crème de menthe and eau de cologne. He was, in addition, a serial importer of Moths – six DH60s and one Puss Moth over the course of the last four years of the decade.

JC's ownership of the DH51 – which he christened *Miss Kenya* – did not last long. Having imported it in September 1925, he sold it in June the following year to former racehorse trainer, Tom Campbell Black, who, like himself, had been a member of the RNAS and subsequently became a partner in Wilson Airways. In 1927, JC's second wife, Maia (known universally as Bubbles), had a Cirrus II-engined DH60X Moth

registered in her name. It was this on which she learned to
fly that summer in England. In September, accompanied by
Hubert Broad, she flew it to Venice alongside de Havilland
chairman, Alan Butler, in his Moth and Bad Luck Wimpey in
hers, to attend that year's Schneider Trophy races. Wearing a
fetching mauve flying helmet, the beautiful twenty-three-year-
old Maia joined Philip Sassoon and others to watch the British
team win the first of three consecutive victories in their startling Supermarine S5 (forerunner of the Spitfire). Four months
later, the Moth was crated up and shipped to Mombasa where
it was reassembled in a garage. For reasons unknown, the
Carberrys had the name *Miss Propaganda* painted on its side,
after which the aeroplane was flown by Maia, first to Nairobi,
then to Ngong, where Carberry had cleared an airstrip next to
his substantial bungalow in the Seremai valley. Alas, the place
lived up to its name – in the Masai language, Seremai means
'place of death'. A month later, at the Aero Club of Kenya's
inaugural air show, Bubbles Carberry met her end when the
aeroplane span in from low level. Witnesses say that, before
the crash, Maia jumped from the doomed aircraft. The couple's
daughter, Juanita, who was later a teenage witness in the trial
following the murder of Lord Erroll, wrote that she was certain
her mother's death was an act of suicide to escape JC's cruelty,
though this seems massively unlikely, unless we are also to take
Maia for a murderer. She was flying a passenger at the time.

Carberry did not wait long before acquiring both another
Moth and another wife, though it is important to note that
he did build a hospital – in the shape of an aeroplane – as a
memorial to Bubbles. The Moth he sold on, almost immediately, to Canada. His new, teenaged bride, June, a South
African of humble birth, lasted longer. Indeed, she outlived

him and the marriage endured, despite her infidelities. Once, Carberry, coming back early to find her entertaining a friend in bed, gathered a bag full of rocks, ran to his plane and pelted the fleeing motor car from the air. One likely reason for their longevity as a couple was the fact that June was one of the few people who ever stood up to him. With too much lipstick, peroxide hair, 'fleur-de-tête eyes, chorus girl make-up' and 'terrifying deep bass voice', she chain-smoked and, like him, drank (mainly brandy and soda) prodigiously. Needless to say, the Muthaiga Club snobs looked down on her for being common and Juanita portrayed her as being cruel, like her father. But many remembered her warm-heartedness.

Another two Moths were registered to Carberry in 1928, but these he operated only for a short time, again selling one of them on to Canada almost immediately. He then acquired a Metal Moth in late 1929, operating this for two years. According to one friend, Carberry was 'not wicked but naughty', a man who took delight in 'pretending to be more of an ogre than he really was'. Given, though, his open support for Hitler – to whom, in 1940, he publicly proposed a toast (for which he was reported to the police, though they chose to overlook the incident) – it is clear that there was more to his bad reputation than some liked to admit. He would also, on occasion, boast of having committed two murders and was known for his utter disdain of native Kenyans. It is not the least surprising to learn that, after the war, he spent a year in prison for flouting the currency regulations then in place. It was to have been three years with hard labour, but the sentence was reduced on appeal. In another world, he would have spent the rest of his life there.

If John Carberry was a key, if dubious, player in the history of aviation in Kenya, there were several other Moth owners and operators who had a lasting impact on that history. Florence (Florrie) Wilson, famous for her skill as a billiards and snooker player – she had her colonial bungalow home built round a full-sized table – was one of them. When her husband died, Carberry offered to fly her back to England in one of his larger aircraft (a Fokker Universal). In the event, he was unable to do so and instead the pilot was Tom Campbell Black (future co-pilot of the de Havilland Comet that won the 1934 MacRobertson Trophy Air Race). So delighted was Florrie at the speed and ease of her flight that, on return to Kenya, she invested £50,000 in the eponymous Wilson Airways, which, beginning with a single DH60 Moth nicknamed *Knight of the Mist*, quickly grew to more than a dozen aeroplanes.

By 1930, more than forty Moths were operating across the African continent. The one best known to posterity is the Gipsy-engined DH60G owned by heartbreaker and big-game hunter, the Hon. Captain Denys Finch Hatton. The Oscar-winning film, *Out of Africa* starring Robert Redford and Meryl Streep, based on Karen von Blixen's memoir of her love affair with him and with Africa, features some of the most romantic flying sequences ever shot. Acquired by Finch Hatton in late 1930, the Moth served partly as a means of personal transport but, more seriously, as a means of scouting for game.

Denys Finch Hatton was the second son of the Earl of Winchelsea, while his paternal grandmother was a daughter of the 2nd Earl of Mansfield, through whom she was related both to Jane Austen and to Dido Belle, a freed Jamaican slave brought up as an English gentlewoman by the childless 1st Earl. His mother was the only child of the much cuck-olded Admiral of the Fleet, Sir John Codrington – himself a descendant of one of Nelson's captains at Trafalgar and also a member of one of Britain's most prominent slave-owning families. During the seventeenth century, they had acquired two important plantations in Barbados which, in the early eighteenth, they bequeathed, not without irony, to the Society for the Propagation of the Gospel in Foreign Parts. A condition of the bequest was that the income provide for the education of the labourers who worked on the plantations and who were branded with the word 'Society' on their chests. Although by Denys' time slavery had long been abolished, his mother's family retained a connection with Codrington College, which now supported the training of West Indian clergy.

Having first come to Africa in 1910, Denys F. H. spent the war years firstly serving in Cole's Scouts, an irregular unit comprising British and Somali troops under the command of his friend Berkely Cole, and then as an aide-de-camp to General Hoskins who commanded the 1st East African Division. In 1917, he was accepted for flying training with a view to transferring to the RNAS. He had wanted to learn to fly ever since attending the first British air races at Dunstall Park racecourse in Wolverhampton just before leaving for Africa in 1910. Bad weather for the duration of the meeting had meant limited and, when attempted, generally unsuccessful flying, and the crowds were treated to a number of spectacular crashes, fortunately none of them fatal. It was enough, however, to inspire in Finch Hatton a lifelong passion for aviation. But although he qualified successfully at Cairo in 1917, the young nobleman did not in the end take up a position with the air services and it was not until 1929, following the Prince of Wales' first visit to Kenya, that he again took up flying seriously.

Another major figure in the history of Captain de Havilland's

Moth in Kenya is Beryl Markham. Her claims to fame rest on three things. Firstly, on her remarkable achievement in being the first woman to fly solo from England across the Atlantic to America; secondly, on her autobiography *West with the Night* – praised by Ernest Hemingway for being 'written well, and so marvellously well, that I was simply ashamed of myself as a writer'; thirdly, on the fact that she had simultaneous affairs with Edward, Prince of Wales and his brother, Harry, Duke of Gloucester. There is much more that could be said about her – among them the fact that she did not actually write the book. Her (third) husband did. For now, suffice it to say that, without her contribution, both the history of Kenya as a British colony and the culture it produced would have been dramatically poorer.

Born in Rutland in 1902, Beryl (née Clutterbuck) moved with her family to Kenya at the age of two. There, she was abandoned by her mother before she had reached her fourth birthday and left in the care of her racehorse-training father, an ex-cavalry officer. He immediately subcontracted responsibility for her to his African servants. By the time he took a mistress some months later, Beryl had made herself a home among the native Kipsigis people, who tied a cowrie shell round her wrist to ward off evil spirits and accepted her frequent presence among them such that she soon spoke Swahili better than she spoke English. The young Beryl absorbed their culture, too. Indifference to fear and endurance of physical pain were, jointly, the most highly prized Kipsigis virtues, while loss of face was the thing most abhorred. Each of these traits characterised Beryl's existence to its lonely, humiliated end in penury, alcoholism and dementia.

Because she was so young at the time of her mother's

absconding, Beryl assumed that the woman her father took in subsequently was her mother, only discovering the truth when she was eight. The treachery of her parents marked her for life – as, it must be said, did the time she spent with her African friends. People came to say of her that she was a nymphomaniac. It would be fairer to say that her upbringing hardly equipped her to appreciate the value of monogamy.

When Beryl married for the first time, shortly before her seventeenth birthday, it was to a man more than twice her age. Jock Purves had fallen for her when she was just thirteen and, in a tacit agreement with her father, had supported her since then until she was of marriageable age. Unsurprisingly, the bargain was a bad one for all concerned. Within six months, the marriage was over and Purves hit the bottle. They did not divorce immediately and, by the time they did, the door into which her husband was said to bang a brass nail for each of her indiscretions was decorated with a swirling pattern.[2] That may have been an exaggeration, but her appetite for sex was almost as great as her longing for a man whom she could respect. The closest she ever came to such a person was in her relationship with Denys Finch Hatton, with whom she fell in love as a little girl at the races. She first slept with him when she was nineteen and, by that time – astonishing in today's world – a successful trainer of racehorses. Yet she wanted more from him than just the delight of sexual intimacy and she spent the next eight years doggedly pursuing him – even to the extent of building a dishonest friendship with his then lover, the – as yet unpublished – writer Karen von Blixen. She got there in the end, thanks to Captain de Havilland's Moth.

That it took so long is fortunate from a literary perspective. Had Beryl carried him off immediately, we would not have von Blixen's memoir *Out of Africa*, one of the most sublime evocations to have come from the colonial period. The book owes much of its poignancy to the fact that, by the time Finch Hatton acquired his custard-and-cream coloured Moth (the aircraft's markings in the film are historically inaccurate), von Blixen had, to all intents and purposes, lost him. Unfortunately for herself, she was the homely type who, although she disdained convention, craved domesticity. Beryl Markham had just the opposite temperament.

Baroness Karen von Blixen, daughter of a wealthy Danish family and later also known for *Babette's Feast* and her *Seven Gothic Tales* (both written under the pseudonym Isak Dinesen), had been attracted to Africa principally by its untamed beauty. She was both an intellectual and an aesthete. Having married a cousin, Baron Bror von Blixen, in 1912, she had moved to Kenya with him at the beginning of the First World War. There, the couple had established a – largely unsuccessful – coffee farm. Africa gave Tania Blixen (as she was invariably known) a sense of complete abandonment to nature: 'Here at long last one was in a position not to give a damn for all conventions, here was a new kind of freedom which until then one had only found in dreams.'3 Unfortunately, her husband took this freedom from convention as just the excuse he needed for indulging in a series of affairs, leading to the couple's eventual divorce in 1925, though any disappointment she may have felt about this gave way to her passion for the handsome lothario, Finch Hatton, with whom she lived, on and off, for the next eight years.

He based himself in her home, kept his books and gramophone records there, and came and went as he pleased. Karen, meanwhile, managed the farm while he pursued his career as big-game hunter and guide to wealthy tourists. It was an arrangement that suited them both at first. Sharing not only a love of the Ngong Valley where they lived but also similar interests in art and literature, they were well matched. The problem arose only because, as she approached middle age (she was two years older than Finch Hatton and was almost forty when they began their relationship), her emotional needs grew too much for him.

Her opponent, meanwhile, was closing in on her target. In the interval between first sleeping with him and getting him to move in with her almost a decade later, Beryl Markham had become universally acknowledged both as a peerless horse-woman and as having a genius for identifying and training winners. Her leading patron was Lord Delamere, one of the founding members of the colony. Notwithstanding – perhaps to some extent because of – her infatuation with Finch Hatton, in 1927 she married the vastly wealthy Mansfield Markham, second son of the 1st Baronet Markham, whose family owned a string of collieries in the north of England. They honeymooned in London and Paris, where her striking looks were finally matched by the trappings even her enemies would concede they deserved. Extravagant jewellery and a trousseau of dresses by Lanvin, Chanel and Worth brought out the soignée beauty for which she became famous. It was never likely to last but the marriage brought her firmly into Finch Hatton's world. When, late the following year, he was chosen to lead the Prince of Wales on safari, she knew exactly what she must do.

She began with the low hanging fruit. The palace had decided that the prince should be accompanied for the first part of his visit to the colony by his younger brother, Harry, Duke of Gloucester. It was he with whom Beryl began a protracted affair and through whom she came to have a more intermittent affair with the future king. It is not clear that Edward and Beryl ever spent the whole night together during the safari itself, but it is indisputable that, if she did not bed him as such, she certainly – if the verbs exist – motor-vehicled, railway-carriaged and shrubbed the equally avid Prince of Wales. On one occasion, he climbed out of his bedroom window at Government House in order to meet her for a tryst. Challenged by a guard who did not recognise him, he had considerable difficulty persuading the man of his identity.[4] Their relationship was given a fillip when Beryl provided a winner for him to ride at the Eldoret races – albeit that the race itself was fixed, with the others all dropping their hands to let him through.

Quite apart from her tremendous appetite for sex, it is clear that Beryl's royal relationships were conducted with more than half an eye to impressing Finch Hatton. She was good enough for royalty so he'd better sit up. But before she could pursue him further, Beryl had to deal with the small matter of the child with which she was already five months pregnant by the time of the royals' arrival (it did not show at first). Her solution was to travel to London where, following the birth – and with Mansfield's agreement – she would hand her son over to his paternal grandparents.

On her arrival in Southampton at the end of 1928, she was met on the wharf by the Duke of Gloucester, in fulfilment of his promise to do so. Setting her up in the Grosvenor Hotel, he was in constant attendance on her right up until little Gervaise appeared in February 1929. The gossips gleefully counted on their fingers to see whether he could have been the father. Alas for them, it was impossible. It might not have been Mansfield's, but it certainly wasn't Gloucester's. In any case, the unfortunate child was immediately taken into custody by its grandmother. Recovering her health quickly, Beryl again entertained openly with the duke from her suite in the Grosvenor Hotel while her husband plotted divorce. When Mansfield's solicitor informed the palace of his intention to cite the duke as co-respondent, Harry, whose mother, Queen Mary, was incensed by his behaviour, agreed immediately to settle £15,000 on his mistress. This was to be held in trust for her lifetime and pay her a monthly income. The arrangement was that Harry would take financial responsibility for Beryl – in addition to providing for her while she was in London – just so long as Mansfield dropped his case and Beryl left England. Unfortunately for Beryl, the money was invested in bonds and gilts, rather than the stock market, such that the income – which was paid faithfully to the end of her life in 1986, long after the duke had died – never exceeded £750 a year.

She duly left the country towards the end of 1929, but not before Denys F. H. put in a sudden and unexpected appearance. He had come to England partly to renew his pilot's licence and partly to escape Tania von Blixen, whose possessiveness was, by this time, proving too much for him. Having recently flown in one of the Kenya Aero Club Moths (donated by Lord Wakefield), Denys had immediately understood the utility of light aircraft in the bush, both for speedy communications and for spotting and tracking game, and he was set on acquiring his own aircraft. This was the very moment when de Havilland went public with the news that the Prince of Wales had bought a Moth. It was at this moment too that Beryl understood that she should learn to fly. Tania was a homebody and would never be able to compete with her if she did. At once, she booked her first flying lessons in one of the London Aero Club's Moths.

They stopped only when she learned that the Prince of Wales, who'd had to cut short his first safari on account of a health scare involving the king, was determined to go back to Kenya to complete it, again appointing Finch Hatton as leader. She had better be on hand.

By the time Edward P. (as his staff referred to him) had resumed his safari in February 1930, he had transferred his affections – if only temporarily – to Beryl's friend, Lady Enid Furness (setting aside the tumbles he took with one or two others). But that was of no concern to Beryl. Finch Hatton continued to be the object of her desires (setting aside the tumbles she also took with one or two others; one partner at that time described an encounter with her as a 'most startling and erotic' experience). Denys, too weak simply to make a clean break with Tania, was procrastinating. He wanted it to be her decision to part, not his, and their relationship survived long enough for him to go back to England and return, in the autumn of 1930, with the Moth about which von Blixen was to write so movingly.

Where Denys went, Beryl followed unerringly. Leaving her horses in the care of her father, she sailed for England and brazenly picked up with Harry as if Queen Mary had no valid opinion in the matter. This time she spent more than six months in London (without seeing her son even once, it must be said). Denys, meanwhile, stayed with, among others, Philip Sassoon at Trent Park while he awaited delivery of the Metal Moth he had ordered. Unfortunately, a crash on returning from a trip to Ireland in August necessitated buying a replacement. Although the original was repairable, Denys wanted to get back to Kenya as soon as possible, so the wreck was sold to Nigel Cohen, an undergraduate at King's College, Cambridge. Unfortunately,

Cohen was not a natural pilot, taking more than twenty hours to go solo. When, eventually, he got his ticket the following year, he took up aerobatics, nonetheless. Although, when fitted with the lighter Genet engine and flown by skilled RAF pilots, the Moth could sometimes be persuaded to execute an outside loop – often referred to as a bunt – in the hands of a novice, this was an extremely risky manoeuvre. It seems that Cohen was attempting just such a stunt when his starboard wing failed and he was killed in the ensuing crash.

Finch Hatton's Gipsy-powered DH60 was delivered in September 1930 and immediately he sailed with it to Mombasa. Beryl, meanwhile, had spent the summer mostly in the company of the Duke of Gloucester. She did, however, remain on intimate terms with the Prince of Wales, whom she would entertain from time to time at the Royal Aero Club in Piccadilly. On at least one occasion, the prince bought a whole cartload of white flowers for her from the man whose Shetland pony stood outside its entrance. At the London Aero Club's summer party, he consorted openly with her. But really, though she probably would not have admitted it even to herself, this was all for Denys and, as soon as he left, Beryl packed her bags and followed.

Describing the miracle of flight, von Blixen wrote of how 'language is short of words for the experience', and how, 'when you are sitting in front of your pilot, with nothing but space before you, you feel that he's carrying you upon the outstretched palms of his hands, as the djinn carried Prince Ali through the air and the wings that bear you onward, are his'. She describes how, in *ndzige* (the locust), Denys' nickname for the Moth, they would 'visit the Eagles' and watch them 'careening and throwing themselves onto one wing and then to the other'. 'I believe,' she wrote, 'that that sharp-sighted bird played with us. Once, when we were running side-by-side, Denys stopped his engine in midair, and as he did so I heard the eagle screech.' She also says that she and Denys flew together almost every day. She must have meant every day they were together. By this time, this was not very often. He likely flew with Beryl just as frequently – her tactics having succeeded brilliantly. Now in the last months of his life, Denys moved into Beryl's cottage in the grounds of the Muthaiga Club (whose members dubbed it 'the way of all flesh') and they became lovers in the true sense of the word. She admired him for his combination of adventurousness and erudition. He felt a freedom in her company that the neurotic Tania could not give. And while he could speak about poetry with Tania as an equal, he clearly enjoyed introducing Beryl to the life of the mind. Years afterwards, she spoke of how he 'half taught [her] how to live'.[5]

If Finch Hatton had finally fallen in love with Beryl, he was by this time also thoroughly smitten with the Moth, announcing that next time he went to England, he would fly it there. In the meantime, he used it as often as he could. By the spring of 1931, the big-game hunter had largely lost interest in shooting and was preparing a photographic safari which needed to be planned and reconnoitred. When he announced his plan to fly upcountry, von Blixen asked to go with him. At first, he agreed, but then he changed his mind. It would be a rough trip involving nights out in the bush. This conversation with Karen took place two days before he actually set off and provides the poignant moment when, in the film, Robert Redford bids farewell to Meryl Streep and drives off – only to come back with a book of poems he had forgotten to give her. He stands with one foot on the running-board reading from it:

I saw grey geese flying over the flatlands,
Grey geese vibrant in the high air
Unswerving, from horizon to horizon ...

The next day, Denys invited Beryl Markham to go with him.
The rotter! She, however, was persuaded – so she later said –
not to go by both her maid and by a mutual friend, who seemed
to have had intuitions that evil was abroad. As a result, Finch
Hatton took one of his Kenyan servants instead.

Flying direct to Mombasa, as Finch Hatton landed, the
propeller picked up a piece of coral, something that happens
quite easily when moving over loose ground. The propeller
tends to suck up any chippings lying on the surface, hence the
need always to check your blades whenever you suspect this
may have happened – in addition to checking them before
every flight. It does not take much damage to cause severe
vibration. In the event that a blade fails, it is inevitable that
the ensuing gyroscopic forces will wrench the engine from its
mount, causing a catastrophic rearward shift in the centre of
gravity that renders the aircraft uncontrollable.

In this instance, we know that Finch Hatton thought the
damage severe enough to order a replacement propeller from
Tom Campbell Black at the flying club. What is not clear is
whether it was actually delivered before the aeroplane's fatal
accident. According to one account, there was a large crack in
one of the blades on the day of the crash. This suggests that
the replacement propeller may not have been fitted and that
Denys had decided that he could continue with the damaged
one for the time being.

The night before the accident, Finch Hatton stayed with
some friends to whose house he had recently taken the Prince

of Wales. When Uncle Denys offered a joyride to his hostess the following morning, the younger of her two daughters threw a tantrum, begging her not to go. So instead, Finch Hatton's servant got in and they set off. The Moth did a couple of circuits of the airstrip and then turned, climbing, in the direction of Nairobi. Some moments later, the engine was heard to falter and the horrified onlookers watched as, about a mile distant, the plane fell from the sky. A plume of black smoke marked the place of impact and, by the time the first people could reach it, the blaze was so fierce that they could do nothing but look on in torment and dismay.

16

The Record-Breakers: Stunting All Over the World

It is but human nature that, as soon as a record has been set, someone will want to break it. Francis Chichester and Amy Johnson both had the idea of beating Bert Hinkler's London to Australia record of fifteen and a half days, set in May 1928. Both failed. The first person to do so in a similar aircraft was C. W. A. Scott, in a DH60 Moth. He did so by meticulous planning and preparation – the first of the professional record-breakers.

Like Amy Johnson, Scott's family was well-to-do, but without high connections. His father, an outstanding classical musician who contributed much to the revival of interest in plainchant and early modern music, was the founder and conductor of the London Philharmonic Choir, but the family did not move in the same circles as many of the early Mothists. And while Scott did spend two years at Westminster School, he did not take to it. Despite having something of an artistic temperament – he showed promise both as a musician and as a poet – he gave up his studies for a job in the sugar industry in what was then British Guyana. There he subsisted 'in an atmosphere of toil and oppression, home-sickness and malaria' for a year before his parents bought him out of his contract and gave him the fare home. On arrival back in England, he took a job as a clerk with a firm of yacht outfitters but soon grew bored. With almost as little thought as he had given to his West Indian sugar escapade, he enlisted in the RAF in 1922.

Tall and well built, Scott became RAF boxing champion during his time as a cadet at Duxford. Later, when he had taken a flying job in the Australian outback, he would some-times play classical piano in the bar of an evening. It is said that if pushed too far by locals teasing him for his Pommie accent and graces, he could knock a man down without spilling the drink in his other hand.

During his training, Scott made a name for himself as a master of the Sopwith Snipe, regarded by many as a death-trap. This was on account of the powerful gyroscopic forces produced by its nine-cylinder Bentley rotary engine. The point being that a rotary engine, unlike a radial – or, for that matter, any other configuration – turns around a stationary crankshaft, taking the propeller with it. This confers a strong tendency for aeroplanes fitted with this type of unit to rotate in sympathy with the engine, necessitating firm pressure on the rudder to keep an even keel. Another feature of rotaries was that they could only be run at full power. The pilot, instead of throttling back as the aeroplane came in to land, had to cut the engine by switching off the ignition and, in case of needing to go around, hope to be able to restart it in the air.

Scott was quickly recognised as an outstanding pilot.

Unfortunately, this went to his head. The very day after obtaining his wings, he flew an outrageous low-level aerobatic sequence that ended with him stalling his aircraft at 30 feet, far too low to recover, and he wrote it off. In spite of this faux pas, he went on to be selected to perform as a member of the RAF aerobatic team at Wembley Stadium during the Great Empire Exhibition of 1924. Remarkably, the routine was flown at night, the aircraft painted black but with small white lights picking out the underside of the wings and fuselage. Approaching in the dark, at a given signal, the three aircraft in the flight would switch on their lights and fly in formation round the stadium. At another signal, these would be switched off and they would mock-attack a target actually within the stadium, their machine guns stuttering with blanks. Each aircraft was also fitted with a rack of half a dozen pyrotechnics which, once ignited on a scratch pad, the pilots would release after a count of three so that they burst just under the tail, imitating ack-ack fire. Meanwhile, on the ground, thunder flashes were set off to simulate the bombs they were dropping. This mock battle concluded, they would switch their lights back on and, in turn, perform a solo aerobatics sequence. Flying six days a week for six months, these demonstrations were, unsurprisingly, extremely popular. Even when, on one occasion, one of the aircraft suffered an engine failure and made a forced landing just before bursting into flames – happily without injury to the pilot – there was no suggestion that anyone's health or safety was in danger.

Another series of shows the following year was less successful, in that, during a single week, there were five separate incidents. One occurred when a pyrotechnic went off in a pilot's hand causing serious burns; another when a newly joined team member was killed when he rolled too close to the ground. Then on the Thursday, the Friday and the Saturday, successive aircraft suffered engine failure. Needless to say, the show went on in spite of these mishaps. Even the pilot with the injured hand continued with his performance, though, by the time he got back to base, he was in such a state that, no sooner had he switched off his ignition than he passed out.

Scott's RAF career was never destined to be a glorious one. He was too much of an individualist and too full of himself to remain out of trouble for long. He was frequently reprimanded for low flying and, having tactlessly made several treetop-level passes over his own station, was eventually put under arrest and court-martialled. Though guilty without defence, he was acquitted on a technicality. But it was not long before he was on another charge, again for low-level aerobatics, and on this occasion he was sentenced to a month of square-bashing back at the RAF depot. Although his sentence was subsequently reduced to ten days, Scott wisely decided at this point to jump, rather than wait to be pushed, and resigned his commission. It was not, he said afterwards, that he had any desire to flout rules or defy authority but simply because, put at the controls of an aeroplane, he could not resist the temptation to wring it out to the maximum extent possible – as close to the ground as possible.

Back on civvy street, the year being that of the General Strike, Scott had few employment prospects. On sheltering from the rain in Australia House on the Strand, he was offered an introduction to the Australian liaison officer in the Air Ministry and, before he quite knew it, found himself bound for the Antipodes with a steerage class ticket and sharing a bath with fifty people. But on fetching up in Melbourne, he found work flying mail for Qantas in one of their DH50s.

It was two years after Scott arrived in Australia that there occurred an event which electrified the country's then six million strong population. In his tiny aeroplane, there appeared among them one of their countrymen, having flown all the way from England 'just to see his people'. This was Bert Hinkler in his Avian. The effect, once the incredulity had worn off, was much the same as that of Lindbergh's appearance in Paris nine months previously. It seemed a miracle. And yet it was something else besides. It showed people that the marvels of modernity were for all the Empire, not just for the folks back in the 'Old Country'. It was therefore with utter dismay that they heard the news that Hinkler had disappeared after heading across the barren wastes of the Northern Territories. At once, Scott went in search of him – only to find that the great adventurer, having got lost, had landed safely at his intended destination the following day.

Two years later, it was Scott who escorted Amy Johnson from Darwin across the Northern Territories and Queensland to Brisbane on the east coast. He was among the crowd that gathered round the oil-smeared, sunburned young woman in her shorts and open-necked shirt in her triumph and saw, as the world saw, 'there was no more modest person in the world than Amy Johnson at that moment'.[1] It was also Scott who attended to *Jason* while she rested. 'Never,' he wrote, 'had I seen an engine in such appalling condition.' Two pistons were completely lacking compression; the spark plugs were screwed in so tight that it took two strong men to remove them; the vent plug in the sump was likewise removed only by the application of extreme force, while the propeller bolts had started to work their way loose.

Unfortunately, the DH50 that Scott flew was considerably

faster than *Jason* and, at one point on the journey down to Brisbane – which they made in several easy stages – he lost her. According to him, one minute she was there just behind him, the next minute not. Reading between the lines, however, one is tempted to suppose that Scott was already caught up in the dream of himself making an epic flight.

To his consternation, before he could put his plan into action, another Australian hero, Charles Kingsford Smith, arrived in Australia from England flying his Fokker trimotor, *Southern Cross*, having broken Hinkler's record by a full six days. If he was to break this record, his planning needed to be supremely careful. Scott set about his business by finding a customer for a Moth who would buy it off him if he would fly it out from London. He then placed an order and had the aeroplane fitted with maximum fuel capacity. With tanks both in the front cockpit and in the locker behind the pilot's seat, this gave 103 gallons in all – sufficient for over twenty hours aloft, or around 1,600 miles in still air. It would be no good beating Kingsford Smith by just a few hours so he needed to be able to cut his refuelling stops to the minimum.

Scott's plan was to fly direct from Croydon to Belgrade on day one and to Aleppo in Syria on day two. Leaving on Wednesday 1 April 1931, he made the first leg in good order but, in bad weather, landed 35 miles short on day two. Successfully refuelling, he nonetheless reached Baghdad on day three. Flying by night, he hoped to make it from there all the way to Karachi on the Saturday but was forced down 300 miles short. Unable to find the airfield at Gwadar, he managed to put down safely in the desert nearby where friendly locals brought water and a goat which they milked for him. As soon as daylight broke, he flew into Gwadar and on to Jodhpur in Rajasthan that evening. This put him 400 miles ahead of Kingsford Smith – roughly six hours – at the halfway point. The next day, despite having to stop to make a running repair on his engine cowling, he covered the thousand miles to Calcutta and crawled into bed at 10 p.m. But by 1.30 a.m. on the Tuesday morning, he was back aboard the Moth. Flying through bad weather over the same hills that had troubled Amy Johnson so much, he refuelled in Rangoon before pressing on to reach Victoria Point by nightfall, having covered 1,300 miles in the day. This put him 570 miles ahead of Kingsford Smith. Leaving at daybreak, he reached Singapore for 2 p.m. There, he refuelled and replenished his oil before pressing on to Sumatra where bad weather forced him down, reducing his lead to 280 miles. Staggering out of bed after a few restless hours, he arrived back at the airport dismayed to find the place enveloped in a thick mist, which delayed his take-off by several hours. In the event, he succeeded in covering more than a thousand miles that day to arrive, in pitch dark, at Bima on the southern tip of Indonesia. There, completely unable to identify the airfield, he flew in circles until, by good fortune, someone heard him and switched on their car headlights to reveal the runway – which lay under six inches of water – a short distance away.

It was now a week and a day since Scott had left England and he was all of 450 miles ahead of Kingsford Smith. The Gipsy had performed faultlessly up to this point and, provided he could get airborne in spite of the waterlogging – and provided that it kept going over the next thousand miles (600 miles of which would be over water) – he was in with a good chance. Unfortunately, he could find no English speaker at that time of night and had only the car's lights by which to service his engine. He therefore did no more than refuel, replenish the oil and clean the oil filter, leaving the rest to luck.

Back with his aeroplane at daybreak, it took four attempts to get airborne. Succeeding at last, Scott flew along the coast initially, when, to his sudden alarm, the engine cut out not once, but, after a short interval, a second time. Fortunately, he was at 3,000 feet on each occasion and the motor picked up before he needed to find somewhere to land. The cause: almost certainly water contamination. Faced with the dilemma of landing to drain any more of it out the system or chancing his arm, it was inevitable that he should chance his arm. Admitting afterwards to being utterly terrified when he set out across the Timor Sea for the longest eight hours of his life, he eventually arrived in Darwin having broken Kingsford Smith's record by just under nineteen hours. It was an astonishing feat of endurance.

Even if *Flight* magazine took only grudging notice of Scott's achievement, the public at large had yet to tire of record-breaking aviators. People turned out in their thousands to greet him wherever he landed and there were brass bands and lunches with lord mayors, speeches, dinners, dances and theatre appearances for weeks afterwards. It was at one of these that Scott was propositioned by an agent of Lord Wakefield. If he was given the aeroplane to do it in, would he turn round and have a crack at the record for the return journey?

Needless to say, he would. What he did not realise at the time was that Lord Wakefield, having noted the extraordinary enthusiasm of the public for the long-distance flights of 'the lone airman', saw an opportunity to create still further interest – and advertising – by organising an unofficial race. Having recently agreed to sponsor another pilot in an attempt on the

Australia–England record, a young Scotsman by the name of Jim Mollison, later to become husband of Amy Johnson, the stage was set for a duel to be fought over its more than ten-thousand-mile course. And should one not complete it, there was a decent chance the other would. Either way, Wakefield Oil would be the winner.

Unfortunately for his lordship – and for Mollison – the all-black Gipsy Moth in which the Scotsman was to make his attempt came to grief on take-off from Darwin. Grossly overloaded with fuel, it failed to clear the telegraph wires at the end of the runway and was completely written off. Fortunately, it did not burn. Scott – who had warned Mollison that, at 500 yards, the runway at Darwin would be too short and he would be better off starting from Wyndham, as he himself proposed to do – now had the field to himself. As usual, there were the customary near-calamities and, again, most of the way it was touch and go as to whether he would break the record. A 90 mph tailwind over the Middle East was a great help but this was more or less undone by contrary winds as soon as he reached Europe. When he reached Marseilles, he ran out of maps and, like Aspy Engineer before him, was forced to dead-reckon the last 600 miles. Thunderstorms around Paris forced him down, completely drenched and hardly able to see, almost to ground level. Finally, with the record in the bag and at 10 feet over the Channel, he was 'singing and shouting and offering prayers of thankfulness'.

There followed a profitable two-week aerial tour of the country. In addition, Lord Wakefield made a gift of the Moth to Scott and he was awarded the Air Force Cross in the king's birthday honours. Alas, he lost his record just a month later and, within a few more weeks, the England–Australia record had gone, too. The first of these went to Jim Mollison in his rebuilt Moth who, when he finally got going, broke Scott's run by a scarcely credible two days. Mollison himself has some claim to being the greatest of Britain's long-distance flyers, as well as the least appealing. He cannot compare to Chichester in terms of genius but, in terms of sheer determination while under immense pressure – fuelled in Mollison's case by brandy and greed – his commitment was unmatched, as was his vanity. His autobiography, *A Playboy in the Air*, has not aged well. Written in faux Cary Grant style, and with self-regarding references to the 'bevvies of beauties' with whom he had relationships, it makes for uneasy reading. It seems certain that his relationship with Amy Johnson was cynical from the get-go and he was unfaithful to her within days of their marriage. Yet, because of it, and because of his exploits in the air, he was, for a short time, the most famous man in Britain.

Scott's other record, from England to Australia, was beaten by all of 102 minutes by Arthur Butler (no relation of Alan) flying a Comper Swift. This, a diminutive single-seater, was more than 30 per cent faster than the Gipsy Moth, though, because of its small size, it had a much shorter range, necessitating more frequent stops.

The only thing for Scott to do was to break back – which, in the same DH60 Moth, he duly did.

Today, it is hard to understand the fervour these long-distance pilots inspired. Many at the time, most notably the editor of *Flight* magazine, arguably the world's most influential aviation journal of the day, questioned the worth of their exploits. But to do so would be to overlook the extraordinary levels of endurance shown by the pilots. It wasn't merely the uncertainties they faced in a world where radio communications were in their infancy and in which meteorology was only just beginning to be developed into a reliable science. The physical demands imposed by the aircraft themselves were extreme. It is one thing to fly an open-cockpit aircraft for an hour or two in clement weather. It is something dramatically different to do so for up to eighteen hours, variously through fog, snow, tropical rain and desert heat, for nine or ten days without let up – Scott wrote how, on arrival in England, he couldn't even hear people shouting at him. Nor should we overlook the fact that the 1930s was a decade made depressing by the continuing worldwide slump. If the professional classes had started to do well, millions lived in a permanent state of enervation, afraid of losing their jobs, often underfed, frequently inadequately clothed and many badly housed. The exploits of the record-breakers were an avenue down which the aspirant masses might escape in their imagination. The aviator was still a prodigy and, like the poet, seemed someone set apart, someone born to a higher destiny, privy to the deepest workings of the natural world; someone who had tasted eternity up beyond the clouds.

If this seems hard to relate to now, compare the 20,000 air passengers carried in a whole year by Imperial Airways at the end of 1929 with the 100,000 daily arrivals at Heathrow less than a century later. Consider, too, that, at the time, there was no television and only the most rudimentary radio service such that, apart from the cinema, almost all entertainment was live entertainment. An afternoon out to greet a famous aviator was an afternoon well spent.

It is with this in mind that we should consider the exploits of Jean Batten, another of the great Mothists of the 1930s. The youngest of three siblings, she grew up in New Zealand among the shadows of her parents' marital breakdown. Her family was of the aspirant middle class – Jean's father was a dentist, her grandfather an NCO in the British army (though Jean was to give him a commission in her autobiography), while her mother, Ellen – 'a really quite frightening figure' according to one acquaintance, 'almost certainly a lesbian' according to another – was an energetic but domineering, possessive and thwarted would-be actress, who would succeed through her daughter if she couldn't do it on her own. When her two elder brothers both emigrated, the young Jean was brought up alone by her mother, firm in the knowledge that she would have to compete with men if she wanted to get on in the world – and that this was something that could be achieved, at least in part, by exploiting the good looks with which she had been blessed. Yet, lest Jean suppose that male attention could be anything more than mere lust, Ellen took her teenaged daughter to see the then notorious film *Damaged Goods*, about a young couple who contract syphilis through having multiple affairs. Men were to be exploited, not succumbed to.

As Jean wrote in her memoirs, the film made a lasting impression on her. So, too, did the succession of one-roomed flats in which mother and daughter lived. But while Ellen was determined that Jean should make a name for herself in the world of theatre and dance, a meeting with Charles Kingsford Smith when she was nineteen years old changed her career path entirely – though it was not the meeting as such, but rather the mocking laughter that greeted her when she announced that she, too, would learn to fly and break records. When she repeated her intention to her father, he was appalled. She was a talented pianist and dancer. Flying was dangerous and expensive. She should stick to what she was doing.

On reporting this back to her mother, the iron in Ellen's soul at last found its outlet. She told her daughter that, together, they would find a way. Her first move was to announce to her ex-husband that Jean had won a place at the Royal College of Music. This was a lie but it convinced him to pay their fare and to give Ellen a small weekly allowance to enable her to maintain the two of them in London. For her part, Ellen sold the family piano and scraped together just enough money to finance some flying lessons for Jean at the London Aero Club. Acutely aware of her daughter's good looks, Ellen made certain that she moved in a milieu where, when the time came, they could best be exploited. As one fellow member recalled, the twenty-year-old Jean was 'an absolute knock-out' who excited the interest of many in the club. What increased her appeal was her attitude to flying, which was entirely businesslike. She did not flirt or show off. Instead, she was quiet and determined.

Jean was later to claim that she took to flying 'like a penguin to water' though, if that were the case, penguins are lousy swimmers. It took her more than twenty hours to go solo. But there were to be no celebrations when she finally did. Her father, having discovered that he had been duped, stopped the allowance. Forced back to New Zealand in the summer of 1931, Jean was surprised when her father – now remarried – agreed to help her with flying lessons in Auckland. It is clear that his animus was against Ellen, not his daughter. While this was welcome, she was by this time firmly set on the idea of being the first woman to fly from England to New Zealand. She was therefore determined to return to England where, she was sure, she would be able to find a sponsor. It was at this moment that her elder brother, John, stepped in. A successful actor, first in America, now in London, the strikingly handsome John Batten starred in some of Britain's first talkies and was just now riding the crest of a wave of popularity. Thanks to him, Jean was able to return and, living in his flat, to resume her flying. Even more promisingly, on board the ship that took her there, she met a young RAF officer, also a New Zealander, by the name of Fred Truman, who fell hopelessly in love with her. On arrival, they flew together as often as he could get away from his duties and he did much to help her improve her skills. For her part, Jean kept her distance. But she gave him just enough hope that, when subsequently he was stationed abroad, she would be there for him when he came back and they would settle down together in New Zealand.

In the meantime, Ellen had managed to pull together the money to come back to England where, in circumstances that are unclear, she had a furious row with her son, as a result of which he never spoke again either to her or to Jean, though they all lived long. Mother and daughter then shared a one-bedroom flat near Heston airport. This was financed by the unfortunate Fred who, expecting Jean to return home to New Zealand as soon as she had qualified for her licence, made over his entire gratuity of £500 to her when he left the RAF and returned to civilian life.

The 'Dear John' letter came shortly after he reached Auckland. Jean, meanwhile, began to cast around for another patron. This she found in Victor Dorée, son of a wealthy linen manufacturer and fellow club member. Several times she went to stay with him at his family house in Hampshire, and when, doubtless with feigned artlessness, she wondered who she might approach to help her buy an aeroplane in which she might make her long-distance flight, Victor immediately announced that he would. This enabled her to buy G-AALG, the Prince of Wales' aeroplane which was being sold on his behalf. He had recently acquired a Puss Moth. The only condition of sale was that Jean vary the colour scheme, which she did by changing the white coach line that ran the length of its fuselage to pale blue.

It was thus, on 8 April 1933, that Jean Batten set off in the direction of the history books. Remarkably, there were at least four other amateur pilots simultaneously chasing records during that week. One of them, Captain Leonida Robbiano – in a Breda, a stylish Italian monoplane, rather than a Moth, but also powered by a Gipsy engine – was only a day ahead of her, having also departed from British soil. He was intent on breaking Scott's record to Australia, as was Bill Lancaster, flying an Avian. Elly Beinhorn, a German aviatrix, was on her way to crashing in the desert, surviving only thanks to the generosity of some Tuareg tribesmen who took her to Timbuctoo, while Lores Bonney, a cousin of Bert Hinkler – who had himself recently gone missing in the Italian Alps (and was later discovered to have died; his Puss Moth having broken up in flight) – was attempting to become the first woman to fly from Australia to England. She got as far as Thailand. Of them all, Lancaster's attempt was the only one that attracted much press attention, albeit not for his piloting. He had recently been acquitted of murder in America after a former lover of his mistress committed suicide in such a way as to make it appear that Lancaster had killed him. That was the story, anyway. Unfortunately, he crashed in the Syrian desert on the second day after his departure, where his remains lay undiscovered for almost thirty years.

Jean, meanwhile, made excellent progress – despite the fact that her Moth was clearly not rigged properly. She was unable to trim it to enable her to fly hands off. It was not until she was almost at Aleppo that she encountered her first seriously bad weather: 'Suddenly, the machine was being tossed into what felt like an upwards roll. Then, with a shudder that made all the wires ripple, it pitched into a spin' from which she recovered with only a few feet to spare.

In Bushire, she caught up with Captain Robbiano – despite the fact that the Italian's aeroplane was much faster than the Moth. Her next stop, as was his, was Karachi, which she was on course to reach a day ahead of Amy Johnson's already very quick time. But, like Robbiano, she was forced down by an engine failure. Tantalisingly, hers occurred within sight of Karachi, though the result was a complete write-off. Unluckily for Robbiano, his, a day later, was over the Bay of Bengal and, while the remains of his aircraft were eventually washed ashore near Chittagong, his body was never recovered.

Given these mishaps, a *Times* editorial condemning the would-be record-breakers was not wholly unfounded: 'It may be asked whether any good can come of further adventures of this kind. The routes traversed are those which have already been blazed by pioneers of the air and present flights can add nothing to human knowledge ... it is time to call a halt to these hazardous exploits'. Not that Miss Batten would have taken any notice, even if she had read it. Abandoning her Moth, she made her way back to England to brood and scheme. Naturally enough, she immediately contacted her hapless patron. Unfortunately for her, it seems that he had, in the meantime, come to his senses and there was nothing further forthcoming from that quarter. A photograph of her standing next to the wrecked Moth in what became her trademark, a white flying suit, had, however, caught the eye of one of Lord Wakefield's agents and a personal introduction to him by none other than

Geoffrey de Havilland succeeded in persuading the oil baron to put up £400. This was not enough, but it was a good start. For a remarkably modest £260, she acquired a much-travelled Moth, G-AARB. Originally owned by an RAF officer based in Jordan, it had been sold by him to an Indian national with whom he flew it to England. Again sold, this time to a French lady pilot who crashed it in Morocco, the Moth had been repaired again and finally wound up in the back of a hangar in Reading.

Still utterly determined to break Amy Johnson's record, the twenty-five-year-old Jean now set her cap at an amiable young stockbroker and fellow Mothist named Edward Walter. They became officially engaged just two weeks after first meeting early in 1933. Fuelled by his ardour and his financial support, Jean Batten set off for Australia on 21 April, just over a year since her first attempt. This time she made it as far as Rome. Having left Marseilles in spite of the remonstration of the airport manager on account of torrential rain, the Moth fought its way to the Italian coast against ferocious headwinds. By now flying in the dark, the future record-breaker crawled on fumes to the Eternal City where her luck finally ran out among the radio masts adjacent to the airport. Down she came, completely unable to see and somehow escaping with damage only to her lower wings, which both needed replacing. Spotting another Moth in the hangar, Batten boldly besought its owner to loan her its set in order to enable her to fly home and start again. She would return them immediately on arrival. He agreed, and for once, she was as good as her word, having, in the meantime, extracted a promise from Edward Walter to lend her his Moth's wings so that she could make a third attempt.

Remarkably, Batten was back in the air within forty-eight

hours of her arrival home. This time, the 'Try it again girl' – as the press dubbed her – had better luck. Europe and the Middle East and India fled by and, by the twelfth day after her departure, she had reached Singapore – a full four days ahead of the Johnson record. Only now did her flight begin to spark the public's imagination. Back in London, Ellen Batten began to be besieged – and to lay the foundations of the Jean Batten myth. She had got as far as she had purely by her own hard work, according to her mother. Simple prudence and dogged-ness had seen her through years of struggle. Yet while we might be tempted to focus only on the betrayals (Edward Walter duly got his letter in the weeks to come) and the obvious gaps in the story, it is important to acknowledge several things. The first is that Jean Batten had matured into an extremely skilful aviator. Her landings and take-offs were invariably expert. Her navigation, if not up to Chichester levels of genius, was nevertheless spot on. Having by this time also acquired her engineer's licence, she was also a more than competent mechanic. But whereas Amy Johnson remained the quintessential girl next door, Batten was, as she well knew, glamorous and appealing both to men (who fancied her) and to women (who fancied being her). No matter that her exploits were mere repetitions of journeys undertaken by others.

When her little Moth landed in Darwin on 23 May, having beaten Amy Johnson's time by more than four days, the press went wild. 'JEANIUS!' screamed the headlines. 'Flight made literally on the wings of love!' – this in reference to Edward Walters' loan. (He never did get them back, though Fred Truman, later confronting her in Auckland, got £250.) As with Amy, there were huge crowds and telegrams in their hundreds, including one from the king. Jean spent a month touring

Australia at government expense and in Brisbane an estimated 25,000 turned out to greet her. Everywhere she stayed, bouquets of flowers, boxes containing hats and parcels of frocks piled up on her bed. Lord Wakefield sent her £1,000. True, her ambition was to fly on to New Zealand, but, like Chichester before her, she was forced to conclude that the distance was beyond the capability of the Moth. Nonetheless, when she arrived at Auckland, her aeroplane having been taken by ship, she was mobbed. The government granted her a bounty of £500 and she packed theatres and cinemas up and down the country. Someone gave her a kitten.*

As with both Scott and Mollison, Jean Batten went on to make several more pioneering flights and, like them, she earned large sums of money from her exploits. Yet not one of the three can be said to have had successful lives thereafter. Scott shot himself (succeeding only with the second bullet), disappointed in love, aged forty-three. Mollison died of cirrhosis of the liver, paradoxically – if not comically – in a temperance hotel bought for him by his wealthy second wife when they parted company – aged fifty-four. Jean Batten continued to live with her mother and even, on Ellen's insistence, turned down an invitation from Charles Lindbergh to make a lecture tour of America, which promised to be extremely lucrative. Living firstly in Jamaica and then in Tenerife, for the last year of Ellen's life they stayed at a succession of European motels, after which she returned to Jamaica. In the seventies, free at last from her parent's baleful influence, she dyed her hair, raised her hemline and embarked on a series of fleeting affairs

---

* Nicknamed Buddy, it became her mascot for a year and flew wherever she went, passing each flight unhappily in the locker.

when attending various aviation-related events organised in her honour. Yet while she gave the impression of an active life, in reality, she lived as a recluse. After her death, alone in a hotel in Mallorca, she was buried in a communal grave and it was more than six years before her family learned her fate.

By the time of Jean Batten's record-breaking run to Sydney, the DH60 Moth was also nearing the end of its production run. There were no more successful stunts, though the last one attempted was in a way the most ambitious – if also the maddest of them all.

17

Into the Silence

What goes up must come down. That which goes high shall be brought low: this is the inexorable law.

The aeroplane's descent is a time of transition, both mental and physical. Physically, you surrender your altitude. Mentally, you prepare yourself for the most demanding phase of any flight: the approach and landing. Throttling back in the Moth, the sound of rushing wind replaces the engine's roar and the aeroplane, realising the game is up, yields to gravity as though acknowledging defeat.

If you want to lose height quickly, you can do so by bringing the speed back to 50 mph – less if there isn't too much wind. You do this by holding the nose up until the speed has decayed sufficiently and trimming accordingly. If you really need to get rid of height, you side-slip, something the Moth does beautifully. To initiate a side-slip, you have to go against your instincts and deliberately cross controls. Left aileron and a boot-full of right rudder to initiate a slip with the port wing down. Right aileron and left rudder for the opposite effect.

It looks very pretty – especially when on a tight, curving approach to land. Just watch you don't get the speed back too far. Enter a stall with crossed controls and you will flip straight into a spin.

On this occasion, however, you don't need to lose height quickly. In fact, it's rather the reverse. You are nearing 20,000 feet, right at the limit of the Moth's ability to climb. Having scrambled slowly up here, buffeted by the wind, determinedly ploughing through patches of cloud and freezing fog to get as high as you possibly can, you are now looking for somewhere to put down. For on this day of all days, you are about to execute one of the most audacious landings in all aviation's short history ...

The son of a mill owner, Maurice Wilson was born in Bradford, West Yorkshire, in 1898 – one of that short span of fatal years that meant you were ripe for planting in the soil of Flanders fields. Having joined up as a private soldier, Wilson quickly rose through the ranks to be commissioned – an officer and 'temporary gentleman' in the cruel argot of the day – in which capacity he won a Military Cross for 'conspicuous gallantry and devotion to duty' during an action that occurred as part of the defence against the Germans' final great offensive of the war in April 1918. At the beginning of the day, his battalion numbered around a thousand men. That night, the roll-call counted just ninety.

Not long afterwards, the young Captain Wilson caught a Blighty and was invalided out of the war. It was not a happy homecoming. Reunited with his family, he found his beloved elder brother, Victor, broken and gibbering from his own war experience. As to the future, Wilson was hopeful of obtaining a wounded soldier's war pension, but in this he was disappointed. Struggling to find work, he eventually ended up in the garment trade. In 1922, he married – though he was barely making ends meet. Soon after, he hit on the idea of making a new life in New Zealand, setting sail towards the end of 1923. The idea was that he would send for his wife just as soon as he could get himself established.

Regrettably, by the time Maurice's bride, Beatrice, caught up with him, he had fallen in love with another woman. Abandoned and completely without support, the unfortunate Beatrice sought a divorce, returning to England, while Maurice remained and remarried. His new wife was a successful dress designer and together they grew their business to the point where they enjoyed what counted as a fashionable existence. Yet Wilson – like so many of that fateful generation – dogged by the horrors of what he had endured, never really settled. When his wife decided on a visit to the fashion capitals of New York, London and Paris, in 1930, he did the same to her as he had done to Beatrice but in reverse. She went on ahead. He failed to join her, instead making for California in hope, it seems, of finding help for his ongoing trauma from the burgeoning spiritual healing movement that was, even then, proving so profitable to Mohan Singh, aka Hari Ram.

In this, Wilson was unsuccessful and, having crossed the American continent, he eventually took a ship bound for England where, having had a brief affair with a dressmaker en route, he finally set foot in his homeland seven years after departure. On a visit home, his mother, infirm and lonely after the death of her husband and two of her three sons, implored him to stay. But he would not, instead making his way to London and from London to South Africa and back, having brief onboard affairs on each leg of his journey, each of them again with women in the garment trade – a fact that becomes significant later. Then, at some point between his return in summer 1932 and the New Year of 1933, he had an epiphany.

He later claimed that he had met a mysterious healer who directed him to put his faith in God and fast for thirty-five days in order to 'purge himself of all extraneous matter physically and mentally'.[1] On the final day, hardly in control of his faculties, Wilson realised that he had done what he had set out to do. He had cured himself! And not only that, he came to the realisation that he was a man of destiny. On the first of January 1933, he made a resolution.

What that resolution was needs to be seen in the context of what was happening in Britain at the time. The British and other European empires had reached their maximum extent, even if the logic of 'raising up' their subject peoples was making them increasingly hard to govern. By now, the great age of exploration that followed in the wake of empire was drawing to a close. The north and south poles had been conquered, the source of the Nile discovered and every ocean traversed in all directions. The conquest of the air was now complete. There remained only one major unattained trophy: the conquest of Everest.

Then, in October 1932, the Houston Everest expedition was announced. Having as its object an overflight of Everest to reconnoitre possible routes up, its leader was a young RAF officer, the air-mad Douglas Douglas-Hamilton, future 14th Duke of Hamilton, who was later at the centre of one of the more bizarre escapades of the Second World War. It was Douglas-Hamilton whom Rudolf Hess, Deputy Führer of the Nazi Party, claimed he had come to visit with a peace proposal when he parachuted out of a hijacked Messerschmitt in May 1941. Briefly under suspicion, the duke quickly restored his good name – beyond having seen him at the 1936 Berlin Olympics, he had never actually met Hess – and went on to have a distinguished career in public service.

Unable to persuade the government to sponsor his proposed expedition to Everest, Douglas-Hamilton had approached the redoubtable Lady Houston to provide the necessary bounty. Well known as a committed aviation enthusiast, she had recently financed the winning 1931 Schneider Trophy team.

Born Fanny Lucy Radmall, the future Lady Houston began her career as a chorus girl who went by the stage name of Poppy. Quickly becoming mistress of the owner of one of England's largest breweries, she developed a taste for money that saw her marry into three successive and ever-larger fortunes to become both the second richest woman in the land and a generous philanthropist. During the war, she founded a rest home for nurses serving on the Western Front – for which munificence she was created a Dame of the British Empire. Subsequently, she stood bail for the suffragette Emmeline Pankhurst. Paradoxically, perhaps, she was also a fierce nationalist, who once hung an illuminated sign from the rigging of her yacht, *Liberty*, that read 'DOWN WITH MACDONALD THE TRAITOR', to protest what she saw as the scandalous neglect of London's air defences by the then prime minister – though, as an admirer of Hitler, it is not entirely clear where she thought the threat lay. In any case, the Everest expedition was to be, in every sense, her crowning achievement. When, a few years later, her friend Edward VIII abdicated the throne, she died – it seems literally – of a broken heart. She had wanted him to remain king and assume control as dictator of Great Britain.

With funding in place, it was the now so-called Houston Everest expedition that inspired Wilson in his resolution as he sat alone in his London digs on New Year's Eve: *he would be the first man to stand on the summit of Mount Everest!*

He would do this by hitching a ride on the wing of Douglas-Hamilton's aeroplane and parachuting onto the mountaintop.

If this idea was as mad as it was impractical, the scheme Wilson came up with when his few friends had convinced him that there was not even the slightest chance he would be able to join the expedition – he had no contacts, let alone any credentials – was even madder. He would fly there himself, climb as high as he could get, crash-land on the mountainside and undertake the last few thousand feet on foot. And, not only that, he would time it so that he reached the summit on his birthday, 21 April (he was as sentimental as most narcissists are), just seventeen weeks away.

He had not a minute to lose.

The first thing he needed to do was to acquire an aeroplane. Then he would learn to fly it. He would get fit. And he would buy some kit.

Having followed up several small ads, he soon became, for £550, the proud owner of a DH60G Moth, which he had emblazoned with the name *Ever Wrest* – get it? Shortly after taking possession of his Moth, Wilson joined the London Aero Club, where he became the pupil of its chief flying instructor, now Nigel Tangye. Like the illustrious trio of Chichester, Johnson and Batten before him, Wilson needed fully twice the average number of hours before going solo. If this was somewhat unusual, it was nothing like as unusual as Wilson's flying kit. He insisted on wearing breeches and gaiters over hobnailed boots at all times, his rationale being that, since he was going to be climbing in them, he had better get used to wearing them. It also meant that he was dressed for his exercise between sorties and, from early morning to late evening and sometimes at night too, he would stomp round the airfield perimeter. Fellow flying club members who tried to socialise with him by offering pints of beer in the clubhouse would be met with the response that he was 'an apple and nuts man'. Following his fast, he had become obsessed with diet and was fanatical about what he would eat and when, and he would invariably refuse their offers.

For day after day, Wilson practised circuits (taking off, flying round the airfield and landing), until his confidence and competence both gradually began to improve. At the same time, he continued to work on his fitness, at one point climbing alone in Snowdonia and, at another, walking in the Lake District during what remained of the winter. He did not deem it necessary to take any climbing instruction, however, even though, by then, there were many clubs that taught the basics of rock climbing. The one other thing he did do was make a parachute jump – in order, as he said, to test his courage. He landed badly, but passed the test.

As for flight planning, he bought all the relevant charts, carefully plotting his course and his refuelling stops. He would take the shortest possible crossing of the Mediterranean and fly in easy stages. To cater for the possibility of coming down in the desert, he purchased three unbreakable water flasks. Apart from these, his specialist kit was minimal. From Fortnum & Mason, he bought the best coat and woollens then available, also a cooker, a lightweight tent and the latest kind of sub-zero sleeping bag. For the final assault on the summit, he bought a small supply of oxygen. But ropes, ice axe and, most unwisely of all, crampons, he decided to do without.

Although he made no secret of his plan to fly to Everest – and many, including Tangye, tried to dissuade him – it was not until the end of March that he went public with his scheme. At first, he was hopeful that he would secure a deal with one of the papers, but they were sensibly unpersuaded of his likelihood of success. Nevertheless, on the Sunday before his scheduled departure, one paper ran with the headline: 'MOST AMAZING AIR ADVENTURE EVER ATTEMPTED'. Unfortunately for Wilson, the details it gave of his plans alerted the Foreign Office, which began at once to set in motion various bureaucratic hurdles to ensure he could not put them into action. This was not out of any concern for his safety, but rather out of concern for diplomatic relations with the countries he intended to enter, most critically those of Nepal and Tibet, both of them notoriously fickle in their dealings with Westminster. It had taken months of negotiations to obtain permission for the Everest overflight.

Meanwhile, Wilson left Stag Lane to visit his mother in Bradford. En route, he spent a night at Bridlington where he had landed on a rugby pitch, parking between the goal posts. Alas, he suffered an engine failure on his next leg and was compelled to make a forced landing. This ended with the aeroplane upside down in a ditch, its pilot sitting suspended in his harness. Did he curse? Maybe not. Maybe he saw the incident as merely the workings of an unkind fate, which he, as a man of destiny, must simply face down.

While his aeroplane was in the repair shop, Wilson took one piece of good advice, and had *Ever Wrest* fitted with strengthened undercarriage and oversized tyres. When, at last, all was ready – his kit packed and stowed, his maps all marked up and folded – there was no fanfare. A small party of well-wishers gathered to see him off, among them Jean Batten, who was, just then, between her second and third attempts to reach Australia. Standing together in the spring sunshine, they watched with mounting horror as Wilson taxied to the wrong end of the runway. Surely, he would realise his mistake! But no, opening the throttle wide *Ever Wrest* began hurtling past them downwind.

Using the whole length of the runway, it lurched uncertainly into the air. Had the wind been any stronger, Wilson would have run out of runway. As it was, having executed a farewell circuit of Stag Lane, he set course, via Heston to clear customs, for the German Black Forest town of Freiburg. He wrote later of his exultation at flying over the Channel. What, though, did he think about as he overflew the Western Front, still scarred and pockmarked fifteen years on?

Bad weather over the Alps the next day forced him back to Freiburg. His heavily laden aircraft could not be persuaded above 7,000 feet. For the Everest trip, he would need only minimal fuel so this did not concern him greatly. Deciding, for once, that discretion was the better part of valour, he changed his plan, and, as soon as the weather was clear, he set out for Marseilles on the south coast of France. The press meanwhile reported him lost.

On reaching the Mediterranean coast, Wilson flew along the Cote d'Azur before cutting the corner of the Gulf of Genoa and flying 130 miles over water directly to Pisa. Landing at the Italian air force base adjacent to the city, he was thrilled to be royally entertained in the officers' mess. 'So far,' he wrote, 'the trip is a piece of cake.'

Two days later, arriving in Tunis, Wilson discovered there was no fuel available so he made for Bizerte to the north. But there, he found himself completely unwelcome. He would be held under arrest if he did not immediately go away. His only option was to return to Tunis where he must be able to get hold of some fuel eventually. To his delight, he found some abandoned fuel drums round the back of a hangar, to which he helped himself. Retribution was swift. Although he made it successfully to his next stop at Gabès, almost as soon as he was airborne once more, his engine began to vibrate horribly. Losing power, he wheeled round, barely making it back to the airfield before it quit entirely. The cause? Water. Evidently, the fuel he had purloined at Tunis had been contaminated.

In spite of these various setbacks, Wilson made it to Cairo within a week of his departure. There, however, he faced fresh obstacles. The permit he claimed to have arranged to enter Persia had not arrived. As a result, despite his efforts to persuade the local (British) authorities to facilitate his transit of the land of the Peacock Throne, he was refused assistance.

But they could not stop him from flying on to Baghdad. Fate might smile on him more kindly when he got there. He was a Man of Destiny, after all. As it turned out, there was no help for him in Baghdad either. The consulate informed him that there was no possibility of a permit to enter Persian territory. There was nothing for it now but for him to go back the way he had come. Nothing daunted, Wilson began to plot. His reason for routing via Persia was on account of his limited range. He didn't have the maximum tankage that Batten and Co. had. If, on the other hand, he were to transit what were then known as the Trucial States (which included Oman, Dubai and Abu Dhabi) as far as Bahrain, he might just make it into India.

Filled with renewed hope, he went off in search of a map. Unfortunately, he only had ones that covered the northern side of the Persian Gulf and, like Aspy Engineer, he had to make do with a school atlas and a hastily scribbled sketch copied from a wall chart. According to this, he would be around nine hours in the air. Undaunted, he set off. There followed two occasions when, having nodded off, he woke to find himself hurtling out of control towards the sea, recovering only just in time. As he neared the end of his flight, Wilson began to feel light-headed. One wonders how much water he had drunk. But at the eight-and-a-half-hour mark, he saw in the distance the shadow that presaged landfall. He'd made it to Bahrain.

His troubles were by no means over. Before he could leave next day, he would need a fuel chit and, for that, he must contact the local authorities. They had, in the interval, been firmly instructed not to help. It was explained to him that, if he was going to India, the nearest place he could land without special clearance was at Gwadar. What was the maximum endurance of his aeroplane? Around ten hours. That would carry him around 750 miles in still air. How far was it to Gwadar? Fifty miles beyond that. No one but a maniac or a fool would attempt such a thing. The merest puff of wind against him would see *Ever Wrest* run dry somewhere over the eastern reaches of the Persian Gulf. No, his only chance was to fly north to Bushire. If he did that, he might, after all, be granted a transit permit by the authorities. Alan Cobham and Amy Johnson had both been that way, after all.

Wilson realised this was a trap. If his wheels so much as touched Persian soil, they'd have an excuse to arrest him and impound his aeroplane. But two could play that game! Ruefully accepting the British consul's advice, he signed an affidavit agreeing to proceed to Bushire, replenished his tanks, lined up and took off.

Airborne, he must have laughed to himself as he executed a 180 and set course for India. Who did they think he was? It was certainly true that Gwadar was beyond the normal limit of his still-air range. But if he throttled back a bit, he could easily increase it by the required 7 per cent. Full of misplaced confidence, he set off. Never mind that the mean daytime temperature in that part of the world is anywhere between 35 and 40 degrees centigrade. Never mind that the moment he had cleared the east coast of the Oman peninsular, there would be nothing but the mirror of the sea radiating the sun's rays back up at him or that, with the view ahead just a haze of grey, fatigue would put him in mortal danger. The fact that, somewhere around the halfway mark, his engine quit without warning was perhaps the best thing that could have happened to him in the circumstances. It would have given him a shot of adrenaline such as probably he hadn't experienced since the day he won his MC.

Keeping his head in the awful silence, he flicked the magnetos off, pumped the throttle several times, switched them back on again and prayed. The engine sputtered, he eased out of the dive but it died again. One more chance. Same routine. The sea fills his forward view. He pumps the throttle; he flicks the switches back up. He prays.

And God hears him! His engine bursts back to life with a roar and *Ever Wrest* soars high above the man-hungry waves.

That scare must have helped, and so must the cramp that gradually developed in his legs. Wilson was a tall man and the cockpit of the Moth gives little room for manoeuvre. He spent the last part of the journey in agony, relieved only when, at last, after almost nine and a half hours in the air, he spotted the little promontory that, if his calculations were right, should denote the port city that was his destination. Sure enough, there, in the gathering dark, he could just make out Gwadar airport – a wide, flat expanse, with sundry hangars and administrative buildings dispersed around the perimeter.

That night, he slept in the open, next to the faithful *Ever Wrest*.

But now he had to get to the mountain. He would do as the Hamilton-Houston expedition had done and launch his attempt from Purnea, 1,600 miles away in the far northeast of India, routing via Karachi, Hyderabad, Jodhpur and Allahabad. On arrival in Karachi, he gave his first major interview to the press when he met with a reporter from the *Daily Express* – then the highest circulation newspaper in the world. Its headline gives a good indication of Wilson's mania. He was going to climb Everest sustained by 'Deep breathing and one meal a day.' Following his thirty-five-day fast at the end of the previous year, he had proven that, by eating less, he would be able to 'breathe down to my stomach, taking in a vastly increased supply of oxygen', thereby obviating the need for an elaborate diet. Mention is also made of 'rice and dates', of which he would take enough to last fifty days.* 'There is no stunt about it,' he added. 'It is a carefully planned expedition, which is certain of success although the orthodox minded might consider it madness.'[2]

Alas, Wilson's quixotic odyssey by air was soon brought to an end. He made it to Purnea only to be told that permission to overfly Nepal most definitely would not be granted. Unabashed, he went by train and car into Nepal in hope of

---

* By contrast, Eric Shipton, who led the 1936 expedition to Everest, says that a team of four would eat 140 eggs in one day.

persuading the twenty-seven-year-old king, Bikram Shah, to give him a chance. Unsurprisingly, his mission failed. He now had another problem to contend with. He had very little money. If he really was not going to be able to fly there, well then, he would go on foot. But that would cost a fair bit. He'd need to engage porters to carry his (albeit meagre) food and equipment and to show him the way. He began to look for a buyer for *Ever Wrest*. In the meantime, he wired his mother for funds and made his way to Darjeeling, the Himalayan hill station from which each of the recent British expeditions had set out. He was sure to be able to find people there who would help.

From Tiger Hill, which stands a few miles outside Darjeeling, Wilson had his first sight of Everest. The view is extraordinary. Because of the curvature of the earth, you look down on the summit as if it were below you, almost exactly 100 miles away. Resuming his regime of long walks and limited nourishment, Wilson confined himself to a single bowl of porridge a day. He also had to be careful not to arouse suspicion of any unauthorised attempt to enter Tibet, which enforced a strict no-foreigner policy unless by prior – and seldom given – permission. Any who relied on the Tibetans' famous commitment to non-violence were liable to be cruelly undeceived – as were several Catholic missionary priests murdered earlier in the century and Father (now Blessed) Maurice Tournay was to be in 1949, shot by hostile Buddhist monks while trying to cross the border. It was not only the Tibetan authorities that Wilson had to fear, however. The local British authorities were entirely supportive of the Dalai Lama's policy and kept a close eye on anyone who seemed liable to make trouble. His lodgings were raided more than once by local police.

In December 1933, Wilson completed the sale of *Ever Wrest* to its new owner, a planter by the name of Cassell. At the beginning of the same month, he embarked on another epic fast, breaking it on Christmas Day having eaten nothing for three weeks – this in preparation for the ordeal that lay ahead.

For the next ten weeks, Wilson bided his time. In March, he hired three local porters and bought a pony. Learning that Buddhist monks were exempt from the need of a permit to enter Tibet, it made obvious sense to Wilson to travel disguised as one himself. To that end, he acquired a costume consisting of an elaborate hat and a brocade waistcoat worn under a long gown. Unfortunately, standing at six foot one, he was well above average height for a Tibetan and, whenever he came in contact with other people, he was compelled to shuffle along with bent knees to keep himself down to a more plausible height. In order to decrease further the likelihood of detection, he decided that he and his party would travel by night.

Setting out on 21 March 1934, the two Sherpas went on ahead while Wilson, the pony and his groom followed some distance behind. Averaging a little under 20 miles per day, they made excellent progress. Within three weeks, they had entered the Ronbuk valley and made contact with the monastery at its head. This, standing at over 16,000 feet, had been recently built by its abbot, Dzatrul Rinpoche, a highly regarded teacher of the esoteric Nyingma tradition. The Rinpoche himself seems to have taken a liking to Wilson. Although he regarded efforts to climb Chomolungma – as Tibetans call Everest – to be entirely pointless, he appreciated Wilson's light touch. The British had an uncomfortable tendency to kill the local fauna for food – sometimes even for fun.

The abbot's other concern was with the local spirits, or

srungma. When the Ruttledge Everest expedition had passed through, it had been necessary for him to organise a number of rituals of appeasement after their departure.[3] But one man would hopefully not upset the spirits too much.

Unfortunately, Wilson seems not to have appreciated the honour he was shown. He described a religious festival he witnessed as nothing more than a 'big cheroo' and complained that the people were 'filthy'. As for the abbot, he merely refers to him as a 'dear old man'. By contrast, a climber on the 1935 Everest expedition described him as 'beyond question a remarkable individual . . . full of dignity', who was 'treated with the utmost of respect by the whole of his people'. Indeed, there are many even today who revere the teachings contained in his masterwork, *A Guide to the Thirty-seven Practices of a Bodhisattva*.

Two days after their arrival, Wilson and his party set off to climb Everest. As he had been the previous year, Wilson was determined to reach the summit on his birthday. To begin with, all went swimmingly. The weather was fine, the walking was easy and they managed over a thousand feet a day for the first two. Leaving his Sherpa party at base camp, he pressed on alone. But the third day was 'hell', as was the fourth. Then it began to snow. On 21 April, his birthday, he realised he wasn't going to make it. He was low on food and reliant on getting to Ruttledge's Camp III where, so the porters told him, there was a large cache of supplies to which he could help himself. But the weather was clearly against him. He would have to go back down and wait until it cleared.

Following a fourteen-hour trek – itself an impressive achievement for a man of thirty-six, with little food and zero mountaineering experience – Wilson made it back down to

Ronpuk, falling at least five times and having 'often had to let myself go, tumbling over and over until I hit something'.[4]

A lesser man – certainly a wiser one – would have given up at that point. But Wilson hadn't flown all the way to India and walked two thirds of the way up Everest to call it quits. Clearly, what he needed was a better plan. He would enlist the help of his Sherpas to get him up to Ruttledge's Camp III and only go solo after that. Skinning it this way, he felt sure, would greatly increase his chances of success. If he could get to Camp III, there'd only be 8,000 feet to go and he'd be in with a sporting chance. In the meantime, he would rest up and recuperate. On 12 May, he set out once again. Now fully acclimatised and climbing over 2,000 feet per day, this time he made it in good order to the camp where, sure enough, he found 'plum jam, honey, butter … anchovy paste from Fortnum and Mason, sugar, Ovaltine, Nestles milk and other treasures from heaven'. It seems his dietary strictures had gone out of the window at this point.

Replenished, he looked up with renewed hope. But, with the immediacy that characterises the Himalayan weather, the elements precluded further progress and he remained stuck for a week. On the 21st, he set out from the camp in the company of one of the Sherpas who agreed to accompany him as far as the North Col where he would begin the final leg of his journey.

But the local deities were clearly displeased. Four days later, he was again beaten back and retreated to the camp where the Sherpas awaited him. For another four days, he remained in situ. On 29 May, he set off again, determined to make it up to the next camp. He failed once more but pitched his tent for the night, rather than turn back. 'Strange,' he wrote, 'but I feel that there is somebody with me in the tent all the time.'

On the 31st, he woke to brilliant sunshine and struck a hopeful note in his diary: 'Off again, gorgeous day.'

Maurice Wilson's body was found a year later by Eric Shipton and his team. He had pitched his tent at around 21,000 feet and got into his sleeping bag one last time, never to awake. The tent had, in the intervening months, blown away. But his rucksack containing his journal lay next to him undisturbed. They pitched his body down a nearby crevasse – though whether with a prayer for his soul is not recorded.

Could Wilson himself have been successful had he succeeded in getting his Moth halfway up the mountain? The question is not worth asking. The more interesting question is: what drove this madness? Was it the horror of war unresolved? Was it the desperate egotism of a man who fancied himself destined to do something great? Was it some kind of psychological impulse born of embarrassment about his secret enthusiasm for cross-dressing? That was always the rumour about Wilson, the truth of which has been put beyond reasonable doubt by his most recent biographer. Or was it, rather, the romantic view of the aviator as Nietzschean Übermensch, capable of moulding reality to his will, carried to its logical and pitiful conclusion?

18

Works of Mercy

B y the time that Maurice Wilson set off on his crazed
Everest adventure, the last of the classic DH60 Moths
had rolled off the production line. Its immediate successor, the
Moth Major, was in almost every respect identical, save for its
Gipsy Major engine. This latest iteration of Frank Halford's
design inverted the cylinders, placing the crankshaft on top,
rather than below – his thinking being that the engine itself
had no notion of whether it was the right way up or not. As
a result of this reconfiguration, besides the increase in power
of a further 10 hp over the Gipsy II, the Moth Major had
substantially improved visibility over the nose. Another consequence of inversion was to obviate the need for the exhaust
pipe running down the side of the fuselage. In its place, a
much shorter (and lighter) pipe could be installed underneath.
Whether this was an improvement in terms of aesthetics is a
matter of personal opinion. Many would say that it was not.

Some 154 Moth Majors (technically designated the
DH60GIII) were built, before, in response to RAF

requirements, the basic design was substantially modified to become the DH82 Tiger Moth. Although sharing many common parts and still recognisably a Moth, this variant – which proved in time to be one of the most successful aircraft designs ever – differed from its predecessors in many small ways, but in one that was visually significant: its upper wings were both moved forward and, to compensate, swept back slightly in order to enhance egress from the forward cockpit in an emergency. It also came fitted with the latest development of the Gipsy engine series. In time, with a higher compression ratio, this gave 135 hp, and, with aluminium cylinder heads, 140 hp.*

A remarkable hybrid DH60/DH82 known as the Queen Bee remained in production until 1941. This was, in effect, a full-sized drone. Controlled entirely by radio (although it could also be flown manually from the front cockpit), the Queen Bee was used as a target for gunnery practice.

So far as sporting light aircraft were concerned, there were now many contenders for the private enthusiast's attention, not least de Havilland's own Puss Moth and, latterly, the Leopard Moth. The first of these was a comfortable two- or uncomfortable three-seater cabin monoplane which had found favour with the royal household. The Duke of Gloucester had one, while the Prince of Wales had two. GDH's own favourite was the DH85 Leopard Moth which had comfortable seating for three, the pilot sitting ahead of two passengers. Introduced in 1933, this featured the Gipsy Major engine with which it won that year's King's Cup at a speed of almost 140 mph.

---

* Its apotheosis, designed for use in the Saunders-Roe Skeeter training helicopter, was the Gipsy Major 50. With a turbocharger, it produced an astonishing 220 hp.

By this time, too, the craze for flying had abated considerably. All the major records had been set and broken at least
once and the racing circuit had largely become the preserve of
professionals. Wealthy private owners now hired pilots to fly
their aeroplanes for them, rather as they hired jockeys to ride
their racehorses. Sassoon, the Prince of Wales and his brother
are all cases in point. There was still a romance attached to
the aviator but the whole business of flying was becoming
increasingly technical. Less and less did the aeroplane seem
a daring and wonderful means of seeing the world. If not yet
quite commonplace, it was emerging as just another tool in the
workshop of modern industrial society. If there remained one
area where light aircraft were still, in the late twenties and early
thirties, being used in a hitherto largely untried role, it was in
what we might call 'works of mercy'. It had long been realised
that, in particular circumstances, aeroplanes were uniquely
suited to bringing succour to the afflicted – to delivering aid to
those in want or stricken with illness; to rescue those injured in
battle or imperilled by advancing enemies. An early example
of the Moth's participation in a rescue mission came in the
summer of 1928.

When, in January of that year, three DH60s equipped
with skis had arrived in Sweden, a crowd of 40,000 – which
included the crown prince and other members of the royal
household – had turned out to watch them being put through
their paces. Following this event, the Stockholm flying school
operating the Moths trained a remarkable twenty-two pilots
to licence standard in just the first seven weeks of operation.
This necessitated more than 4,000 sorties off the frozen lake
from which they operated.[1] So impressive was the aeroplane
that, in July of that year, the Swedish Air Force chartered

one of the club's Moths to attempt a rescue of Captain Einar Lundborg, one of their pilots who had become stranded north of the Arctic Circle. In what might have been described as a comedy of errors if it had not claimed the lives of several gallant men, Lundborg had become the latest victim in a series of disasters precipitated when the *Italia*, a huge semi-rigid airship built along the lines of Germany's Zeppelins and Britain's R101, came to grief while conducting scientific studies at the north pole.

Unfortunately, the Italian expedition was beset with obstacles from the start and enjoyed only one wholly fine day during its time in the Arctic. On its way back to base, facing a headwind that reduced its speed over the ground almost to zero, the airship's propellers began to accumulate ice. As this ice broke off, it formed projectiles that began tearing holes in the envelope, necessitating constant repairs from inside. Worse came when the ice began to affect elevator control. Eventually they jammed in the full downward position, causing the nose of the *Italia* to rise uncontrollably. Even with the engines cut by the captain, Umberto Nobile, the craft rose to 3,000 feet where, although he was able to re-establish control temporarily, Nobile realised that a crash was inevitable. Fortunately, when disaster finally struck, the occupants of the gondola, himself included, found themselves more or less unscathed. Unfortunately, those still within the envelope were trapped as it reascended and drifted off, never to be seen again.

Thanks to the presence of mind of one of the trapped crew members, chief engineer Ettore Arduino, who immediately began hurling emergency supplies out of the injured craft, Nobile and the other crash survivors – which included his fox terrier Titina – at least had the possibility of staying alive until rescue came. Among the equipment was a Colt revolver which soon came in handy when they were visited by a polar bear. Also salvaged was a portable radio transmitter. This turned out still to be working, though reception of its S.O.S. signals was impeded by journalists who monopolised the various wireless stations that might otherwise have detected them. As a result, it wasn't until several days later that a twenty-one-year-old Russian radio ham happened to pick up a signal from the stricken crew.

In the weeks following the crash, flights over the ice cap were undertaken by Italian, Norwegian, Swedish, Finnish, French and Russian aircraft. The Italian government also hired a Norwegian whaler when it became apparent that the expedition's support ship could make no headway through the ice and two Russian icebreakers also joined in the search. Despite the support ship's incapacity, it launched an abortive mission using dog sleds to find the survivors.

Other rescue efforts included one led by Roald Amundsen, the great Norwegian polar explorer who had beaten Captain Scott to the south pole in 1910. Disastrously, the flying boat carrying him became yet another victim of the disaster, disappearing somewhere in the Barents Sea with the loss of all lives on 18 June. Two days later, one of the Russian icebreakers became stranded.

Eventually, a full twenty-five days after the *Italia* went down, the crash site was found by one of the Italian aircraft. Unfortunately, the supplies it dropped were destroyed on impact, having been thrown from too great a height and speed. It was another two days before a further mission was able to replenish the survivors' dwindling resources. It was soon after this first success that Captain Lundborg, a veteran of the

Finnish civil war and of the Estonian war of independence, accompanied by Lieutenant Schyberg as observer, brought in a Fokker trimotor to rescue the injured Nobile. Leaving Schyberg behind, he evacuated the expedition leader (and his dog) but, when he came back for the other injured men, his Fokker came to grief on landing. As a result, the number of those stranded increased to six. This was still one fewer than actually survived the airship crash. But three men, two Italians and the Swedish meteorologist and physicist Finn Malmgre, had earlier broken away from the other crew members in an attempt to trek overland to safety. The Italians ultimately survived, picked up by the Russians, but not the Swede. Back home, the two survivors never entirely threw off the rumours that they had either abandoned or – as some suggested, had actually eaten – the unfortunate physicist.

Not until 6 July, more than six weeks after the crash, did Lieutenant Schyberg finally appear in one of the Stockholm flying school Moths. Dangerously warmed by the summer sun, the ice floe was by now very fragile but, finding an area on which to put the Moth down and take off, he nevertheless succeeded in flying Lundborg out to safety. By the time he returned to the crash site, the floe on which the survivors stood was beginning to break up. Deciding that it was too chancy, he returned to base. As a result, the survivors were compelled to remain another seven days before being picked up by the Russian icebreaker, *Kasin*.

The whole affair was a great embarrassment to the Mussolini government and, although the remaining crew returned home to a hero's welcome, it was the end of the expedition leader's career and yet another nail in the coffin of the dirigible airship. If there was any good that came of it, it redounded to the

English company that had supplied the one aircraft shown to be light enough to be able to operate – within limits – on the Arctic's treacherous summer ice.

If the rescue of Lieutenant Lundborg was an intimation of the sort of mission in which light aircraft could be deployed, another use to which the Moth was put in the late twenties and early thirties looks, to modern sensibilities, at best, decidedly eccentric. Some time in 1926, the Reverend Leonard Daniels, a British war veteran who had emigrated to Australia, conceived the idea of using a Moth for missionary work in the Australian outback. His parish was larger than England, with roads that made travel by car slow, perilous and uncomfortable. An aeroplane was clearly a better proposition. To this end, therefore, he began fundraising on a trip to Britain, quickly accumulating sufficient funds to be able to put in an order for a Cirrus II-engined DH60X. Lord Wakefield, backer of Amy Johnson among others, put up half.

Given the way he exploited the courage and skill of the record-breakers to the advantage of his oil business, Wakefield's donation seems, at first sight, somewhat unlikely. Yet the man was far from the caricature of the canny northern businessman that he is sometimes taken for. Born as long ago as 1859, Charles Cheers Wakefield (Cheers was his mother's maiden name) founded his oil company around the turn of the twentieth century.[2] Of the many patents that he filed, one, the addition of castor extract to the company's products, was to make him a fortune. Castrol became, for a time, the world's leading brand outside America. A visionary with regard to the future of aviation, he famously claimed, as early as 1909, that aeroplanes would soon be travelling at speeds in excess of 120 mph, carrying passengers, goods and mail across continents and that there would be air taxis taking travellers to any one of dozens of aerodromes up and down the country, lit, at night, by neon signs identifying each by name – even though, at the time, it was all that anyone could do to get a single person off the ground, and that it was hardly more than a year since Henri Farman had won the Grand Prix d'Aviation in France for a flight that had lasted all of one minute and twenty-eight seconds. But Wakefield understood clearly what the future held.

A committed churchman – Wakefield was a Nonconformist who took his duties seriously, generously funding a huge number of charities for disadvantaged children and being the main benefactor of the Toc H, the international Christian social movement that went on to set up a network of service-men's clubs during the Second World War and after. He was made lord mayor of London in 1915 and in that year put up a prize of £500 for the first person to shoot down a Zeppelin over British soil. Convinced that, within a few years, flying would be a hobby, like motorcycling and driving, he put money towards Alcock and Brown's successful transatlantic flight and, in 1923, also put up much of the prize money at the Lympne aircraft trials. The following year, it was his company's DH50 that won the 1924 King's Cup. Two years after that, Wakefield sponsored Cobham's pioneering flight to Australia and then, in 1929, Cobham's country-wide aerial 'Tour of Britain'. In addition, Wakefield set up numerous flying scholarships to assist young men from disadvantaged backgrounds to join the RAF. His donation to Reverend Daniels was therefore in support of two causes very close to his heart: flying and spreading the gospel.

As for Daniels himself, he, like Denys Finch Hatton, had

joined the RNAS and trained in Cairo in 1918. Having emblazoned the fuselage of his Moth with the legend *Church of England*, he operated the aircraft successfully for several years before it was damaged beyond economical repair during a heavy landing in 1932. It was subsequently rebuilt and had a brief career cattle rustling before being crashed again and resold.

Another missionary who quickly saw the value of aircraft in the Australian bush was Keith Langford-Smith. His ambition from a young age was to spread the Word throughout Arnhem Land, the geographically remote and hostile region lying to the east of Darwin. Unlike Daniels, Langford-Smith did not have Wakefield's ear and instead raised funds entirely in Australia. Also unlike Daniels, Langford-Smith did not have the benefit of service training. Indeed, he almost failed in his undertaking before it began as the result of an accident in the gym. This left him, like GDH's father, with one leg substantially shorter than the other and he failed his first medical. Although both a highly enterprising young man – he was just twenty-two when he set out to raise the necessary funds – and a considerable wit, his plan was not universally approved by other members of the Church Missionary Society. In his memoirs, Langford-Smith recounted exchanges with some of the more senior members of the Church Missionary Society:

'If God had meant us to fly, he would have given us wings,' said the old man.

I gently pointed out that he himself not only travelled at 40 mph in his car, but also did not hesitate to take a sea trip for his health, and yet, so far as I knew, God had omitted to supply him with either wheels or fins ...[3]

On another occasion, I noticed most of my audience consisted of lonely looking spinsters, and I told them of the shortage of white women in the north and the matrimonial possibilities of Darwin. Unfortunately, one old lady took offence at my words, said thoughtlessly for a joke, and got up and started for the door. There was an awful silence, such as follows a joke that has fallen flat. I realised that, unless I could recapture the sympathy of the audience, the lecture would be a failure. Feeling it was just as well to be hung for a sheep as a lamb, I told the retreating lady that 'really there is no hurry. The boat to the North only leaves once a month.' Fortunately, the audience roared with laughter.[4]

In the same book, Langford-Smith gives a good sense of what it was like learning to fly before the advent of air traffic control. Coming in to land at a busy airfield:

> someone side-slipped past my starboard wing, and appeared so close that I involuntarily ducked my head. It was hopeless trying to keep out of the road. These other pilots were more experienced than I was, and more used to aerial traffic, and none of them would be anxious to have a collision, so I thought if I went straight ahead they would keep out of my way. Sure enough after I nearly took the rudder off an Avro, and by a miracle avoided a collision with a club Moth, a clear gap seemed to open up right before me, every pilot giving me such a wide birth that landing was an easy matter.[5]

When he had eventually accumulated sufficient funds to buy a second-hand DH60G, which he named *Sky Pilot*, and was ready to fly up north, the Bishop of Melbourne turned out to bless the Moth. This proved to be of only limited value as the engine developed a fault within a day of setting out. Fortunately, the problem proved to be minor and Langford-Smith was able to continue after adjusting the timing, giving joyrides along the way. He continued this habit on arrival in Arnhem Land – including often to the aboriginal people among whom he worked. Unsurprisingly, his ministry was not always welcome among the Indigenous communities. Landing on the shore on one occasion, he was met with a shower of spears, 'one of which pierced my bottom starboard wing'. Regrettably, Langford-Smith was unchristian enough to take his revenge by flying 'low over their heads' and in the case of one, chasing him 'for about half a mile along the beach, until he threw himself into the sea'.[6]

If the activities of the bush missionary pilots seem hopelessly misguided to modern sensibilities, it is important to recognise that they were, nonetheless, an indispensable precursor to the vital aid provided by the various flying doctor services that, today, operate in many of the world's remotest regions. Reverend Daniels and Keith Langford-Smith were quick to see the utility of aircraft in this role. Both would fly sick passengers from lonely farmsteads and bush settlements to hospital. Transporting medical personnel and equipment across the outback became a standard feature of the missionary pilots' lives.

Another missionary who recognised the value of aircraft was John Flynn, the Presbyterian minister who founded what became the Royal Flying Doctor Service in 1928. Its first aircraft was a DH50 leased from Qantas and operated from Cloncurry in Queensland. Yet another pioneer in the field was Nancy Bird Walton. Born in 1915, Nancy (Bird was her maiden name – she married an Englishman by the name of Charles Walton) was taught to fly by the great Australian pioneer Charles Kingsford Smith, who declared her one of his best pupils. Qualifying for her A licence at the age of just nineteen, she went on to become the youngest woman in the British Empire to hold a commercial pilot's licence. As soon as she qualified, and using money bequeathed by a great aunt together with a loan from her father, Nancy Bird bought the Gipsy I Moth originally owned by Lady Isobel Chaytor, the fashion guru who had brought it over from England. Teaming up with her friend Peggy McKillop – whose aerial honeymoon, a few years later, took her from London to Moree in New South Wales – Nancy founded an air taxi and barnstorming company which toured the country, often astonishing her customers. Many had never seen an aeroplane before, let alone one piloted by a young woman standing no more than four foot ten inches tall.

In 1935, Nancy was approached by Reverend Stanley Drummond, a Methodist minister, to help establish what became the Royal Far West Children's Health Scheme (in which capacity it continues to this day). At first operating her own Gipsy, Nancy was subsequently supplied with a DH83 Fox Moth which, with its cabin capable of accommodating two stretchers, became for many years the standard equipment of the various air ambulance services.

If, though, there was one person who epitomised the can-do attitude conferred by the advent of the aeroplane in the Australian outback, it was Dr Clyde Fenton. For reasons best known to himself, when Reverend Flynn inaugurated his flying doctor service, he forbade doctors from piloting aircraft themselves. Perhaps this was to ensure that they were spared the stresses of operating aircraft in addition to having to operate on patients with minimal equipment and often in difficult circumstances. This did not satisfy Fenton who, between qualifying as a doctor in 1925 and – briefly – joining the RAF in England in 1929, first made an attempt by car, with his brother as co-driver, on the east coast to west coast record. When this ended with a crash in southern Australia, his thirst for adventure saw him buy and assemble a single-seat aircraft in which he taught himself to fly. It is not clear what type this was, but it may have been one of three DH53 Humming Birds exported to Australia. Certainly, one of them was bought by a doctor. In any case, he soon crashed this, too, before taking up a short-lived position practising medicine in Darwin.

Fenton's time with the RAF was short, as was the marriage he contracted while in England. In 1933, he was back in Australia where he began looking for a position as an *actually* flying doctor. Not finding one, he set about raising funds to buy a Gipsy Moth. Quickly succeeding, he took a job as medical officer at Katherine, a remote settlement in the Northern Territory. Unfortunately, he crashed this aeroplane within a matter of weeks on landing at a cattle station. His passenger recalled how, watching him exit the upturned Moth was like watching toothpaste being squeezed from a tube. The two of them then had to wade across crocodile-infested rivers to reach safety.

Nothing daunted, the soon-to-be-legendary Dr Fenton went on to operate various other aeroplanes, including at least one more Gipsy Moth, which he named *Robin*, and a DH83 Fox Moth, surviving several more crashes as he continued to practise medicine and bring succour to some of the most remote communities in the world. Tall, lean and bespectacled, Fenton was known for his keen wit, his kindness, his 'compulsive

acceptance of challenge' and his courage 'to the point of recklessness'. His devotion to his calling was absolute. Idolised by
the people he served, he was given successive public awards,
culminating in an OBE. This was despite the fact that he had
an abiding contempt for the aviation authorities. He was in
the habit of landing, when in need of refreshment, in the main
street outside Katherine's one and only pub where he would
sink schooners of beer. He was also not above flour-bombing
the town's unsuspecting inhabitants from time to time. On
another occasion, he was fined 200 Australian pounds for
'endangering public safety' when he made repeated low passes
over the open-air theatre, including once 'between the front
circle and the screen'.[7]

The territory he covered compelled Dr Fenton to travel
enormous distances, on one occasion flying 400 miles at night
to operate on a farmer with a burst appendix. The local ambulance crew had to climb the pole to which the windsock was
attached in order to be able to shine a torch on it to indicate
the wind direction. On another occasion, having flown 900
miles to the aid of an injured airman, he immediately turned
round and flew another 2,000 miles to treat a man suffering
with tetanus. Flying by day and even by moonless night – on
at least one occasion in his pyjamas – through tropical rain and
through sandstorms, the man was unstoppable. Once, having
treated a toddler that had been gored by a buffalo, he went out
and shot the creature. On another occasion, while up at 2,000
feet he noticed a four-foot-long brown snake sliding along the
bottom of the cockpit in the direction of the rudder pedals.
The third most venomous snake in the world, collapse from its
bite can occur within as little as two minutes and death follows
within hours. Fenton immediately climbed onto his seat and

put down on the nearest plausible piece of ground using only the joystick for control, successfully pulling off a rudderless arrival (no mean feat in itself) and leaping from the aeroplane before it had come to a standstill. He subsequently dispatched his unwelcome visitor with a hammer.

In 1936, Fenton flew his Moth to Shantou on the east coast of China in order to bring his mother home after his sister had died there in childbirth. Having no extra long-range tank, he devised a method of refuelling while airborne by controlling his aeroplane with his knees and refilling the main tank using jerry cans. On arrival in Bangkok, he was asked for his aeroplane's certificate of airworthiness, which he did not have. Producing instead the flight manual, he was able to persuade the official to let him pass. After landing in China, he was arrested but set free on the grounds that his mission demonstrated 'filial piety', only to be grounded when passing through Hong Kong on the way home. This time, he managed to persuade the official to let him 'test' the aeroplane, enabling him to return home to a hero's welcome in Darwin. Having served as a wartime flying instructor in the Royal Australian Air Force, he joined the Department of Health in Brisbane, settled down and got married. Twice. Not long after his death, in his eighty-first year, his original Moth, by then in private ownership, was purchased by public subscription and installed as a permanent memorial at the Katherine Museum where it may be seen to this day.

There are doubtless many more stories of the DH60 Moth that could be told but let Dr Fenton stand for the last of the great pioneers. When war came in 1939, the majority of active DH60s in private ownership was impressed by the War Office, both in England and throughout the Commonwealth. Only a minority came out at the other end. Some had, in the meantime, been crashed and physically written off. Others had simply languished in the back of a hangar and, when hostilities ceased, were deemed uneconomical to put back in flying order and were administrative write-offs, cannibalised for parts or simply left to rot before being cleared out. Some survived as curiosities, eventually to be restored and become objects of nostalgic affection. A very few continued to work for a living. Clyde Fenton's was an example, his aircraft serving for several years as a glider tug before being sold again into private ownership.

Certainly the most famous DH60 still airworthy is G-AAMY, the aircraft used for the flying sequences in *Out of Africa*. Originally built at de Havilland's licensees in Lowell Massachusetts, it was used for a time as a company demonstrator. Passing through several pairs of hands, the aeroplane was wrecked landing – paradoxically, but so the record tells us – in a snow-covered hayfield in Colorado in 1941. Thereafter sold as an educational project for $25 (less its engine, presumably), it was again sold, by now just a collection of bits, to an engineer in Florida who, apparently using parts cannibalised from three other Moth projects, fitted it with an American-built Wright Gipsy engine and restored it to flying condition in 1964. Subsequently, it was sold and bought again on an almost annual basis before it found a home in Maryland for almost ten years until, in 1979, it was acquired by the British Moth engineer and de Havilland enthusiast Cliff Lovell, who imported the aircraft to England. It was while in his ownership that the aeroplane was shipped to Africa for its historic role in the biopic of Karen von Blixen's doomed love affair with Denys Finch Hatton. Astonishingly, it took sixty hours of flying to produce the two minutes or so that appear in the film, the shot of it flying over a flamboyance of flamingos being purely serendipitous. The day's actual filming was over and it was pure chance that the helicopter camera-ship was in situ at that precise moment.

A year after G-AAMY came back from Kenya, she was again sold, this time to another well-known Moth enthusiast, the larger-than-life Roger Twisleton-Wykeham-Fiennes (a cousin of Ralph's) whose enthusiasm for old aeroplanes was said by some in the flying fraternity to have been exceeded only by the success of the aviation-ability bypass operation he was said to have undergone. This seems harsh but is perhaps borne out by the fact that in 1998, Fiennes disappeared over the Channel in his Tiger Moth. No trace either of the aeroplane or its pilot was ever found. Inevitably, there is an alternative view – that he had 'done a Lucan' on account of various bad debts and questionable business ventures. With sightings reported as far apart as Poland and Cuba, there are some who believe that, having reported himself approaching mid-Channel, he dropped down below radar height and diverted back to France. Still others believe that it was a straightforward act of suicide done out of despair.

Amy, as the film-star DH60 is known, had meanwhile passed from Fiennes to sometime owner of Aston Martin, Victor Gauntlett, before being sold into Dutch ownership in 1996. A forced landing five years later was followed by major work to the notoriously unreliable Wright Gipsy engine. In 2014, the aeroplane was again sold, this time at auction in Paris for an unprecedented quarter of a million dollars to a Kenyan entrepreneur who planned to use it for 'Out of Africa' tours at his private game retreat at Nanyuki. At this point, though the engine rebuild had successfully restored the aeroplane to flying condition, it was deemed underpowered for its intended role and was instead fitted with a Gipsy Major engine turned the right way up and reconfigured as a Gipsy II. Now a satisfactory performer even in the hot and high altitudes of the Kenyan bush, for reasons that are not entirely clear, Amy never did see much service as an aerial tour provider and she was again sold in 2024, having been shipped to America for a high-profile auction at Sotheby's 'ModaMiami' event. Going under the hammer, this time for an astonishing $527,000, the funds raised were to be put into creating a new rhinoceros sanctuary at her former home. The new owner is Roger Brandts, CEO of a German fashion brand named – wait for it – Fynch Hatton.

Of the roughly fifteen hundred examples of the DH60 built (the exact number is not entirely clear), just fewer than sixty are currently airworthy, although the number is not stable. Every so often, another one is reduced to a collection of parts while yet another is resurrected. The oldest airworthy Moth is the Cirrus-engined G-EBLV, number eight off the production line in 1925, which is operated by the Shuttleworth Collection. Around fifty more survivors are, like Dr Fenton's, exhibited in museums round the world. Of these arguably the most famous, Amy Johnson's *Jason*, hangs suspended from the ceiling at the Science Museum in Kensington, London.

The last production DH60G was registered in March 1934 and the last production Moth Major a year later. Setting the later variants aside, the classic DH60 had a production run of just under nine years during which it saw service on every continent and in almost every country of the world. Moreover, while they remained in production, and for years afterwards, Moths were flown in every setting conceivable. Often they suffered from poor fuel quality and lack of maintenance.

They were mishandled due to ineptitude on the part of over-confident and under-trained pilots. Propellers broke, flying wires snapped, tyres burst, the undercarriage failed. Fabric got torn, wing ribs were broken, tail skids fell off. They were ground-looped, flipped over, stood on their heads, bashed into each other and into more solid objects. They were landed up trees, on mountain tops, in the sea, in rivers and creeks and snowdrifts. And while there were plenty of fatalities, in actual fact the vast majority of crew survived.

It is true that Geoffrey de Havilland's dream of creating the Model T Ford of the air was never likely to succeed. Thanks to the vagaries of wind and weather, flying small aeroplanes was always and ever shall be too demanding, too uncertain, too hazardous for it ever to be more than a minority interest. Not until the Comet, the world's first successful jet airliner did GDH, in the end, attain his vision of bringing fast, safe and reliable air travel to within the reach of all. Yet the DH60 was an indispensable step along the way. Without question, it is the aeroplane – thanks to the exploits of the extraordinary men and women who flew them – that did more than any other to banish the idea that flight would always be reserved to the privileged few. You did not need to be high-born. You did not need to be a genius. Yes, you had to find a way into the cockpit and yes, you needed a modicum of skill. But once both these were acquired, all you needed was a tank of fuel, plenty of oil and, with a set of Gipsy wings, the world was yours for the taking.

Acknowledgements

The writer who receives as much help, cheerfully and un-stintingly given, as I have received in writing this book is fortunate indeed. In particular, I should like to thank Stuart McKay, secretary of the de Havilland Moth Club and him-self the author of what will remain the standard history of the DH60 Moth, for kindly answering innumerable ques-tions and for saving me from a number of egregious mistakes; Henry Labouchere, 'the Moth whisperer', who has not only rescued me from the frequent mechanical impediments that restrict one's flying of old aeroplanes (failed magnetos, broken tail skids and damaged rudders due to bad landings, among others) but is also almost certainly the world's lead-ing authority on operating the de Havilland Moth series; Tim Barron for lending me several titles from his personal library as well as for information about his grandfather, C. W. A. Scott; Malcolm Fillmore of Air-Britain for answering frequent questions of detail and for generously sharing his research; Tony Pilmer of the National Aerospace Library, for not only responding to my many queries but also for hunting down references and pointing me in the direc-tion of a large number of useful resources; Terry Mace for

answering various queries relating to his excellent resource
A Fleeting Peace; my friend Ralf Kramer of the Bayerische
Staatsbibliothek for unfailing assistance whenever I came
unstuck in my research and for passing on web-based material that was beyond my reach and competence; Alan Brown,
senior library assistant at the Bodleian Library, Oxford, for
help in tracking down elusive titles; Merwan Engineer, to
whom I owe a special debt of gratitude for furnishing me
with Aspy Engineer's wonderful account of his flight with
R. N. Chawla to England and for putting me in touch with
Aspy's son, Cyrus Engineer – this not to mention the many
thoughtful emails he sent in response to my enquiries about
Zoroastrianism and other matters tangential to the project;
Perveen Engineer who supplied me with further information about his relative in the form of an article in *Hamazor*;
Zerbanoo Gifford for introducing me to the editor of the
Parsi magazine *Parsiana*, which also published an account of
Aspy's triumph in the Aga Khan Trophy; Tim Williams –
another great exponent of the marque – who gave me
information about J. R. D. Tata (whom he once met when the
great man held up a jumbo jet for an hour in order to speak
to him) and about Man Mohan Singh; Captain Nigel Reid
for so generously taking me up in his DH60, G-AAWO; my
cousin Miranda Gunn who dug out her mother's logbook
and flying album and passed on her reminiscences of various
family members' flying stories; Sarah Rickett, another cousin
(and a goddaughter of Alan Butler), who also shared some
extremely useful stories about – and photographs of – her
father's and uncles' various aeroplanes; Mark Lucas for encouraging me in the idea that it ought to be possible to find a
publisher for such a book as this; Richard Beswick at Little,

Brown for proving him right; and, finally, my wife Linda and my children Rosie, Eddie and Theo who have put up with my long absences (physical or not), ill humour, tetchiness and general bad behaviour all in the name of writing (whether or not it really had anything to do with the matter): I love them more than I can say.

A Note on Sources

This book is intended as a popular history for the general reader. As such, it is not intended as a definitive scholarly study. In view of this, I have not held myself to the rigorous standards of my two books about the Dalai Lama. Instead, I have cherry-picked and adapted mainly from secondary and contemporary journalistic resources. For knowledge of flying, I have relied on my own experience of many hundreds of hours flown in various vintage types, notably the DH82A Tiger Moth. For knowledge of the general aeronautical landscape of the era, I have also relied heavily on my personal reminiscences growing up as a member of an intensely air-minded family. My father was co-designer and manufacturer of the half-eponymous Britten-Norman Islander. He himself was a graduate of the de Havilland Aeronautical Technical School. My uncle Torquil owned the finest collection of de Havilland aircraft in private hands and I am greatly indebted to him for his generosity not only in loaning his Tiger Moth but also for providing hangar space and unfettered access to his airfield in Gloucestershire. My grandfather (who succeeded Sir Philip Sassoon as Squadron Leader of 601 Squadron), his two brothers and sister were all Moth owners and I have a few stories from my grandmother that were formative: one of these was her remark – when I told her (more than four decades ago) that I had just read Beryl Markham's book *West with the Night* (we always talked about our latest reading) – 'Oh, Beryl Markham! The last time I saw her was in the arms of the Prince of Wales under the wing of your grandfather's Puss Moth.' That would have been at the London Aero Club's summer party in 1930.

Readers interested to do so will find listed in the bibliography the titles of each of the works that I consulted in writing this book, as well as the websites to which I had – in some cases – frequent recourse.

One of the things I found was that quite a few of the first-hand accounts I used were written in a style that made direct quotation difficult. As a result, I have taken the liberty of occasionally adapting not just reported speech but in some cases the prose, too, in order to make quotations more readable. I have also not disdained to use the magazine articles published by organisations such as the Smithsonian Institution. Neither of these techniques would have satisfied the stern academics under whom I studied at university but I trust that my readers will forgive – and possibly even thank – me. Accordingly, I have given references in the endnotes only when it seemed strictly necessary.

The standard work on which any historian of the type must rely is Stuart McKay's outstanding book *The DH.60 Moth*. The de Havilland Moth Club (www.dhmothclub.co.uk), of which he is secretary, is also an extraordinary resource for anyone interested in the de Havilland Moth series of light aircraft, notably through its quarterly magazine. The club's chief glory is, of course, the individual members whose collective knowledge of the marque is breathtaking in its extent.

Also indispensable is the mammoth, minutely researched and in every way extraordinary Air-Britain database, which gives a brief history of every single known example of the type. Another vital resource of similar quality and excellence is the list of early British owners and operators, again compiled by researchers at Air-Britain under the leadership of Malcolm Fillmore. A very useful database on early British aircraft registrations can be found on the website of Air History UK. The work of each of these individuals and organisations is remarkable for the passion, care and enthusiasm that shines through their work. As any popular historian ought to admit, the kind of endeavour of which this book is an example would not be possible without the uncounted hard yards put in by those who do the basic research and, in most cases, are willing to share the fruits of their labours freely to anyone who cares to ask.

Of course, all preliminary research today begins with Wikipedia. Though often sketchy and frequently inaccurate as to details, it can nevertheless be very helpful in pointing to other sources. I tried using perplexity.ai for further help in this regard but, frankly, found it, as yet, not superior to Wikipedia and, on the whole, less accurate. The newspaper and magazine archive to be found within the Internet Archive's *Wayback Machine* is, however, indispensable; many, if by no means all, relevant early editions of *Flight* and *The Aeroplane* can be found there. I also found the Australian site at trove.nla.gov.au extremely helpful. Of course, the various dictionaries of national biography (notably those for America, Great Britain, Ireland and Australia) were tremendously useful – even if they, too, are not, on further inspection, always wholly accurate.

A more particular resource is de Havilland's in-house magazine *The DH Gazette*, copies of which are quite hard to come by, but some of which can be found at the National Aerospace Library in Farnborough. Similarly useful are back copies of every Moth enthusiast's favourite magazine, *The Moth*, published by the de Havilland Moth Club. These contain an extraordinary wealth of information relating to the various types and variants of the Moth series as well as an abundance of magnificent photographs.

For a more detailed account of the sources I used, I sketch below the major ones for each chapter.

Chapter One: Is it Right or Left for England?

Here I have quoted freely from Apsy Engineer's private reminiscences.

Chapter Two: 'You really think you know enough? To build a flying machine?'

The principal source for this chapter is GDH's very well-written and engagingly modest autobiography, *Sky Fever*.

Chapter Three: Captain

Again, the main resource is *Sky Fever*. For further information about the hilarious Pemberton Billing and about J. W. Dunne, see the relevant *Dictionary of National Biography* entries.

Chapter Four: The de Havilland Aircraft Company

Here the standard work is C. Martin Sharp's *DH: A History of de Havilland*; also useful for particular types is A. Jackson's

De Havilland Aircraft. Alan Butler's wife, Lois, was my father's godmother, my cousin Sarah Rickett was one of Alan's god-daughters and the Butler family was something of a feature of my childhood. Their son, David, was my brother's godfather and, incidentally, the leader of the opposition to Ian Smith's Rhodesian Front. Some think the car crash in which he was killed was not an accident.

Chapter Five: Design Number 60

For details of the design and construction of the type, an excellent summary may be found in *The Airplane*, part 112, 1992. The same publication has a similar overview of the DH60 Moth's great rival, the Avro Avian (though the Moth outsold it by a ratio of five to one).

Chapter Six: 'The most practical and successful light aircraft the world has ever seen'

There are several good sources for Sophie Eliott-Lynn, the Irish *DNB* having probably the best short summary. Written almost in the style of G. K. Chesterton, her book of poems, *Kenya Nights*, was not notably successful but it has a certain wistfulness that speaks to her later career. See also the biography by Lindie Naughton. For Tiny Borwick, see especially the interview with her at www.youtube.com/watch?v=EN-RAGs33yNM. For information about the King's Cup air races, Terence Boughton's *Story of the British Light Aeroplane* is useful.

Chapter Seven: Far Horizons

For an outstanding overview of aviation in the twenties, see especially *The Spectacle of Flight* by Robert Wohl. It is a tragedy that he did not live to complete the projected third volume of his cultural history of aviation. Another indispensable source is the – frankly terrifying – proto-fascism of le Corbusier's *Aircraft*, in which we are invited to rejoice at the prospect of the coming 'machine age'. It reminds us that, as well as being a time of great adventure in the air, this was the era of eugenics, institutional anti-Semitism and nationalism. For a more cheerful take on the period, see Dick Bentley's own account of his flight to the Cape and back, listed in the electronic sources.

Chapter Eight: The Obstinacy and Determination of Forty Devils

Although now largely forgotten, Lady Mary Bailey is the subject of Falloon's biography. Her exploits are, of course, covered extensively in contemporary sources. Abe Bailey's life is well documented, as is his art collection bequeathed to the South African people. For those easily sidetracked, the remarkable story of *Drum* magazine is also easily accessed. For those interested in cricket scores, *Wisden* is, of course, indispensable.

Chapter Nine: Flying Gypsies

Violette de Sibour's lively account of her year's peregrination by Moth is quite scarce and there is no online version that I am aware of. I read it in the Bodleian Library where the staff were as helpful as any library staff could possibly be. The book itself was almost certainly dictated but, read alongside Waugh's *Vile Bodies*, you get a good sense of the period – both of its frivolity and of the great opening up of society that followed the First World War. Philip Sassoon's book is neither as well written nor as informative as one might have hoped, while one can only gasp in astonishment at the lack of reflection contained in Friedrich Karl Richard Paul August Freiherr Koenig von und zu Warthausen's book.

Chapter Ten: Bad Luck Wimpey and the Moth Maniacs

Many of the great aviatrices left accounts of their exploits, notably Pauline Gower and Mildred, the Hon. Mrs Victor Bruce. Again, they lack much in the way of reflection, especially self-reflection. On the other hand, one supposes that if Mrs Bruce had thought very deeply about her famous Fox Dive, she might not have done it. Apart from his book *The Third Route*, Philip Sassoon published nothing and, in fact, one cannot help but feel that he deserves a more ambitious biography than any he has received to date. The anecdote about his flying can be found in *The Flying Sword*, which also gives a useful picture of the early years of 601 Squadron, of which he was Squadron Leader.

Chapter Eleven: The Empire Strikes Back

I am greatly indebted to the Engineer family for so generously sharing material relating to the great Aspy. J. R. D. Tata's biography is available online, as is quite a lot of other useful material relating to the Aga Khan Trophy, through the archives of the Tata Group. Man Mohan Singh's life is well documented in various online resources produced by the Sikh community. He features in some Pathé News footage of Indian pilot volunteers at the beginning of the Second World War. Information about Mohan Singh, aka Guru Hari Ram, can easily be found on the internet, the most comprehensive article being that published by the Smithsonian Institution.

Chapter Twelve: Moth Rastafari

The main source for this chapter is to be found in an excellent French resource at crezan.net, while Evelyn Waugh's atmospheric account of the coronation in *Remote People* – not by any means his best work, though it has its admirers – is still in print as a Penguin Modern Classic. The life of the amazing Hubert Julian is well documented. Entering his name on the Bodleian's SOLO search engine turns up a good number of sources, of which the Smithsonian Institution's article provides a very good summary. He, too, surely deserves a serious biography.

Chapter Thirteen: *Jason* and Johnnie

The standard life of Amy Johnson by Constance Babington Smith has not been surpassed, although Luff's more recent biography provides a wealth of material relating to her caddish former boyfriend, Hans. A trawl through press reports on the *Wayback* Machine gives a very good feel for the enthusiasm Britain's first real celebrity aroused among ordinary people.

Chapter Fourteen: The Lonely Sea and the Sky

Francis Chichester wrote a number of books relating to his crossing of the Tasman Sea. The best of them is his autobiography. For a useful check, and especially for information regarding his unfortunate first wife, Leslie's very readable biography is worthwhile. The Royal Institute of Navigation has many excellent resources with respect to sextants, Bygrave slide rules and the various methods of solar navigation.

Chapter Fifteen: Out of Africa

The lives of Denys Finch Hatton, Beryl Markham and Karen von Blixen are all well documented. Of course, von Blixen's magnificent (though not unproblematic) autobiographical account of her time in Africa, *Out of Africa,* is indispensable. Beryl Markham's book is, as Hemingway recognised, also outstanding for lots of reasons. It deserves a scholarly examination in its own right (to explore the whole question of ghostwriting and whether, among other things, the work of ghostwriters should not be classified as fiction) but, in the meantime, see James Fox's *Spectator* review of the Lovell biography. The excellent scholarly resource on Europeans in East Africa compiled by Peter Ayre continues to be expanded. It has entries and further sources for each of the characters discussed in the chapter.

Chapter Sixteen: The Record-Breakers: Stunting All Over the World

Each of those mentioned in this chapter (Scott, Mollison, Batten) left accounts of their record-breaking flights. Scott's is the most entertaining, though he protests his innocence too much to be wholly credible. Jean Batten's own book is dreary and self-aggrandising (while the Mackersey biography of Batten is a remarkable piece of detective work). Mollison comes across as thoroughly dislikable in everything written by and about him. Had he no redeeming features?

Chapter Seventeen: Into the Silence

I have borrowed the chapter title from the excellent book on Mallory and the quest for Everest by Wade Davis. The latest biography of Wilson is, of course, indispensable but so too is the earlier work by Roberts, if only to flesh out some of the flying details. For a brief account of the Tibetan Nyingma tradition and of the *srung ma*, see my own history of the Dalai Lama institution, *Holder of the White Lotus* (Little, Brown, 2008).

Chapter Eighteen: Works of Mercy

The history of the Australian Royal Flying Doctor Service is well documented, that of the early airborne missions less well so. I was unable to find Reverend Leonard Daniel's book, but his obituary tells as much as the general reader needs to know. Dr Clyde Fenton deserves at least a whole chapter in any history of the aeroplane in Australia: he sums up very concisely a particular moment in Australian history. For details of surviving DH60s, the de Havilland Moth Club is, inevitably, the primary resource.

Bibliography

Of course, there are many sources of background material that I do not list here, though I must mention the works of the peerless Antoine de Saint-Exupéry, the outstanding *Flight Without Formulae* and *Aircraft Construction* by A. C. Kermode, the wonderful *Teach Yourself to Fly* by Nigel Tangye, the atmospheric *The Grasshoppers Come* and *A Rabbit in the Air* by David Garnett and the incomparable *Sagittarius Rising* by Cecil Lewis. Le Corbusier's *Aircraft* provides an ugly counterpoint.

Aslet, Clive, *The Last Country Houses*, Yale University Press, New Haven and London, 1982

Batten, Jean, *Alone in the Sky*, Airlife Publishing, Shrewsbury, 1979

Blixen, Karen (Isak Dinesen), *Out of Africa and Shadows on the Grass*, Penguin, London, 1985

Boughton, Terence, *The Story of the British Light Aeroplane*, John Murray, London, 1963

Bruce, The Hon. Mrs Victor *Nine Lives Plus*, Pelham Books, England, 1977

Caesar, Ed, *The Moth and the Mountain*, Penguin Random House, London, 2020

Chichester, Francis, *The Lonely Sea and the Sky*, Hodder & Stoughton, London, 1964

Collins, Damien, *Charmed Life: The Phenomenal World of Philip Sassoon*, William Collins, London, 2016

Cruddas, Colin, *Those Fabulous Flying Years: Joy-riding and Flying Circuses Between the Wars*, Air-Britain (Historians) Ltd, Tonbridge, 2003

Elkins, Caroline, *Imperial Reckoning: The Untold Story of Britain's Gulag in Kenya*, Henry Holt & Company, New York, 2005

Falloon, Jane, *Throttle Full Open*, digital edition, Lilliput Press, 2012

Fox, James, *White Mischief*, Penguin, London, 1984

Hannah, Donald, *'Isak Dinesen' and Karen Blixen: The Mask and the Reality*, Random House, New York, 1971

de Havilland, Sir Geoffrey, *Sky Fever*, Airlife, England, 1979

Jackson, A. J., *British Civil Aircraft 1919–1972: Volume I*, Putnam, London, 1973

——*De Havilland Aircraft since 1909*, revised edition, Putnam, London, 1987

Koenig von und zu Warthausen, Friedrich, *Wings Around the World*, G. P. Putnam's Sons, London, 1930

Langford Smith, Keith, *Sky Pilot in Arnhem Land*, J Hamilton, London, 1936

Lala, R. M., *Beyond the Last Blue Mountain: A Life of J. R. D. Tata*, Penguin Books (India), New Delhi, 1993

Leslie, Anita, *Francis Chichester*, Hutchinson, London, 1970

Lovell, Mary S., *Amelia Earhart*, Abacus, London, 2009

——*Straight on Till Morning*, Abacus, London, 2009

Luff, David, *Amy Johnson: Enigma in the Sky*, Crowood Press, Marlborough, 2002

Mackersey, Ian, *Jean Batten: The Garbo of the Skies*, Macdonald & Company, London, 1990

Markham, Beryl, *West with the Night*, with an introduction by Martha Gellhorn, Virago, London, 1984

McKay, Stuart, *de Havilland DH.60 Moth*, Midland, Leicestershire, 2005

Moulson, Tom, *The Flying Sword*, Macdonald, London, 1964

Naughton, Lindie, *Lady Icarus: The Life of Irish Aviator Lady Mary Heath*, Ashfield Press, Dublin, 2004

Raleigh, Walter, *The War in the Air: Being the Story of the Part Played in the Great War by the Royal Air Force: Vol. I*, Clarendon Press, Oxford, 1922

Roberts, Andrew, *Churchill: Walking with Destiny*, Penguin, London, 2019

Roberts, Dennis, *I'll Climb Mount Everest Alone: The Story of Maurice Wilson*, Faber Finds, London, 2010

Sassoon, Philip, *The Third Route*, William Heinemann, London, 1929

Schiff, Stacy, *Saint-Exupéry: A Biography*, Alfred A. Knopf Inc, New York, 1994

Scott, C. W. A., *Scott's Book*, Hodder & Stoughton, London, 1934

Sharp, C. Martin, *DH: A History of de Havilland*, Faber & Faber, London, 1960

de Sibour, Violette, *Flying Gypsies: The Chronicle of a 10,000 Mile Air Vagabondage*, G. P. Putnam's Sons, London, 1930

Smith, Constance Babington, *Amy Johnson*, Sutton Publishing, Stroud, 2004

Stansky, Peter, *The Worlds of Philip and Sybil*, Yale University Press, New Haven and London, 2003

Trzebinski, Errol, *Silence Will Speak*, William Heinemann,
    London, 1977
——*The Lives of Beryl Markham*, William Heinemann,
    London, 1993
Waugh, Evelyn, *Remote People*, Penguin, London, 1985
——*Vile Bodies*, Penguin, London, 2000
Wheeler, Sara, *Too Close to the Sun: The Audacious Life
    and Times of Denys Finch Hatton*, Jonathan Cape,
    London, 2006
Wohl, Robert, *A Passion for Wings*, Yale University Press,
    New Haven and London, 1994
——*The Spectacle of Flight*, Yale University Press, New Haven
    and London, 2005
Ziegler, Philip, *King Edward VIII*, Collins, London, 1990

Articles and Journals

Macdonald, A. W., 'The Lama and the General', *Kailash*,
    vol. 1, no. 3, 1973, pp. 225–234
The Aeroplane, 'The Gipsy Moth Light Aeroplane',
    March 1933
The DH Gazette, 'Hatfield', 1926–1934

Websites

www.airhistory.org.uk/gy/reg_G-E1.html – superb
    Air-Britain publication listing all known early British
    aircraft, the registration numbers, construction numbers,
    owners and operators
www.caa.co.uk/aircraft-register/g-info/search-g-info/ – for
    contemporary British aircraft registrations

air-britain.com/pdfs/production-lists/DH60.pdf – provides short histories of each and every DH60 (and its derivatives) known to have been built, whether in Britain or abroad. An astonishing piece of work

www.youtube.com/watch?v=3alTlYCuv38 – Man Mohan Singh features among the young Indian volunteers to the RAF during the Second World War

www.afleetingpeace.org – 'Golden Age Aviation in the British Empire'

www.crezan.net/pag_aby/abyssinia_avi_dh60.html – article in French on the Haile Selassie Moth

www.europeansineastafrica.co.uk – featuring biographical information about many European settlers in Kenya

www.baesystems.com/en-uk/our-company/heritage – a comprehensive resource for material relating to many British aircraft types

static1.squarespace.com/static/5c65dd81af46834afd07e40a/ t/603418bb2a597102c3e4ea34/1614026949936/ lives+retold+bentley+richard.pdf – resource for Dick Bentley's story

archive.org/details/Flight_International_Magazine?sort=-publicdate – early editions of *Flight* magazine

aviation-safety.net/wikibase – an excellent resource for details of air accidents

www.flyingdoctor.org.au/about-the-rfds/history/john-flynn-bio/ – invaluable resource on Australia's Royal Flying Doctor Service

ingeniumcanada.org/channel/articles/the-remarkable-story-of-leonard-daniels-the-archdeacon-of-up-a-gum-tree – entertaining account of early airborne missionaries in Australia

www.europeansineastafrica.co.uk – outstanding resource on
    the European colonial period
Early owners and operators of all aircraft types in Britain
    prior to the Second World War, Bernard Martin at
    Air-Britain, https://air-britain.com/web/da-civil/

Endnotes

Chapter One

All quotations taken from Aspy's own typewritten account, kindly provided by his family.

Chapter Two

1. de Havilland, *Sky Fever*, p. 33.
2. Ibid.

Chapter Three

1. *Sky Fever*, pp. 93, 95.
2. Ibid., p. 104.

Chapter Four

1. Raleigh, *The War in the Air*, p. 132.

Chapter Six

1. *DNB* entry.
2. www.thisdayinaviation.com/tag/lockheed-orion-9d-special/

Chapter Seven

1. McKay, *de Havilland DH.60 Moth*, p. 92.
2. McKay, *de Havilland DH.60 Moth*, p. 41.
3. jlpc.co.za/pdf/personalities/Story_Richard_Reid_Dick_Bentley_Pioneering_Spirit_JLPC.pdf

Chapter Nine

1. de Sibour, *Flying Gypsies*, pp. 9–12.
2. Ibid., p. 30.
3. Ibid., p. 223.
4. Ibid., p. 228.
5. Ibid., p. 259.

Chapter Ten

1. Ziegler, *King Edward VIII*, p. 178.
2. https://aviation-safety.net/wikibase/24981.
3. Cruddas, *Those Fabulous Flying Years*, p. 15; Air Britain.
4. https://trove.nla.gov.au/newspaper/article/276137119.
5. Ibid., p. 177.
6. (G-AALG, c/n 1411).
7. See *Rusty Tack* ENTERPRISE number 124, published by the de Havilland Moth Club
8. Wheeler, p. 234.
9. Moulson, *The Flying Sword*, p. 29.
10. Ibid., p. 28.
11. Aslet, *The Last Country Houses*.
12. Adapted from an advertising leaflet; Cruddas, p. 32.

Chapter Eleven

1. henrypoole.com/individual/
   hh-maharaja-sir-bhupinder-singh-patiala/
2. www.smithsonianmag.com/air-space-magazine/
   mohan-singh-aviator-of-mystery-180962015/
3. Tim Williams, personal conversation with the author.

Chapter Twelve

1. www.smithsonianmag.com/air-space-magazine/
   the-black-eagle-of-harlem-95208344/
2. Waugh, *Remote People*, p. 45.
3. doi.org/10.1093/anb/9780198606697.article.2001868
4. www.jstor.org/stable/j.ctt1pd2ktb
5. www.crezan.net/pag_aby/abyssinia_avi_dh60.html

Chapter Thirteen

1. Luff, *Amy Johnson*, p. 113.
2. Ibid., p. 190.

3. Smith, *Amy Johnson*, pp. 198–9.
4. Adapted from Smith, p. 204.
5. Ibid., p. 206.
6. Ibid., p. 206.
7. Ibid., p. 257.

Chapter Fourteen
1. Chichester, *The Lonely Sea and the Sky*, p. 67.
2. Ibid., p. 69.

Chapter Fifteen
1. Elkins, p. 11.
2. Lala, *Beyond the Last Blue Mountain*, p. 66.
3. Quoted in Hannah, *'Isak Dinesen' and Karen Blixen*, p. 15.
4. Chapter 8 of Trzebinski, in her biography of Beryl Markham, has all the gruesome details.
5. Wheeler, *Too Close to the Sun*, p. 247.

Chapter Sixteen
1. Scott, *Scott's Book*, p. 148.

Chapter Seventeen
1. Roberts, *I'll Climb Everest Alone*, p. 23.
2. Caesar, *The Moth and the Mountain*, p. 145.
3. See A. W. Macdonald, *The Lama and the General*.
4. Roberts, p. 123.

Chapter Eighteen
1. McKay, p. 55.
2. tochcentenary.wordpress.com/2022/12/03/a-most-generous-man-the-story-of-charles-wakefield/
3. Langford-Smith, *Sky Pilot*, p. 182.
4. Ibid., pp. 185–6.
5. Ibid., p. 190.
6. Ibid., p. 234.
7. www.abc.net.au/news/2022-08-13/nt-clyde-fenton/101303864, see also trove.nla.gov.au/newspaper/article/48350343, 30 May 1940.

Index

Tatler, 137
Taurus Mountains, 180
Thompson, Lord, 183
Tigris, river, 152
Time magazine, 81
Times, The, 58, 252
Timor Sea, 244
Toc H, 282
Tournay, Fr Maurice, 270
Townsend, Marchioness of, 138
Trafalgar, Battle of, 225
transatlantic flight, first, 11
Travers, Major, 176
Trenchard, Lord, 34, 131
Tripoli, 94, 162
Trucial States, 266
Truman, Fred, 250, 254
Tuareg tribesmen, 251
Tunis, 265–6
Tutschek, Adolf Ritter von, 57
Twisleton-Wykeham-Fiennes,
    Roger, 291

unemployment, 10
United States Army Air Service, 35
Universal Negro Improvement
    Association, 168
Urquhart, 'Sligger', 144

Valley of the Kings, 84
Venice, 128, 200, 222
Vickers Vimy, 147
Victoria Falls, 83, 85, 95–6
Victoria Point, 243

Wakefield, Lord, 139, 141, 176, 231,
    244–5, 252–3, 255, 281–3
Walter, Edward, 253–4
Walton, Nancy Bird, 285–6
War Office, 289
Warthausen, Baron Friedrich Karl
    Richard Paul August Koenig von
    und zu, 116–17, 305

Watts, Emily, 125
Waugh, Evelyn, 169, 192, 305–6
weather forecasts, 5, 131, 194
Wembley Stadium, 239
Westland Wapiti, 178
Westland Widgeon, 77
Westland Woodpigeon, 121
White Mischhief set, 219
Wilhelm II, Kaiser, 30
William the Conqueror, 13
Williams, Reginald, 66
Williamson, Margaret, 193
Wilson, Beatrice, 259
Wilson, Florence, 224
Wilson, Maurice, 258–75, 308
Wilson Airways, 221, 224
Winchelsea, Earl of, 224
wing loading, 46, 52
wing warping, 47–8
Winter Olympics (1936), 120
Woburn Abbey, 125–6
Wohl, Robert, 304
Wolseley Tool and Motor Car
    Company, 19
Women's Amateur Athletics
    Association, 62
Women's Auxiliary Army Corps, 62
Women's Dixie Derby, 73
Women's Olympiad, 63
women's suffrage, 10, 126, 261
Women's Tax Resistance League,
    126
Women's World Games, 63
Woodhead Pass, 124
world speed record, 78
Wright, Orville, 27
Wright brothers, 20

Yorkshire Evening Post, 183

Zeppelins, 26, 45, 123, 178, 278, 282
Zoroastrians (Parsis), 146, 149,
    151–2